Contents

Tables

The upstart earl

The upstart earl

A study of the social and mental world
of Richard Boyle
first Earl of Cork
1566–1643

NICHOLAS CANNY

*Professor of History in the National University of Ireland
at University College, Galway*

CAMBRIDGE UNIVERSITY PRESS

Cambridge

London   New York   New Rochelle

Melbourne   Sydney

CAMBRIDGE UNIVERSITY PRESS
Cambridge, New York, Melbourne, Madrid, Cape Town, Singapore, São Paulo, Delhi

Cambridge University Press
The Edinburgh Building, Cambridge CB2 8RU, UK

Published in the United States of America by Cambridge University Press, New York

www.cambridge.org
Information on this title: www.cambridge.org/9780521244169

© Cambridge University Press 1982

First published 1982
This digitally printed version 2008

A catalogue record for this publication is available from the British Library

Library of Congress Catalogue Card Number: 81–21687

ISBN 978-0-521-24416-9 hardback
ISBN 978-0-521-09038-4 paperback

Do Morwena:

Aoibhinn, a leabhráin, do thriall
I gceann ainnre na gciabh gcam.

Preface

Since, unlike Plutarch, I write history and not lives, I should warn the unsuspecting reader that this work was neither conceived nor executed as a biography of Richard Boyle. Rather it has been designed as a series of studies based on Boyle's life experience which are intended as a contribution to a series of debates of general importance that are currently engaging the attention of historians in many countries. Each chapter, with the exception of the first which is introductory, is capable of standing on its own, but the book was also conceived as a whole and will hopefully be accepted as a contribution to understanding the mores of planter society in early-modern Ireland. To that extent this work is a logical continuation from *The Elizabethan Conquest of Ireland*, and a foretaste of what is to come in a book on a broader canvas, on which I have been engaged for several years, to be entitled *Ireland in the English Colonial System, 1580–1650*.

The composition of the book was very much a Galway achievement in that the research was undertaken during the vacation periods of the years 1975–9 and the writing was done in time stolen from my leisure activities. During those years I have been constantly vigilant to spare my students from mention of Richard Boyle, but the ideas that run through the book have been tried out on unsuspecting colleagues, graduate students and undergraduates. Furthermore the various works on social and intellectual history that are mentioned throughout the book have been the standard fare in my special option courses.

What was originally conceived as the final version of the book was completed in May 1979, but two events persuaded me to rethink some aspects of the work. The first of these was an invitation to present a paper on 'The Family Life of Richard Boyle' to the September 1979 conference of the Economic and Social History Society of Ireland. In the process of reducing what was a chapter in a book to acceptable lecture format I came to recognise several deficiencies in the chapter, and some comments from my audience further convinced me of its inadequacy. The most valuable contribution for me, in what was a lively discussion, was provided by Aidan Clarke who drew my attention to 'The Letter Book of George, Earl of Kildare', the existence of which was not even known to the staff members of the Public Record Office of Northern Ireland, who have custody of the document and who were present at the conference. This combination of factors persuaded me that I should defer publication until such time as I had an opportunity to re-fashion 'The Family Life'.

The second event that provoked misgivings was the publication in *The New York Review of Books* of an extremely laudatory review by Christopher Hill of J. R. Jacob's book, *Robert Boyle and the English Revolution: a Study of Social and Intellectual Change*. The review convinced me that the book was of central importance to my concerns, but I was unable to satisfy my curiosity because of a prolonged postal dispute in Ireland that did not permit the importation of books. Rather than suspend all activity until such time as the dispute was settled I decided to proceed with my work but I lived in dread lest the Jacob book rendered my work unnecessary. When I eventually procured a copy in September 1979 I was happy to discover that the structure of Robert Boyle's mind as outlined by Professor Jacob was very close to that which I had depicted for his father, which gave me confidence that both were correct. However, Professor Jacob's account of the formative influences on Robert Boyle aroused misgivings that I had previously voiced in the context of reviewing T. C. Barnard's *Cromwellian Ireland*, over the association of the Hartlib Circle with Ireland and with Irish Protestants. This rekindled doubt persuaded me that I should substitute what is now the concluding chapter of this book for what was originally intended as a bibliographical essay.

Research on this book was greatly facilitated by grants in 1976–7 and again in 1978–9 from the Royal Irish Academy under the Royal Irish Academy–British Academy Exchange Fellowship programme. These grants lightened the burden of research expenses for the vacation periods of those years. Assistance was also forthcoming from Gerald and Ursula Aylmer in the form of fellowship and hospitality at York while I was delving in the archives at Chatsworth House and in Sheffield. For this, too, I am exceedingly grateful. No book could be prepared without the assistance and co-operation of librarians and archivists, and I have been particularly fortunate in my dealings with the staffs of the Sheffield City Library, the National Library of Ireland, the British Library and the Kent Archives Office. A special word of thanks is due to the late Mr Tom Wragg and his assistant Peter Day at Chatsworth who did everything to make my prolonged visits to rural Derbyshire as pleasant as they were profitable. My wife Morwena and my daughter Solenn were most considerate over the extended absences of husband and father while the research was being done.

The writing of the first version was done in Galway and I wish to record my thanks to Eibhlín Ní Chnáimhsí for her expert typing. An opportunity was provided me to rewrite the fifth and the final chapters in ideal working conditions when I was invited to become a Member of the Institute for Advanced Study, Princeton for the academic year 1979–80. I wish to thank John Elliott and the other permanent members of the School of Historical Studies for this great honour, and I am grateful to my colleagues, the President and the Governing Authorities in Galway for making it possible for me to accept this invitation.

At the Institute for Advanced Study so many scholars offered advice on different aspects of the work that I find it possible to mention only those who read and commented on the entire text. These are Tim Breen, John Elliott, Drew Gilpin Faust, Geoffrey Hawthorn, Michael Heyd and Anthony Pagden. To these I am grateful for their suggestions even when I did not follow them, and the same holds true of the many more who commented on individual chapters. I wish also to thank Ms Peggy Van Sant and the secretarial staff of the School of Historical Studies who typed the final version with speed and efficiency. I am particularly grateful to Alison Quinn who prepared the index at very short notice, and Dáibhí Ó Cróinín kindly checked my reading of the proofs. The editorial staff of Cambridge University Press have been most considerate, and Ms Linda Randall did much to clarify my expression.

I have followed normal conventions in relation to dates and I have modernised the spelling of quotations throughout. Those who wish to pursue the subject further will be guided by the references, and a comprehensive bibliography to the Irish background is available in T. W. Moody, F. X. Martin and F. J. Byrne, eds., *A New History of Ireland* (Oxford, 1976), III, pp. 634–95.

NICHOLAS CANNY

University College, Galway
February 1982

1

The enigmatic career
of Richard Boyle, 1566–1643

The figure of Richard Boyle has, understandably, loomed large in every account of early-seventeenth-century Ireland, but in more recent years historians of pre-revolutionary England concerned with subjects as diverse as upward social mobility, and the development of modern science, the changing character of the family and the impact of puritanism on behaviour have found occasion to pass comment on Richard Boyle, either alone or in the context of his family.[1] Despite the several acknowledgements of his importance, historians have viewed Boyle from a distance, and would appear to have been repelled by the aura of suspicion which surrounded him in his own lifetime. Consequently, what is known of Boyle comes chiefly from official records, or the frequently hostile correspondence of his contemporaries. These have been employed to reveal the means by which Boyle acquired his property in Ireland, to trace his rise to political power during the reign of Charles I and to investigate how he used his wealth and power to preserve himself against the onslaught of Lord Deputy Wentworth who sought to deprive him of what were represented as ill-gotten gains.[2]

Twentieth-century historians have not been ignorant of the existence of Boyle's own papers,[3] but they have, for a variety of reasons, decided against admitting them as historical evidence. The most obvious of these reasons is that the pietistic self-righteousness that characterised Boyle's well-known 'True Remembrances' stood little chance of winning the sympathy of scholars who were the products of a sceptical or secular society.[4] Furthermore, the repeated uncritical endorsements that Richard

Boyle's interpretation of his own career received from a long succession of admiring writers – some of them in the pay of Boyle's descendants – have further served to convince historians that their initial estimate of the Boyle material has been the correct one.[5]

Historians resident in Ireland, most especially those who belonged to the Catholic Nationalist movement of the nineteenth and twentieth centuries, were less influenced by the first of these considerations, but they too reacted against the credulous tone associated with much of the writing of Richard Boyle, and thus came to despise the evidence on which such accounts were based. Instead they were attracted by the investigation of Richard Boyle's career undertaken by his enemies in his own lifetime.[6] This provided Irish Nationalist historians with plenty of material to support their contention that since landlord property in Ireland had been acquired initially by theft no moral obstacles stood in the way of expropriating that property.

The end-product of this assumption, in so far as it concerns our understanding of the career of Richard Boyle, was the thesis prepared in 1928 by James Carty on 'The Early Life and Times of Richard Boyle' which treated of the method by which Boyle had acquired his property in Ireland. Carty was, however, merely filling out what had already been sketched by T. M. Healy in two books with delightfully emotive titles: *Stolen Waters* and *The Great Fraud of Ulster*.[7] While the real villain in Healy's works was Sir Arthur Chichester, the author made it abundantly clear that he recognised that Chichester was merely employing those methods of defrauding the crown, and ultimately the native Irish proprietors, that had earlier been brought to perfection by 'Lord Cork, prince of patent mongers'.[8]

Now that adventurers such as Richard Boyle and Arthur Chichester were being exposed to attack it was inevitable that Thomas Wentworth, later Earl of Strafford, that indefatigable exposer of corruption among the New English elite, should be recognised as something of a hero by Irish Nationalist writers. As always, T. M. Healy pointed the way when he proclaimed that 'Strafford's head was taken off on the testimony of those whose plunder he had checked.'⁹ The guideline thus provided by Healy was followed slavishly by Hugh O'Grady in his highly eccentric book *Strafford and Ireland*,¹⁰ and the reputation of Boyle fared no better in the many biographies of Wentworth that were composed in England during the succeeding decades, the most notable being C. V. Wedgwood, *Strafford*.¹¹ Indeed, the only historians who strove to see some virtue in Richard Boyle were those who explained away the evidence that exposed his methods by arguing that he was the prototype of a capitalist entrepreneur whose ethical code was beyond the comprehension of such as Thomas Wentworth, whose ambition was thought to be the defence of an aristocratic culture.¹²

This brief historiographical account will help to explain why the surviving Boyle manuscripts at Chatsworth House and in the National Library of Ireland have received such scant recognition from historians, while relatively little attention has been devoted to Richard Boyle's 'Diary' and those of his papers which were published in the nineteenth century.¹³ The consequence of this for Richard Boyle has been that, regardless of the disposition of the historian towards him, the information on him that emerged was bound to be unflattering since it was based on hostile sources. In fact the only relief that his reputation has enjoyed has occurred fortuitously since in consulting Wentworth's papers, which are those most consistently hostile to Boyle, most historians have limited their attention to the eighteenth-century compilation prepared by W. Knowler which studiously omitted the more vituperative outbursts made against Boyle by Wentworth and his associates.¹⁴ Even this relief, as we shall see in the next chapter, was something of a mixed blessing.

However, in 1959 an end was brought to the moralising and historians were compelled to confront the evidence with the publication of H. F. Kearney, *Strafford in Ireland, 1633–41*, and with the completion of Terence O. Ranger's thesis, 'The Career of Richard Boyle, First Earl of Cork in Ireland, 1588–1643'. The portrait of Boyle presented in Kearney's book was no less unattractive than that delineated in previous studies on Thomas Wentworth, but what was new was the conclusion, based on a

close inspection of the surviving manuscripts of Thomas Wentworth, that 'Strafford was close in spirit to his adversary Richard
Boyle, for all the jibes which he levelled at him'. Ranger concurred
with this conclusion but his appraisal of the career of Richard
Boyle, which he made after sifting through the available manuscript material, achieved a balance that was absent in previous
accounts, because it made allowance for the constructive aspects
of Boyle's career while acknowledging the fraudulent means by
which Richard Boyle rose to wealth, power and eminence.[15]
The findings presented by Ranger have certainly added several
new dimensions to our understanding of Boyle but a further ex-
amination of the evidence is justified because some material
relating to Boyle has since come to light, and because recently
developed approaches to the appraisal of historical evidence
enable us to look with greater sympathy at the more personal
sources, and to place Boyle with greater confidence in the context
from which he sprang.[16] This study is intended to shed light on
what Richard Boyle considered to be the proper role of the New
English in Ireland, and what rewards he thought appropriate for
those, like himself, who fulfilled this role. It is also intended to
assist our understanding of how Boyle, who through his own effort
achieved such dramatic economic and social advancement, came
to perceive material success, and to reveal how his outlook on the
world and his relationship with his family and kin underwent
change as a result of his remarkable achievements.

The basic facts relating to Boyle's career are not in dispute;[17]
what was in contention in the seventeenth century, and what has
not yet been resolved, is how these facts should be interpreted.
Richard Boyle claimed descent from the Boyles of Herefordshire
from where his father, Roger Boyle, migrated to Kent and married
Joan Naylor, daughter of John Naylor of Canterbury. Roger
Boyle's occupation is unknown but the Naylors had long been
established in Canterbury and Roger and Joan Boyle settled in
Preston parish outside Canterbury. Their social position in Preston
is obscure but the fact that two of their three sons attended school
and proceeded to Cambridge suggests that they may have been of
yeoman status. Richard Boyle, 'the second son of a younger

brother', was born in Canterbury in October 1566, but unlike his elder brother John who attended King's School, Canterbury, Richard was educated locally at Faversham. This may be explained by the death of Roger Boyle in 1576 but still John and Richard matriculated together in 1583 at Bene't (now Corpus Christi) College, Cambridge. Richard, having failed to take his degree at Cambridge, acquired some legal and secretarial experience in London, and in 1588, a penniless but ambitious young man, went to seek his fortune in Ireland. In 1590 he secured appointment as deputy escheator and was thus strategically placed to discover flaws in the land titles of many proprietors, principally in Connacht and Munster. With the co-operation of other officials he succeeded in having the recently established crown title passed to himself at ludicrously low rents. These gains were augmented by lands in County Limerick which should have come to the crown following the suicide of the owner Edward Apsley, but which Boyle – again through the misuse of office – acquired by his marriage in 1595 to the co-heiress Joan Apsley. Thereafter Munster was the principal theatre of his attention and he extended his property there, this time at the expense of the established church as well as the crown. The death of his wife in child-birth in 1598 was something of a setback for Richard Boyle, but this too had its advantages since it left him free to seek another advantageous connection through marriage, an opportunity which he deferred until 1603. By 1595 Richard Boyle was a landowner of consequence, but it seemed that he could never enjoy the profits of his recent gains because these were threatened on two fronts: by rebellion which was general throughout Ireland in 1594–1603 and which made Boyle's position there untenable between 1598 and 1600; and by the legal charges brought against him by more senior or more scrupulous English officials in Ireland who seemed to consider that the stability of the country, and with it the security of their own property in Ireland, had been upset by Boyle's prying into men's titles.[18] These charges led to Boyle's imprisonment on numerous occasions both in Ireland and England during the later 1590s, and it was only by what today would be regarded as chance, and the support of Sir Robert Cecil and George Carew, that he was able to return to Ireland in 1600. There as a servant of Carew, then president of Munster, Boyle obtained a royal pardon for those of his earlier actions which had exposed him to charges of fraud. Having thus laid to rest the ghost which had threatened to pursue him through life, Boyle was left free – again through Carew's solicitation – to marry Catherine Fenton, daughter of the Irish Secretary, Sir Geoffrey Fenton, and to build his fortune anew, this time based principally on the lands which Sir Walter Ralegh had acquired in Munster by grant from the crown and purchase from the church, and which Boyle bought from him in 1602 for £1,000.

From this new beginning Boyle entered a phase of his career which can be likened to that of poacher turned game-keeper. While he still had a keen eye for the chance of bettering himself, his principal concern was to secure his estates against the prying eye of would-be speculators. This he did, on the recommendation of his father-in-law Sir Geoffrey Fenton, by exploiting a series of government commissions to obtain fresh patents for those of his estates whose titles were in doubt, and to improve upon the tenure by which his lands were held from the crown. The result was that by 1614 practically all of his estates were held by free and common soccage (the best possible tenure from the proprietor's point of view), and his title seemed to be above question in law. Subsequently the terms by which the land was rented from him were adjusted in his favour to such an extent that his normal income in rents improved from £4,000 in 1613 to an estimated £20,000 in the 1630s.[19] By then Richard Boyle enjoyed an income from rents far greater than that of any other subject of King Charles I,[20] which explains why he negotiated yet another comprehensive patent from the crown to ward against every eventuality that might threaten his estates.

Contemporaneous with this improvement in Boyle's estates and financial position, there occurred an elevation to the social position commensurate with such wealth: a knighthood in July 1603; membership of the provincial council in Munster, 12 March 1607; membership of the Irish privy council, 15 February 1613; a barony, September 1616, and the earldom of Cork in October

1620. Thereafter, Boyle extended his influence beyond the province of Munster and secured appointment as one of the two lords justices of Ireland 1629–33, as lord high treasurer of Ireland from 1631 onwards and finally on 28 June 1640 he attained one mark of distinction to which he had long aspired, membership of the English privy council. This upward progression was interrupted when Sir Thomas Wentworth, governor of Ireland 1633–41, investigated how Cork had achieved such spectacular wealth and eminence in such a short time. It appeared initially that the power-struggle which ensued would result in the dismemberment of the vast Boyle estates, but after some major reverses, including the loss of considerable property to the church and a fine of £15,000 to the crown, Cork emerged as the final victor when his testimony at the attainder of Wentworth, by then Earl of Strafford, before the English Houses of Parliament contributed to the conviction of Strafford. Then, on his return to Ireland in 1642, Cork was witness once more to a sudden overthrow of all he had gained, as his lands in Munster were engulfed by rebellion. As a result, many of the English tenants who occupied his estates fled to England, his castle at Lismore was besieged by rebels and his son Lewis was slain in battle. Nevertheless, even to his death in 1643, Cork was convinced that the rebels on this occasion, as in the 1590s, would be defeated, and that their overthrow would result in the further consolidation of his family in their Munster lands.[21]

Richard Boyle's other outstanding achievement was to become the father of fifteen children, ten of whom outlived him. His surviving sons, apart from Robert, the youngest, who was to achieve fame in a different sphere, were to continue the fight for the Boyle territory, and after 1660 these lands were safely under the control of Richard, who succeeded to the title, Earl of Cork; Roger, Baron Broghill, and subsequently Earl of Orrery, and Francis who was to become Viscount Shannon. Cork's daughters also contributed to the lustre of the Boyle family both through the connections which their marriages brought, and through their own talents. For example, Catherine, the wife of Arthur Jones, Viscount Ranelagh, who with her husband fled their residence at Athlone and took refuge in England following the 1641 rebellion, established a reputation there as being one of the leading female intellectuals of her generation, and her residence in exile became a known resort of puritan divines and scientists.[22] Cork's youngest surviving daughter, Mary, gained notoriety for two reasons: firstly because of her defiance of her father's wishes in rejecting a series of suitors that he had selected for her, before secretly engaging herself to marry Charles Rich, a man with poor prospects, being but the second son of the Earl of Warwick; and secondly in later life, as Countess of Warwick (an elevation that nobody in 1641 could have anticipated), when she became an exemplary witness of puritan conviction and virtue.[23] These, however, were only two of the truly gifted children whose upbringing and education were a matter of the greatest concern to their father.

These facts alone bear witness to a career which was remarkable by the standards of any generation. In the pre-industrial era, however, when men encountered greater difficulty than subsequently in breaking loose from the social and economic constraints which generally keep them bound to the condition in which they are born, Boyle's career was truly exceptional. It comes as no surprise, therefore, that the success of Richard Boyle became, in his own generation, such a subject of envy, curiosity and controversy that the ensuing debate merely added to the mystery of how it had been achieved or what it signified.

2

The hostile witness: Boyle's career through
the eyes of his enemies

The facts relating to the career and family of Richard Boyle were never in dispute, but opinion is divided on how they should be interpreted. Seventeenth-century Englishmen, who generally assumed that history taught by example, were convinced that a career which had followed such a spectacular and erratic course must have some metaphysical meaning, but there was no agreement on what it did signify. The political opponents of Boyle in the 1630s alleged that his wealth and power were based on corruption, and that his fall, which they sought to bring about by exposing this corruption, would serve as a lesson to all others who might seek to elevate themselves above their rightful station.

The first to express this view was Sir Francis Annesley, Lord Mountnorris,[1] a former accomplice of Boyle, and, like him, one of the New English who had come to political prominence in Ireland during the first half of the seventeenth century. It was Mountnorris who most resented Cork's appointment as joint lord justice with Loftus, Viscount Ely, for the years 1629–33, but even before then tensions had developed between the two, since Mountnorris, who was primarily an official, was threatened by Boyle's stated intention to participate in Irish politics as a spokesman of the planter interest.[2] The rivalry between the planter and official in government became embittered once Cork, revealing that he had fixed ideas on how best the country should be governed, urged the displacement of Mountnorris as an obstacle in the way of good government.[3] Rather than permit himself to be outmanoeuvred by Cork, Mountnorris called for the appointment of an Englishman as sole governor, and after Thomas Wentworth had been

nominated, he sought to poison his mind against Cork. This
became all the more critical to Mountnorris when it appeared that
Cork had secured himself in the favour of the deputy-elect by
arranging a marriage between his son and heir, Richard, Viscount
Dungarvan, and Elizabeth Clifford, niece to Wentworth's deceased
wife.[4]

The main thrust of the Mountnorris attack was to revive
memories of the means by which Cork had risen to prominence.
The wealth and power of Cork and his confederates in government, asserted Mountnorris, were based on a 'rotten foundation'
which would collapse if Wentworth would 'pursue them with any
strictness of justice'.[5] More specifically, Mountnorris assured
Wentworth that despite the several patents which Cork had had
passed to secure his title to his estates these were still vulnerable
because they included impropriated ecclesiastical property. The
earl's vast estate, which, Mountnorris alleged, was a matter of
such pride to Cork, was in reality 'much more great than good,
and yet far from that greatness which is published', since it
included 'a bishopric or two besides many other church livings...
swallowed up within it, which perhaps in time will be distinguished, and the king's goose will perhaps come up with the
feathers'.[6] What Mountnorris was undoubtedly seeking was the
disruption of the match, but although failing in this he did outline
the strategy that Wentworth was to pursue in his onslaught against
Cork. Furthermore, he anticipated Wentworth in depicting the
supposed character defects of this unscrupulous despoiler of the
church. Cork, he alleged, was factious, corrupt, vain and boastful
of his property and influence, while he was so given to using people
to serve his purposes that not even his children could trust him.
This, claimed Mountnorris, was evident from the several marriage
alliances which Cork had negotiated 'only to serve present turns';
and which were subsequently dissolved.[7]

The information that Wentworth gleaned from the Mountnorris correspondence may have weakened his resolve to encourage the Clifford match,[8] but the deputy was not surprised by the
general thrust of the revelations. These in fact confirmed his
suspicions, shared by many senior officials in England, that the

entire generation of Englishmen who had acquired fortunes in Ireland since the accession of James I had succeeded in doing so by deceiving the crown. Thus Wentworth was not alone in thinking that Ireland was 'a kingdom abandoned for these late years to every man that could please himself to purchase what best liked him for his money'.[9] Not even Mountnorris, as he later learned to his cost, was exempt from Wentworth's blanket condemnation of the New English as 'a strange people their own privates altogether their study without any regard at all to the public'.[10] Wentworth was objecting not to the fact that the New English had treated Ireland as a colony to be exploited, but rather that in exploiting it they themselves had been the sole beneficiaries and that the crown and church had profited nothing. They had, as a consequence, in Wentworth's eyes, forfeited their entitlement to be considered and treated as social equals, and, as deputy, Wentworth invariably regarded the New English as degenerate colonials. At the outset of his career in Ireland, Wentworth likened his intervention among the New English to that of 'the stork (as it is in the fable)...among those frogs'.[11] His time in Ireland gave him no reason to modify this opinion since, towards the end of his deputyship, he reported that he was lost for companionship having forged no friendships in Ireland where he had been 'dropped here into a New World'.[12]

Wentworth's conviction that in dealing with the New English he was treating with colonials, and his concealment of this assumption from them, explains much of what was thought to be erratic, unpredictable and unconventional in his behaviour.[13] However, since in Wentworth's calculus wealth and rank among the New English were taken to be true measures of corruption, it was inevitable that the Earl of Cork should be isolated for particularly disrespectful treatment and disdainful comment. Furthermore, since Cork was reasonably well connected at court and, in any contest with Wentworth, could count on sympathy among England's ruling hierarchy on grounds of age, position and past service to the crown,[14] it was essential to the lord deputy, if he was to succeed in his purpose of presenting the disgrace of Cork as a fearful example to all who might oppose his authority, that he first undermine his credibility in England. Besides that, as Wentworth emphasised on several occasions, he stood little chance of implementing his schemes for Ireland unless he could make it manifest there that Cork was subservient to him. This local consideration was one reason why Wentworth opened his campaign against Cork with the relatively minor issue of the positioning of the Boyle family tomb in St Patrick's cathedral. The ostensible objection to the monument was that its location contravened liturgical regulations but Wentworth revealed his more fundamental opposition to this symbol of Boyle family prestige when he remarked that if it remained in position men would think

> the king's deputy were crouching to a Dr Weston, to a Geoffrey Fenton, to an earl of Cork and his lady, or if you will to a Kinalmeaky his second son, the veriest shark in the realm as they say, or to those sea nymphs his daughters, with coronets upon their heads, their hair dishevelled down upon their shoulders.[15]

This combination of factors ensured that, until he had achieved his ends, Wentworth's comments on Cork were certain to be negative, and whenever he had an opportunity to investigate Boyle's past career he gave precedence to those episodes most likely to bring him into disrepute over those likely to bring revenue to the crown. This explains why as much correspondence is to be found in Wentworth's papers on such unpromising matters as Boyle's early career in Connacht and the Boyle monument, as on such potentially lucrative issues as the impropriation of ecclesiastical lands. The frequent calls on Wentworth by Lords Clifford and Goring for advice on the marriages of their children with those of Boyle also provided Wentworth with an opportunity to comment on Cork's personal life to the further detriment of his reputation.

The importance which Wentworth attached to his confrontation with Cork and his misgivings over the outcome are reflected in the frequency with which Wentworth portrayed his adversary in Gargantuan terms. He was, for example, described variously as 'that great giant' and 'the most violent and passionate man in the whole world';[16] his collection of papers was said to be so great 'that few men in Christendom have besides himself';[17] the tomb which he erected in St Patrick's was reported to be 'the most slanderous and barbarous piece standing···in any church in Christendom'.[18] Continuing in this vein, the various misdemeanours of which Cork was accused assumed similar enormous proportions. The erection of the Boyle tomb was reputed to be 'such a thing···as was neither done nor seen before', and since it was represented as being a symbol of 'the vanity and insolent novelties of the earl of Cork' it was declared idolatrous;[19] the incorporation of Lismore diocesan lands into the Boyle inheritance was described by Wentworth as 'a direct rapine upon the patrimony of the church, a coal taken from the altar', and as such was deemed sacrilegious;[20] the impropriation of the College of Youghal was held responsible for causing what had been 'a light of religion and charity [to become] clouded under a palpable darkness of impiety and rapine';[21] while in the 'anti-Christian' business of appropriating vicarages, Cork was likened to John, Bishop of Constantinople, who if 'but let alone he would have been his universal vicar'.[22]

This series of superlatives should be sufficient to warn scholars that they should not look to the Wentworth papers for any objective statement on the character of Richard Boyle. However, the fact that most of these comments were excluded from Knowler's edition of Wentworth's letters has meant that many historians have failed to recognise a purpose behind Wentworth's comments on Cork. The consequence for Cork's reputation is that it has never recovered from the witty and pungent remarks which appear so frequently in Wentworth's correspondence with Archbishop Laud. This very success of Wentworth and his associates makes it essential that the Wentworth material be reviewed critically in order to establish precisely what message was being conveyed, to test the interpretation against the evidence which derives from other sources and to explain why Wentworth's version of events has enjoyed such lasting appeal among historians.

The study of Wentworth's papers suggests that, in seeking to denigrate Boyle, Wentworth and his correspondents moulded Cork's personality to fit a caricature. The caricature they chose was that of the anti-noble; that is one who despite his elevation to social eminence lacked the qualities of a true noble, and whose life, as a consequence, was a parody of everything noble. This caricature, as we shall see, was a deliberate distortion of the equally simplistic image of himself that Boyle had delineated in his apologia for his career, and Boyle's subsequent reflections on his life were partly in response to the allegations which he knew were being made against him by Wentworth. This dialogue in itself is fascinating, but one attraction which Wentworth's version of events has held for historians – particularly those of the twentieth century involved in discussion over the social consequences of upward mobility – is that the caricature which Wentworth drew of Boyle contained all the elements which such historians expected or hoped to find in the personality of one who had engaged in what was a truly super-human feat of social leap-frogging.[23]

The first element of Wentworth's caricature represented Cork – the impecunious commoner who had risen to the rank of a noble – as one who had, as a result of his dramatic elevation, lost all respect for hierarchy. This feature was cultivated by reference to his 'greedy and insatiable desires' and by his pretentious exhibitionism, which, it was alleged, was proof that Cork, like all other members of the New English elite, considered himself 'great and magnificent' and of 'a much higher stature' than he really was.[24] This point was further sustained by reference to Cork's boasting of his wealth, which was such, it was said, that his 'narrative legends concerning the provident purchases' he had made in Ireland 'and the liberal donations' he had made of them justified him being dubbed 'a Sir Tristram True Stock with a witness'.[25] The most telling point against Cork on this score was the boast which he supposedly made to his son-in-law Kildare – the representative of the oldest noble house in Ireland – that 'he was a better gentleman than any Geraldine'.[26]

The second element of the caricature was that Cork, unlike a man of true nobility who was expected by nature to be generous, open-handed and liberal, was mean, covetous and tight-fisted. Even before he met Cork, Wentworth confronted him with the charge that his haggling over the terms of the Clifford match was 'a proceeding of too great meanness to descend to for any gain or advantage so ever'.[27] Similarly, in commenting on the marriage of Lettice Boyle to George, the son of Lord Goring, Wentworth repeatedly referred to Cork's dishonourable behaviour in complaining over what he considered to be extremely generous terms on Goring's part. Even where there was some apparent evidence of Cork's munificence, as in the endowment of free-schools and almshouses, this was dismissed as a mere cover for spoliation of the church.[28] Cork's attachment to money became so legendary among Wentworth's acquaintances that Lord Clifford reported that he would 'cry out more for the prick of a lancet where money is drawn from his than others would do for a cupping and scarification'.[29]

This particular trait was linked to a third, which alleged that Cork's meanness extended even to his own children. The purpose of this accusation was, seemingly, again intended to portray Cork as the antithesis of a true noble, since it showed him to be attached to money for its own sake, whereas true nobles supposedly appreciated wealth only as a means towards the glorification and enhancement of their house and lineage. In commenting on the household allowance that Cork, then a widower, had provided to his daughter the Countess of Barrymore, Wentworth remarked that 'if she gain by him her luck and fortune shall be better than others and certainly set him far aside his intentions'.[30] Wentworth's observations on Boyle's various marriage settlements illustrated the same point. Of these observations, the most damaging was that on 'his narrow heart' in providing for his heir Viscount Dungarvan. The estate finally allotted to Dungarvan, claimed Wentworth, fell short of that promised on the occasion of the marriage treaty when, he asserted, Cork 'laughed and rubbed those filthy hands of his' and boasted that the estates assigned to his son included 'I know not how many parks and demesnes [which] should be no part of the bargain'.[31] The supposed shortfall permitted Wentworth to draw the conclusion that if Cork performed 'thus nobly and liberally towards his own house and bowels, how will he deal with strangers, or how can honest men ever admit of his company with honour and safety'.[32]

Cork was also portrayed as behaving ignobly towards the church, since he was accused of being a spoiler rather than a defender of ecclesiastical property. In religious matters generally, Cork was shown to be a hypocrite rather than a true believer, and this was sustained by reference to his supposed allegation that Wentworth, by introducing Laudian liturgical innovations to Ireland, was reviving popery. Such a charge, it was stated, was particularly discordant coming from the man responsible for the erection of the Boyle monument which was declared to be more profane and idolatrous than St Patrick's purgatory.[33] Further-more, Cork's spiritual exercises, such as his reading of Perkins' *Cases of Conscience*, and his attendance 'devoutly' at two sermons each week were declared a mockery of Christianity in one who still enjoyed the fruits of church property.[34]

The final element of the caricature, and that most damaging to his reputation, was that Cork could never be trusted to fulfil a promise, and that he covered his misdeeds by lies and half truths. This, at a time when a man's word was synonymous with his honour, was the most devastating criticism of all. In 1635, Wentworth reported that since he first had 'the happiness of his conversation' he had 'never known [Cork] to deliver one truth', and on another occasion, he advised Clifford against seeking any promise from Cork since he was 'sufficiently foresworn already'.[35] Yet again, Wentworth remarked that he had learned from experi-ence 'to believe [Cork] intends to be a business when I see it done', and as a safeguard against Cork's deviousness he advised Clifford to keep, as Cork himself did, a copy of all incoming and outgoing correspondence. As a final insult he supposed that 'for all that' Clifford did not hold Cork's letters 'worthy the pains to read'. Thus as Wentworth portrayed it to Lord Clifford, the only advantage that might accrue from the marriage alliance with the Boyles was that Lady Dungarvan would bear a son 'that so there may be some noble blood inheritable to that great estate'.[36] These descriptions were intended to undermine his subject's credi-bility in England but the fact that Wentworth, in his dealings with Cork, withheld from him the honour due to a noble, and acted upon the advice that he was giving to others, was more damaging to Cork's standing in Ireland than anything that was written. For example, the deputy reported to England how in conversation with Cork, he had referred to those holding impropriated vicarages as 'the most pestilent vermin in the whole kingdom', and how when one aggrieved clergyman sought the recovery of his vicarage he, without warning, 'told my Lord [of Cork] in plain terms the poor man should have justice · · · all this to his face before the whole council'.[37] Other examples of Wentworth's contemptuous behaviour towards Cork are his frequently unannounced visits to dinner at the earl's Dublin residence, and his mocking reports on these occasions to his confidants in England. On the eve of one such visit Wentworth reported of his host that he and the other guests would 'have half a dozen good loud storms from him in despite of who soever says nay'.[38] The greatest insult accorded by Wentworth to Cork was, however, his appointment of John Atherton in 1638 to the vacant see of Waterford and Lismore. Atherton's sole qualification for the post was his appetite for land which, claimed Wentworth, was such that the Earl of Cork would 'think the devil is let loose upon him forth of his chain'.[39]

In assessing Wentworth's view of Cork, allowance should be made for the fact that he, who at the best of times was intemperate, may have been provoked into making the outrageous statements that he did by his knowledge of the self-image that Cork was cultivating. The 'True Remembrances' was first produced in 1623 and updated in 1632, and since Cork made a point of disseminating it widely it is probable that a copy came to Wentworth's attention. Even without its assistance Wentworth quickly became familiar with the cast of his future adversary who, in his very first letter to the deputy-elect, congratulated him on his appointment, and assured him that he in no way begrudged him his elevation since he himself had 'never thirsted after high employments', and looked forward therefore 'the more willingly · · · to retire to [his] former country life'.[40]

Provocation apart, it should be evident from the foregoing remarks that Wentworth at no point was concerned to present a fair interpretation of Cork's career. Instead, his chief purpose in mentioning Cork or associating with him was to denigrate or humiliate him with a view to discrediting him in England and undermining his authority in Ireland. The fact that this was not generally appreciated by historians, many of whom have taken Wentworth's remarks at their face value, is explained by their using the printed edition of Wentworth's letters where the more scarifying passages, which are the key to the whole, are omitted. Furthermore, as was mentioned, Wentworth's comments of Cork have had a special appeal for certain historians because they lent support to some general hypotheses on social developments in early-modern England. Finally, and most fundamentally, some historians have looked in despair to Wentworth as the only reliable source of information on Richard Boyle, because his references and interpretations relate to ascertainable fact, something that cannot be said for Cork's own case which, to the rationalist mind at least, lacks credibility because it depends on the readers' acceptance of special pleading, happy coincidence and divine intervention in human affairs as valid explanations of historical events.

3

The mental world of Richard Boyle

Information on how Cork saw himself or wished himself to be seen is scattered throughout his voluminous papers, but when the various references are pieced together the whole conforms to the pattern which he first delineated in 1623, and updated in 1632, in the short apologia for his career known as the 'True Remembrances'.[1]

Cork appears in his self-portrait to be possessed of a character as simple as that attributed to him by Wentworth, but with a scale of values the direct opposite to that with which Wentworth had credited him. The self-image cultivated by Boyle was that of the virtuous man, free from ambition, whose wealth and possessions had come to him almost by default, and which he cherished only in so far as they could be employed to honour God, serve the king, strengthen the commonwealth and enhance the reputation of his family and posterity.[2] The motto 'God's providence is mine inheritance' which Boyle chose at the time of his ennoblement encapsulated this explanation of his worldly success. However, the knowledge that his astonishing social ascent was a subject of controversy forced him – although reluctantly – to dwell on those episodes which others had alleged to be ethically questionable. Since, on such occasions, he was striving to convince the incredulous or the ungodly of his righteousness, Cork argued his case on secular grounds, but the eschatological view was always the dominant one, and secular arguments were introduced merely to demonstrate that nobody had suffered injustice in the unfolding of God's plan. A study of Boyle's explanation of his acquisition of the Ralegh lands, of his behaviour in Connacht in the 1590s and

of the issues which gave rise to his conflict with Wentworth in the
1630s will serve to illustrate how he dovetailed secular arguments
to comply with the all-encompassing providential explanation of
his career.

The Ralegh lands were acquired legitimately by Boyle, but
nevertheless his enemies of the 1630s frequently hinted that he
had been particularly far-sighted and worldly-wise in his purchase.
More to the point, Ralegh's widow and surviving son considered
that in view of the benefit which had accrued to him Cork should
be compelled, in equity if not in justice, to make some reparation
to them for the unwise sale made by Ralegh.[3] Cork's response to
this particular challenge was that he had 'really paid the full price
and value' of the lands and he called upon the deceased Walter
Ralegh to bear witness to this. The purchase price of £1,000 in
gold was, he claimed, quite considerable in 1602 considering that
the lands were 'then utterly waste and yielded him no profit'.
Furthermore, the money was then particularly valuable to Ralegh
because it helped to procure his release from prison. In any event,
claimed Cork, his outlay was far in excess of the £1,000 since he
had been forced to pay £2,700 to former tenants and to present a
gift of 1,000 marks to Queen Elizabeth to free the land of unwise
'estates and incumberances'. His expense, he insisted, did not end
there, since he was put to yet further charge to obtain letters
patent to remedy 'flaws and imperfections' in his title to the tithes.
Then, as a final settlement, he had presented Ralegh with a
further 1,000 marks towards the cost of fitting him for his last
voyage to Guiana. That Ralegh was then fully satisfied was
evident, claimed Boyle, from his refusal of a further £100 in
French crowns which Boyle proffered him at Sir Randal Cleyton's
house in Cork in full view of a company – the surviving members
of which were close confederates of Boyle. In refusing this offer
Ralegh allegedly took his son Walter by the hand and pronounced
as follows:[4]

> Watt you see how nobly my Lord Boyle has entertained and
> supplied me and my friends, and therefore I charge you
> upon my blessing, if it please God that you outlive me and
> return that you never question the Lord Boyle for any thing

that I have sold him, for I do lay my curse upon my wife and children if they ever question any of the purchases his lordship hath made to me, for if he had not bought any Irish land of me, by my fall it would have come to the crown, and then one Scot or other would have begged it from whom neither I nor mine would have had any thing for it, nor such courtesies as now I have received.

This self-righteous outburst was clearly intended to deflect Lady Ralegh from further pursuing her suit, and when it did not produce the desired result Cork spared no effort, when he next visited England, to have the matter brought to an abrupt conclusion in the law courts.

It is clear from this study of Cork's defence of his title to the Ralegh lands that he believed initially that a graphic account of his ethical behaviour would be sufficient to preserve him from further molestation. On other occasions Cork was aware that a close investigation of his past behaviour would harm rather than enhance his prospects of success in whatever dispute was taking place and he was then forced to advance the propitious outcome of events as proof that the initial transactions had been worthy. This characteristic emerges most clearly from Cork's justification of his activity in Connacht during the 1590s. This business, briefly referred to out of sequence in the 'True Remembrances' as 'some purchases',[5] was obviously not considered by him as a notable stage in his progress towards fame and fortune. Cork's decision to exclude it from among the list of God's benefactions was to some extent justified since the rent from this property constituted a negligible part of his enormous income during the 1630s. Its omission does not imply, however, that Cork acknowledged the episode to be unworthy either of himself or God, as is clear from his assertion in the 1640s, when his title was again being investigated, that it was 'known to all men in those parts' that when Connacht was submerged in the general rebellion of the 1590s he had maintained a garrison at Bealick castle 'even when all the lands were wasted and overrun...and defended and supplied it with men, munition and victual at my own charge'. The supposed defence of this strategically important castle which Cork described, even to the improbable detail of the beleagured garrison being driven by thirst to drink their own urine, was considered by him to justify his ownership of the Connacht lands. Even though the castle was lost on that occasion its subsequent recovery and reconstruction were cited as further endorsements of the worthiness of his motives, and Cork spitefully referred to Lord Deputy Wentworth's acceptance of hospitality at Bealick during his visit to Connacht in 1635 as further proof that the crown was the ultimate beneficiary of even his own most dubious actions.[6]

Cork's self-righteousness and sense of mission did not fail him even when he was indicted by Wentworth for having encroached upon church property. Despite having paid, against his better judgement, a fine of £15,000 in settlement of the suit over Youghal College, Cork never conceded the merit of Wentworth's case against him, and left among his papers his book of evidence which he was satisfied would also convince his posterity of his innocence.[7] Cork insisted, however, that it 'did not much grieve' him whenever any impropriated lands were 'restored to the church from which they were taken', and he reconciled himself to the fine of £15,000, it being 'the rod that punished other men's errors' in himself, and which he therefore 'silently and patiently kissed'.[8] Even then, however, Cork did not admit that the church had suffered any wrong as a result of having had its property appropriated by him. On the contrary, he insisted repeatedly that the ecclesiastical no less than the secular property which had come into his hands had been better employed to godly purposes by him than they would have been by anybody else. Thus, throughout his correspondence, one encounters frequent protestations that the means by which he acquired his property was irrelevant since his principal concern at all times had been 'to give advancement to the affairs of the crown and to the good of this commonwealth, in which to the view of all men' he had 'bestowed good shares of my substance acquired here by God's blessings, for the public works thereof as far as any' other noble in Ireland had done 'at least these hundred years'.[9]

The 'public works' or 'commonwealth work' to which Cork referred included the settlement of his vast estates with English tenants, the erection and peopling of fortified towns, the construction of churches, bridges and defensible castles, the maintenance of preachers and the foundation of schools and almshouses.[10] As early as 1613, prior to his visit to court to negotiate fresh letters patent for his estates, Boyle had it reported to England that he had 'preferred the public good before his peculiar commodity' by introducing 'more and better sort of English tenants than any man in Ireland', and that he had 'shown himself a careful builder up of the churches upon his land and a maintainer of good preachers to teach and instruct his tenants':[11] a verdict which was upheld in the account of the commissioners in 1622 who reported on the various English plantations in Ireland.[12] This witness alone must have satisfied Cork that his life's work was justified in the eyes of God, and he was equally convinced that the crown had suffered no wrong even through loss of rents. That which he paid for his estates was, he averred, 'as great rents...as ever was answered...and as much as was intended he should pay', while he boasted that the subsidies he paid to the crown were greater than those levied on any other subject in the three kingdoms.[13] The ultimate proof of his innocence on this score was his highly stylised and possibly fabricated accounts of five royal audiences in each of which Boyle was received to favour, was commended for his merits and was praised and rewarded for his previous service to the crown and kingdom.[14]

This summary of Boyle's explanations and justifications for these three episodes in his career indicates firstly that he did not draw any clear distinction between secular and religious pursuits, and secondly that worthy ends justified even what appeared the most doubtful of actions. Thus while at one level Boyle was disclaiming accountability for his actions by attributing his success to divine benefactions, he was simultaneously citing the ultimate good that had derived from his stewardship as proof that what he held was in trust from God. This explains why Boyle was able, without appearing contradictory, to explain his entire career in providential terms.

Cork attributed his initial move to Ireland in 1588 to divine intervention since 'it pleased the Almighty by his divine providence' to take him 'as it were by the hand', where the continued 'blessing of God whose heavenly providence' had first 'guided' him to Ireland enabled him to enrich his 'poor estate'.[15] This enrichment, he suggested, came about by three stages: firstly by his marriage to Joan Apsley which brought him land worth £500 per annum, this, as he put it, 'being the beginning and foundation' of his fortune; then by his nomination in 1602 to the clerkship of the council in Munster, which 'was the second rise that God gave his fortune' and thirdly by the purchase for £1,000 of the Ralegh estates, 'then altogether waste and desolate. . . untenanted and of no value to him'. Finally, 'as the crown of all [his] blessings', Boyle mentioned his marriage in July 1603 to Catherine Fenton.[16] Thereafter, Cork saw himself as having been left by God to make use of those benefits which had been given him, and his increased prosperity satisfied him that he still enjoyed God's blessing. The intervention of Wentworth – 'the rod that punished other men's errors' in himself[17] – was interpreted by Cork as a testing time for his faith in God, but subsequent developments, most notably the trial, conviction and execution of Thomas Wentworth, were presented as evidence that Cork had endured the test. Cork accepted as his earthly reward for his resignation to suffering[18] the vindication of his honour before the English upper house, where Wentworth's charges against him were declared 'false and slanderous aspersions'. The Earl of Cork thus had no doubt that it was the hand of God which had effected the reversal of fortunes which brought Strafford 'to the bar upon his knees (I sitting in my place covered)'.[19] He further asserted that this 'dejection' of one who had appeared all-powerful bore witness to God's power, and exemplified 'the uncertainty whereunto the greatest men are subject to'.[20]

When Cork's servants at Lismore learned of Strafford's fall, they were even more convinced than their master that God had intervened on his behalf because this development coincided with the indictment of Radcliffe for treason, the sudden death of Christopher Wandesford and the execution of Bishop Atherton who had been found guilty of sodomy and adultery. John Walley, the steward of Lismore castle, proved himself an apt pupil of his master when he proclaimed that 'the downfall and ruin of all such as [had] risen up or been raised against [the Earl of Cork]', 'when duly considered' did 'plainly declare it to be the powerful work of God'.[21] Walley, too, was as convinced as his master that this further mark of divine favour was the final proof that, from the beginning, Richard Boyle had been specially chosen by 'the omnipotent God' as 'the example for all men to imitate'.[22] Indeed, he thought the evidence of the immediate past so persuasive that he expected that all men would thereafter be afraid 'to attempt any unjust troubles against' his master.[23] In writing to Cork, Walley was sure of a sympathetic audience when he drew the moral that:

> It is the wrathful hand of the Almighty that casts down the proud and lofty from their seats and exalts the meek and lowly; for it could not be thought that the Lord Lieutenant's tyrannising and most intemperate hand in the government of this kingdom would long persist, the violence thereof was so great, and on the contrary it is evident, how the great and merciful God doth daily bless and preserve the just and upright man to make him to flourish, in so much as by his divine providence his enemies shall fall before him and vanish in a moment; hath not the omnipotent God placed your Lordship in the seat of honour and justice to judge him who did thirst after your ruin had it been in his power, and in like manner hath the lord of heaven cast out of your Lordship's way his confederates Radcliffe and Wandesford, the first detected with treason and the other dead even upon a sudden, not two days sick...after these followed the Bishop of Waterford, who though he were not to be ranked with the former in the power of doing ill had as malicious a heart as any of them: he ended his life with a halter.[24]

Even without the prompting of John Walley we can be sure that Cork would not have failed to attribute this remarkable coincidence to God's direct involvement in his affairs, and like Walley he too would have dovetailed this episode to fit the general pattern that he had imposed on his career. Many more examples of such a moving and largely fictional reconstruction of events are to be found among the papers of Richard Boyle but it is not necessary to cite them because it is clear from what has been quoted that in every case the course of events was made to conform to the pattern of the 'True Remembrances' where beneficial consequences and providential manifestations were also mentioned as the ultimate proof that Boyle had at all times acted honourably and in the interests of the public good. The evidence suggests, moreover, that Boyle was not involved in an exercise of covering his misdeeds by citing pious purposes, but was so completely convinced by his own version of events that even those parts which we know to be pure invention assumed a subjective truth for himself. This is suggested by the fact that some of his more graphic professions of innocence were addressed to intimate friends such as Sir Thomas Stafford, or to individuals of no political consequence such as his servant John Walley.[25] Furthermore, in the case against Cork which Wentworth pursued most ardently, that concerning Youghal College, the lord deputy mentioned repeatedly that he knew Cork to be as assured of his innocence as Wentworth was convinced he was guilty.[26] The most compelling evidence that Cork considered himself innocent is the difficulty which his closest relatives encountered in persuading him to compound for £15,000 rather than permit his case, which they considered extremely weak, to go to trial.[27]

The formula which Cork employed to convince others of his innocence and himself of his righteousness was, as was mentioned, an amalgam of secular and metaphysical explanations, but Cork himself clearly considered his ability to explain events in providential terms to be the most persuasive element of his argument. As far as the secular rationalisations are concerned one does not have to look far to trace their origins. Cork's insistence on the superiority of knowledge derived from experience, his claim for exemption from the strict enforcement of the law and his argument for moral relativity were all characteristics of the thought pattern of Elizabethan adventurers in Ireland.[28] The fact that the young Boyle had been pursued by Sir Henry Wallop, a relentless upholder of the crown's interest in Elizabethan Ireland,[29] is proof that Cork had reason to be familiar with the debate that had then taken place between English officials and adventurers in Ireland. The issue in contention, and which was never fully resolved, was the extent to which the normal ethical code of behaviour might be suspended in treating with Gaelic Irish landowners. The adventurers, and Boyle was ultimately the most successful of them, argued that they could never hope to promote civility in the remote areas unless they were declared exempt from conventional restraints, while the officials accused them, whenever they followed their own philosophy, of having themselves succumbed to the barbarism of the Irish.[30] Even if Cork had been totally ignorant of this debate he would have become familiar with it through his reading of Stanyhurst's contribution to Holinshed's *Chronicle*, and of Thomas Stafford's *Pacata Hibernia*, each of which devoted considerable attention to this issue. It is probable that an even more detailed discussion was available in 'Sir Geoffrey Fenton's Manuscript Book of Letters and Acts of State' which was also one of Cork's treasured possessions.[31] By resurrecting and advancing the secular arguments of the adventurers in his own defence, Cork was thus continuing into the seventeenth century the inconclusive debate of Elizabeth's reign. Like the Elizabethans before him, Cork could argue with conviction that any measures to dispossess the native Irish proprietors were justified because dispossession would make spoils available to 'well deserving English servitors' who would promote the 'civilising and securing' of the kingdom.[32]

While these arguments served Cork's purposes admirably, one would expect that he, who was by disposition a pious man, would have encountered difficulty in reconciling these purely secular ideas with his religious principles. That Cork, whose religious opinions would have been formed before he reached Ireland,[33] remained steadfast in these principles is beyond question, and they are likely to have been reinforced rather than diluted during his years in Ireland since the literature to which he most frequently referred in his diary and correspondence was spiritual in nature. Apart from the Bible and an account of a witch trial in Lancashire, Cork's spiritual reading was theologically left of centre. The items that are known to have belonged to him or are recorded as having passed through his hands were William Perkins' *Cases of Conscience*; 'The Practice of Piety'; 'a manuscript book of sermons by Archbishop Ussher'; 'Dr Downham's sermons'; and 'four manuscript books of religion bound up in quarto'.[34] The obvious puritan bias of the material makes it all the more difficult to comprehend how Cork could bring his mind to accommodate itself to so many secular rationalisations. That he was able to do so is explained by his ability to subsume the totally secular *apologiae* of the Elizabethans into providential explanations. By thus adorning secular arguments in pious garb Cork made them more palatable to himself and possibly more plausible to his audience.

The invocation of providence as an explanation for accidental or chance happenings in this life was so commonplace among sincere Protestants in the early seventeenth century that it had come to be considered irreverent or profane not so to attribute them.[35] Providential explanations of this character are scattered throughout Cork's papers,[36] but, as was noted, Cork also deployed the providential argument to provide a comprehensive explanation for his entire career. It was at this level that reference to the intervention of providence took the place of, or complemented, secular rationalisation, and this formula certainly assisted Cork in overcoming the tension between the secular and the sacred in providing a justification for his career. How Cork arrived at his peculiar formulation is not clear, but on closer scrutiny it appears that the providential model with which he operated bears a striking resemblance to the Florentine Renaissance concept of the man possessed of the indefinable quality of *virtù*, turning to his advantage the inexplicable and unpredictable intervention of the fickle goddess Fortuna in human affairs; the difference being, of course, that in Cork's case *virtù* becomes Christian virtue and Fortuna is transformed into providence. That the resemblance was more than coincidental is suggested by the fact that Cork was aware of at least the general structure of Florentine political thought from his reading of Geoffrey Fenton's translation of Guicciardini's *History of Italy*, a copy of which was one of Cork's prized possessions.[37] Even if we are reading too much into the evidence in suggesting that Cork was seeking to reconcile the irreconcilable by theologising Machiavelli, his model clearly served the same purpose as Machiavelli's would have done. Within it

Cork was able to argue that his material success was proof that he was endowed with virtue, and that this in turn explained why providence continued to favour him. Furthermore, within his eschatological framework Cork was able to overcome the fundamental Christian objection to acceptance of the principle that the end justifies the means so long as he could demonstrate that the ends which had been achieved were virtuous ones. It could well have been the imperative of demonstrating that his deeds led to virtuous ends which explains why, after he had made his fortune in Ireland, Cork pursued his commonwealth and charitable works with such dedication, why he recorded each such achievement so meticulously in his diary and why he broadcast them so loudly to the world.

Since, it seems, it was Cork's success which compelled him so frequently to resort to providential explanations to account for his actions, it is implied that his Irish experience forced him to become more self-consciously puritan than he would otherwise have been. His lively interest in, but rather unsophisticated view of, contemporary continental politics would also seem to have been influenced by his Irish experience. Certainly he perceived the continental Protestants engaged in the Thirty Years' War to be in as precarious a position as their counterparts in Ireland, not because of any insufficiency in themselves but because Protestants elsewhere – especially English Protestants – would not support their efforts to consolidate and extend true religion.[38]

The tolerance in Ireland of so many places of pilgrimage and of surreptitious mass-houses and nunneries, which would have caused offence to any convinced Protestant, also seems to have driven Cork to religious extremes which he might never have reached had he remained in England. During his periods as lord justice it was Cork who was principally responsible for bringing an end to what he regarded as the toleration of idolatry and he took special pride in the closure of religious houses and the destruction of St Patrick's purgatory.[39] The houses which devolved to the government on the dispersal of the religious orders were pointedly employed by Cork as houses of correction and training for the destitute.[40] This was in keeping with Cork's attitude towards charity which was also sharpened as a consequence of his experience in Ireland where, as he saw it, 'the greatest part of the main body of the nation consists of idle persons'.[41] Cork's general disposition towards the giving of charity became so utilitarian that he ceased to draw a distinction between what he previously had described as 'commonwealth work' and his 'works of charity'.[42] There are some instances when Boyle gave what he described as 'relief' to people who were destitute, but these were invariably former servants, and as a general rule he considered giving alms to be no charity.[43] On the few occasions when he did give money to beggars it was to provide them with the necessary training or materials to enable them to resume their work and abandon begging.[44]

These dimensions of Richard Boyle's religious thinking would seem to have been heightened because of his experience in Ireland, but in other respects his latent puritanism was toned down and even compromised because of the peculiarity of the Irish circumstances. Thus, despite his alleged opposition to an elaborate liturgy, Boyle acquiesced in the liturgical changes promoted by Wentworth, and throughout his career he cultivated Archbishop Laud, the principal architect of the new liturgy. On one occasion this cultivation went beyond the usual gifts of runlets of whiskey and Waterford frieze to the arrest and despatch to England of a Londoner who had given voice in Munster to opinions critical of Laud's policy. Furthermore, despite his obvious opposition to centralisation in ecclesiastical affairs, Boyle never openly opposed the office of bishop. The presence in Ireland of some puritan prelates, such as Archbishop James Ussher and Bishop George Downham, must also have made it easier for Cork to accept an episcopal church.[45] Equally important was the fact that until 1635 he ensured that only close relatives were appointed to the principal church livings within his local sphere of influence. Thus, in 1617, Cork secured the appointment of his older brother John Boyle to the vacant bishopric of Cork, and in 1619 he succeeded in having a cousin, Dr Michael Boyle, nominated to the neighbouring see of Waterford and Lismore. Another cousin, Dr Richard Boyle, occupied the deanship of Lismore until 1620 when, following the untimely death of John Boyle, he was promoted to the bishopric of Cork. The ensuing vacancy in the deanship of Lismore was duly filled by Boyle's maternal cousin, Robert Naylor, and Naylor would in turn have been advanced to the see of Waterford and Lismore in 1635 had it not been for Wentworth, who in his determination to end the Boyle monopoly nominated the infamous John Atherton to the position.[46] However, following Atherton's execution in 1640, Boyle again sought to fill what he regarded as this sensitive vacancy with the totally reliable Dean Naylor.[47]

During the short interval when Cork lost control of local ecclesiastical appointments his worst fears and suspicions of the episcopal system materialised. Cork must have privately fumed against the centralisation of ecclesiastical appointment when John Walley described to him how, during his absence in England, 'the churchmen' in Munster 'like hungry wolves...now look and run round about where to snatch and catch a prey, not regarding either right or wrong, but where they set on they must be served, and no people so ravenous as they, for they are grown insatiable'.[48] Furthermore, when in 1640 Bishop Atherton's 'most filthy and odious sins of sodomy and adultery' were 'laid open to the world', and he was found guilty of offences 'so many and the manner so vile and detestable as no modest tongue can make relations thereof', it appeared that Cork's case for local control of the church had been vindicated.[49] Despite the satisfaction that he must have derived from the disgrace of Atherton, and the pleasure which he must have taken in Walley's cynical search for a leper whose presence in the lazar house at Lismore would have frustrated Wentworth's case for revoking a particular parcel of church land,[50] Cork never exposed his private feelings on church affairs to public view. On the contrary, Cork, in public life, identified with the episcopal system and the centralised method of appointment to church livings. Indeed Cork was so careful to conceal his true feelings on these matters that at the very time he was privately fulminating against Atherton's appointment he was soliciting Archbishop Laud to effect a reconciliation between himself and Wentworth.[51]

Cork was equally reserved in offering opinion on life at court and inconsistent in his attitude towards the court. He, like all Englishmen who had been touched by puritan teaching, fostered an intense spiritual climate within his own household, was extremely selective about the households to which he would commit his children for their upbringing, and was cautious, almost to the point of indecision, in choosing tutors for his sons.[52] Besides that, the Boyle children were carefully protected from those vices which were considered most likely to bring them to perdition in the next life and to poverty in this, namely gambling, indebtedness, the reading of romantic literature and ostentatious living.[53] One would expect that any man who so carefully protected his children from contamination would wish to keep them clear of the court, and it would not be surprising to find him a critic of life at court. That Cork had private reservations about moral standards at court and was not convinced that it was a fit place for his children emerges from a passing comment by his daughter Mary that her youthful 'resolution to become a courtier' was an ambition that she kept 'secret' from her father since she realised it had no prospect of realisation while he lived.[54] Cork himself was careful to conceal his reservations, but he was so well able to overcome them whenever an advantageous marriage prospect beckoned that he devoted considerable energy and even more money to arranging marriage alliances for his children with the relatives of prominent courtiers, and most especially with the children of those belonging to the faction of the infamous Duke of Buckingham.[55]

Inconsistency and double-thinking also characterised the political attitudes of Richard Boyle. This was particularly evident in Cork's response to the treatment accorded him by Thomas Wentworth. Instead of openly opposing the lord deputy and the system which he represented, Cork surprised English observers, including Archbishop Laud, by continuing to speak highly of Wentworth and seeking a reconciliation with him;[56] this despite the fact that Wentworth had sought not only to deprive him of his property but had engaged in the policy of public denigration of Cork which was discussed in the second chapter. While Cork's initial response may be explained in terms of its being the most specious one in the circumstances, he was still slow, when circumstances changed, to take his revenge on Wentworth. What eventually drove him to come forward as a witness against Wentworth (by then Earl of Strafford), claimed Cork, was a desire to defend himself against the charges relating to Youghal College, which Strafford had dishonourably revived, rather than to seek the disgrace of his former adversary.[57]

Cork's entertainment in London of all the Irish witnesses who presented evidence that led to Strafford's impeachment casts doubt on this disclaimer,[58] as does his expression of satisfaction when Strafford was found guilty. Whatever of that, Cork did not permit his differences with Strafford to involve him in the English constitutional conflict between king and parliament. Instead, he studiously avoided taking sides, and advised his sons to do likewise.[59] We should not draw from this the inference that Cork was uninterested in or ignorant of the course of events in England. On the contrary, he made a special study of political developments there and considered himself so fully informed that he could assume to instruct and advise his fellow planters on what was happening.[60] His interest in these matters is made clear from the third body of literature which found its place among his sparsely furnished bookshelves, that concerned with British politics. The items mentioned as having been in Cork's possession were the 'Collected Works of King James I'; the 'Book of the King's Advices to Prince Henry'; a 'paper book' of the speeches and proceedings of the 1628 parliament; King Charles' 'Book of his Relations of the Scottish Proceedings'; writings on the proceedings against Strafford 'and other passages of parliament'; and finally, 'The History of Edward IV'. One of his account books reveals most interestingly how the collection concerning Strafford 'and other passages of parliament' came into being. On 2 December 1640 Cork, then in England, paid 2s 6d to 'a clerk that brought Mr Pimm's first and second speech [sic] in parliament'; on 26 December 1640 he paid 6d 'for the remonstrance to the parliament'; on 13 March 1641 he paid 3d for the 'proclamation for banishing papist priests'; on 27 March 1641 he paid 6d for 'the book of articles against the earl of Strafford' and on 10 May 1641 he paid 8d for two books which were answers 'to Strafford's speech in parliament'.[61]

Although obviously well-informed on British politics, Cork avoided commitment and maintained only an academic interest in what he described as 'all the remarkable occurrents', and 'the state and affection of the people' of England.[62] Cork was so successful in concealing his sympathies that it might well be argued that the only use to which he put his knowledge of events in England was to turn the king's financial difficulties to his advantage. Thus Cork's financial gifts to King Charles, an interest free loan of £15,000 in 1628 and a free gift of £1,000 in 1640, were given when the king was most badly in need of money and when Cork could expect to reap the highest reward in return for his timely generosity.[63]

Cork again proved himself inconsistent in the hostility which he displayed towards the Scots when they opposed the king who was seeking to extend to Scotland the self-same liturgical changes which Cork allegedly found offensive in Ireland.[64] Perhaps the aspect of Cork's behaviour which is most incomprehensible to the modern mind is that he, who in so many respects fits present-day definitions of a puritan, was so innocent of being one, and was so hostile to the puritan movement that he could employ the expression 'puritanical rascal' as a term of abuse.[65] That Cork also fostered an antipathy towards puritanism among his children is suggested by the example of his daughter Mary who remarked that prior to her departure from Ireland she was 'stead-fastly set against being a puritan'.[66]

Many in seventeenth-century England who today are described as puritans were, like Cork, not conscious of being such, and many self-professed puritans behaved during the circumstances of the English civil war in what today would appear to be an inconsistent or even illogical manner. It would be difficult, however, to find one in seventeenth-century England whose personality was such a bundle of inconsistencies and illogicalities as that of Richard Boyle looks to have been. That Cork's actions and responses seem illogical, or even opportunistic, is explained by the fact that we are given to considering his reaction to events in England in an English context. When viewed from an Irish perspective, however, the seeming inconsistencies become comprehensible, since it emerges that Cork did not have available to him in Ireland the range of possible responses that were open to members of the political nation in England. In fact it appears that Cork, like other planters in Ireland, had little option but to behave as he did since, circumstanced as he was, he was compelled to react to rather than act upon political developments in England.

The peculiarity of the Irish circumstances to which reference has been made is that English planters in Ireland were in an extremely precarious position, surrounded as they were by a hostile and resentful population who had been so recently dispossessed of their property. Those, like Cork, who had witnessed the facility with which the English plantations in Ireland had been dispersed during the 1590s were extremely conscious of their own insecurity. Nonetheless, as has been argued elsewhere,[67] the New English were so successful in convincing themselves that their future in Ireland was secure that they did not perceive themselves as an embattled minority. This seeming exercise in self-deception was achieved principally by viewing themselves in what might anachronistically be described as a United Kingdom context. By doing so, they were able to convince themselves that in the event of any external attack or internal disturbance their dominance would be assured since they could always rely upon support from England if their own resources were not sufficient to the task. Cork himself was so attracted to this perspective that for much of his career in Ireland he kept his contact with the Dublin government to an absolute minimum and came to consider his plantations in Munster as a logical extension of the English west country.[68] With the purpose of making this sectional view a reality, Cork populated his estates in the vicinity of Lismore and Youghal with Englishmen, and moulded the local environment to an English model.[69]

Environmental appearances did little to change political realities, however, and Cork, like the majority of planters in Ireland, was forced at all times to uphold the *status quo* in England because any threat to stability there would have reduced to nothing the calculation on which his security and self-confidence as a planter rested. Whatever his theological preferences or inclinations, and whatever his resentment at the treatment accorded him by 'the oppressing earl of Strafford',[70] Cork was obliged to remain steadfast in his loyalty to King Charles because to have done otherwise would have contributed to the developing instability in England and would thus have jeopardised the security of his own possessions in Ireland. In the light of this, we can better understand the behaviour of Cork previous to the outbreak of hostilities in England, and we can also better appreciate his cry of anguish at 'the lamentable (and ever to be, by all true English hearts lamentable) battle of Edghill. . . fought between the English'.[71]

Disunity within the ranks of the English political nation spelled disaster for the New English planters who were forced, for the first time since the late sixteenth century, to rely upon their own resources. The settlers in Munster, as it happened, were better able to defend themselves against the Irish rebels than the planters in the other provinces,[72] but their preoccupation with their own defence meant that they reacted to events in England by looking for support to whichever grouping appeared to be in control there. Thus the fact that Cork, until his death in 1643, continued to identify with the king should not be taken as evidence that he was a royalist, but rather that for him the king still represented authority. When, subsequently, the balance in England shifted successively in favour of parliament, the lord protector, and finally the exiled King Charles II, Cork's successors in Ireland, but especially Roger, Baron Broghill,[73] who was principally concerned with the defence and resumption of the Munster lands, gave allegiance to whichever force happened to represent stability in England and hence security for the planters in Ireland. Had Cork lived it is likely that he would have done as Broghill did, but neither father nor son should be condemned for political opportunism since, concerned as they were with their Irish property, they could not afford the luxury of choosing sides in the contest in England.

Reading through Cork's papers one gets the impression that his well-concealed sympathies lay with parliament and the puritans in the years leading up to the revolutionary turmoil.[74] That such was the case is further suggested by the positions taken by those of Cork's children who found themselves in England during the civil war, and who were at liberty to make a decision about which side to take, based on their understanding of the relative merits. Cork's eldest surviving son Richard was of course not a free agent since he had acquired substantial property in England, and eventually an English title, through his marriage to Elizabeth Clifford. The part which he played on the royalist side during the civil war was thus in a sense as the representative of his wife's family and interest.[75] The exiled Catherine, Lady Ranelagh, as was mentioned, devoted her years in England to supporting puritan scientists and divines,[76] while Mary Boyle, once she found herself her own mistress in England, shed her antipathy towards puritanism as readily as she did her desire to become a courtier. She, as was mentioned, blossomed into a fully fledged puritan and, as Countess of Warwick, became a visible witness to upright puritan standards.[77] The most revealing case is that of Robert Boyle, who, on his return from the continent in mid 1644 to war-torn England, was first inclined to join the royal army. Then a chance encounter with his sister Lady Ranaleagh, which he subsequently came to consider providential, deflected him from his intention to enlist for the king and thus saved him from 'the generality of those he would have been obliged to converse with [who] were very debauched and apt as well as inclinable to make others so'.[78]

Lest the foregoing suggest that the loyalties of Cork were absolutely determined by circumstances, it should be mentioned that another factor which influenced his continued loyalty to the English monarch, even after the provocations of Wentworth, was that Cork had come to accept that only the crown and court could extend to him the marks of social recognition and acceptance which were so essential to one who had striven constantly to elevate himself in the social hierarchy. Indeed, in the circumstances of the early 1640s, when many erstwhile supporters of the king had defected to parliament, the time seemed so propitious for the fulfilment of Cork's social ambitions that siding with parliament must have seemed almost unthinkable to him. The king then, for the first time, made it clear that he fully accepted Cork as an equal among his peers. It was then that king and queen assisted Cork in arranging a series of socially advantageous marriages, and they were pleased to attend at the festivities associated with the ensuing weddings.[79] Then also, King Charles invited Cork to attend in the upper house at Westminster during the trial of Strafford, and nominated him as a member of the English privy council.[80] Furthermore, there was the prospect, which was cherished by Cork's intimates if not by himself, that with the downfall of Strafford he would succeed to the vacant lord deputy-ship of Ireland.[81] As he was thus placed within an ace of achieving still further advancement it is easy to understand why Cork did not permit his animosity towards Wentworth to influence his traditional allegiance to the crown.

This study of the mental world of Richard Boyle suggests that although possessed of an alert mind he was far from being an original thinker. His brief study of the law and his secretarial experience in England certainly served Boyle well in advancing himself in Elizabethan Ireland, but he merely perfected methods to acquire property which had already been employed by previous adventurers in Ireland. The secular justification advanced by Boyle to cover this and other dubious activities was likewise the well-worn *apologia* of the Elizabethans which he could have picked up orally or through reading the literature on Ireland in his possession. Boyle's knowledge of the law would again have been of use to him in consolidating his estates during the reigns of the first two Stuarts, but we know that he was prompted to take the measures he did by his father-in-law, Sir Geoffrey Fenton.[82]

Thus it would seem that his sharp ear and keen eye for what was happening about him were as important as any body of literature in forming the mind of Richard Boyle. Furthermore in assessing the influence of reading matter on him one should take cognisance of his admission to Dungarvan in 1643 that he had 'no faith to believe in printed papers, nowadays they are so uncertain and stuffed with untruths'.[83] Boyle's puritan cast of mind was probably formed in his native Kent – where puritanism was well entrenched[84] – and while this seemingly spurred him to greater effort in promoting the educational and evangelising aspect of the plantation effort it also appears to have made it difficult for Boyle to identify fully with the secular rationalisations of the Elizabethans. It has been argued that Boyle overcame this difficulty by playing down the crude and eclectic justifications of the Elizabethans in favour of a comprehensive explanation of his career. This he arrived at, it has been suggested, after he had reconciled the Florentine notion of how the goddess Fortuna could be controlled with the Protestant idea of how providence could be harnessed to exert a benevolent influence on the human condition.

Boyle's all-explaining scheme, which might best be described as spiritualised Machiavellism, was seemingly the product of the reconciliation between these two apparently irreconcilable concepts. This exercise in mental gymnastics is in itself testimony to Cork's ability to turn familiar arguments to serve new ends, but in other respects the intellectual positions which he adopted came little short of being the programmed responses of an Irish planter to events in England. Furthermore, the imperative of social advancement sometimes set him on a particular course of action and closed his mind to the various options and possibilities open to him.

All of this makes it clear that Cork was an infinitely more complex character than was suggested by Wentworth when he constructed his caricature of him. Nonetheless, Wentworth's interpretation of his career has commanded greater respect from most recent historians because it has had the advantage over Boyle's version of events in being based on ascertainable, albeit carefully selected, facts, where Cork relied upon reference to divine intervention. It is essential to recognise, however, that what might appear unscientific by today's standards may not have appeared so in the seventeenth century. In this particular instance the notion of providential intervention in human affairs was so far from being considered unscientific that acceptance of it could actually serve as a stimulus to scientific investigation.[85] Furthermore, in seventeenth-century Ireland, where so many planters feared that the country would revert to what they considered to be the state of barbarism from which they had recovered it, these providential explanations, which today appear unscientific and hence unconvincing, would have been as persuasive as they were consoling.[86] This suggests that, in respect to the context of Boyle's mind, Wentworth was correct in assuming that his subject was a typical member of the New English elite in Ireland; he stood apart from them only in being more disciplined, more persevering, more dedicated to duty as he understood it, and hence more successful.

4

xxxxxxxxxxxxxxxxxxxxxxxxxxxxxxxxxxxxxxxxxxxxxxxxxxxxxxxxxxxxxxx

Social ascent and social adjustments in the career of Richard Boyle

One reason why, in recent years, some English social historians[1] have expressed interest in the career of Richard Boyle would seem to be that his meteoric rise from Kentish obscurity to enormous wealth, an Irish peerage and membership of the English privy council was without parallel in his own generation. The fact that these historians have referred to rather than analysed the experience of Boyle, and that they have cited it in support of what are now generally accepted opinions on the supposed decline of the aristocracy in pre-revolutionary England,[2] would suggest that these historians have been convinced by the campaign of vilification launched against Cork by Thomas Wentworth which was discussed in the second chapter.[3]

What has previously been said of Richard Boyle's political views does not accord with Wentworth's representation of him as a man who had no regard for hierarchy. On the contrary, as has been shown, Richard Boyle was invariably a supporter of the *status quo* in English politics and it could be argued from the perspective of Ireland that Cork's claim for a greater role for the planter in Irish political life was intended to enhance the reputation of the newly created aristocracy there.[4] Furthermore, the most convincing refutation of Wentworth's assertion came from Cork himself who protested that he had first learned to be obedient before he studied the art of government.[5] Throughout his career, Cork invariably appeared to be consciously obsequious rather than rebellious, as when, in discussing his relationship with Wentworth, he assured Archbishop Laud that he never considered 'it wisdom or safety to provoke or give offence to any man of power that is

armed with grace and authority'.[6] In social matters Boyle as Earl
of Cork was so far from being a leveller that he readily conceded
the deficiency of a newly created title, and sought to make good
its shortcomings. Besides that, one of Boyle's principal concerns
throughout his life was to forge alliances with and seek admission
to the social rank next above his own. This led ultimately to the
Earl of Cork seeking acceptance as a courtier of Charles I, and in
pursuit of that elusive goal he resigned himself to acceptance of
rebuffs, insults and humiliations.

Once Boyle had attained the rank of earl he set his mind to
overcoming the three major obstacles which he seems to have
accepted were rightfully placed in the way of his receiving full
recognition and respect from his peers. These were that he was, as
he himself termed it, 'a new man'[7] recently elevated from an
impecunious background; that the title itself suffered the dual
defect of being Irish and newly established, and that he himself
lacked confidence in his new role, particularly in his dealings with
members of the English aristocracy.

In his effort to overcome the first of these, Cork resorted to the
well-worn stratagem of seeking or fabricating a noble ancestry for
himself. The only lead in the grail-like quest for a distinguished
progenitor was 'a great gold ring with the arms of the Boyles in
crystal and colours' with which he had been presented in 1588 on
his first departure to Ireland by his kinsman Richard Boyle of
Maismoor in Gloucestershire.[8] It was seemingly on this slender
evidence that Cork erected his pretence to be a scion of a family
which was 'ancient and well-descended' but 'almost worn out'
until revived by himself.[9] The coat of arms chosen by Cork on his
elevation to the peerage was seemingly that depicted on this ring,
and in 1620, shortly after he had been created earl, Cork sent to
William Camden the Kentish antiquarian 'the achievement of
my arms and other instruments' in the hope that working from
these Camden could trace a noble pedigree.[10] Since no further
mention was made of the pedigree, nor of any progenitor more
ancient than a great-grandfather, one can assume that the powers
of detection of even the great Camden were not sufficient to that
task. One Mr Lylly of the office of heraldry in London was also

unsuccessful in the quest for a notable Boyle ancestor, but displayed an ingenious turn of mind in uncovering a deed, dating from the reign of Richard II, which made reference to an earldom of Cork.[11] The failure of these antiquarians to uncover a distinguished Boyle or Naylor ancestor may explain why the engraving on the tomb in St Patrick's cathedral, described by Wentworth as Cork's 'pedigree',[12] depicted Lady Cork's ancestors rather than Boyle's own. This decision was sensible since by the standards of the New English elite in Ireland Lady Cork was indisputably from a distinguished background. Her father, Sir Geoffrey Fenton, who had gentry connections in England, had served long as secretary and member of the privy council in Ireland.[13] On her mother's side, Lady Cork was a grand-child of Dr Robert Weston, formerly Dean of the Arches who had served as lord chancellor in Ireland 1567–73 and had earned a well-deserved reputation for probity and moderation.[14] This connection was doubly fortunate for the ancestor-impoverished Earl of Cork, since it enabled him to claim kinship for his family with Sir Richard Weston, lord chancellor and subsequently treasurer in England, and one of the more influential courtiers of Charles I.[15]

Cork also sought to compensate for his lack of distinguished forebears by ostentation. The tomb in St Patrick's cathedral, Dublin, deserved the superlatives which Wentworth used to describe it, but this was only one of four such elaborate monuments which he had constructed during his lifetime. Of the remaining three, one was at Preston in Kent where his parents were buried, another at Deptford in Kent where Roger Boyle, his first-born son, was buried and finally the tomb at Youghal where several Boyle kinsmen, and eventually the Earl of Cork himself, were interred. Such was his endeavour to erect memorials to himself and a non-existent ancestry that he well deserved Wentworth's contemptuous criticism that Cork should be rewarded with an honorary membership of the guild of tomb-makers in London.[16]

Lacking, as he did, a noble ancestry, Cork also lacked an extended kinship group which he likewise considered to be one of the essential attributes of a noble house. To compensate for this

Cork, almost from the moment of ennoblement, set about establishing contact with his relatives scattered throughout England,
some of whom were so distant and impoverished that they would
almost certainly have remained unknown to him had he not
become a noble.[17] To these, Cork offered a small share in his
wealth and prestige, in return for which he expected unqualified
loyalty to himself and his descendants as the focal point of the
newly constituted kinship group. Many of Cork's closer relatives
were invited to occupy land or positions in Munster where their
presence must have conveyed the impression of strong group
solidarity. Cork's sister Elizabeth married Piers Power, who held
a lease of Balligarran, and their son Roger, or Hodge, Power
seems to have been adopted as a kind of page into the Boyle
household. His other sister Mary and her husband Richard Smith
were granted a lease of the lands and castle of Ballynetra, and
Smith's knighthood was due to Cork's instigation.[18] Cork's older
brother John Boyle was a successful clergyman in England but it
was Cork's financial support which made it possible for him to
attain to the D.D. at Cambridge in 1614, thus qualifying him for
the bishopric of Cork which became vacant in 1617.[19] Three
cousins in clerical orders Drs Michael and Richard Boyle and
Robert Naylor were invited to occupy strategic church livings in
Munster, and of these we learn that Dr Richard Boyle had previously been a schoolmaster at Barnett, earning £20 per annum.[20]
Cork's endeavour and expense in soliciting a series of ecclesiastical
posts for his relatives was certainly not motivated by a disinterested
concern for his kin; but the fact that he would entrust these
positions, of such strategic importance to himself, to none other
than close kin is a measure both for his pessimistic view of mankind
generally[21] and of the importance which he had come to attach to
the kinship connection. When, subsequently, one of these hand-
picked appointees, Richard, Bishop of Cork, was persuaded by
Wentworth to serve as witness against Cork in the matter of
Youghal College, the earl's fury knew no bounds. This was provoked not so much because of misplaced trust, but because 'the
perfidious bishop' who owed his advancement to Cork's effort had
proved himself 'a faithless and unthankful kinsman'.[22]

That particular prelate recognised the need to have himself removed from Cork's sphere of influence and secured translation to the archbishopric of Tuam where he continued to enjoy Wentworth's favour. Those relatives who remained true to the Boyle interest could, however, depend on their loyalty being reciprocated, and if they served him well were assured of support also for their posterity. Thus when in 1639 he designated a cousin Joshua Boyle to act as his attorney Cork reminded him that 'the fortunes and happiness' of him and his posterity 'would have a great relation' to the faithful discharge of the 'confidence' he reposed in him.[23] Cork's papers are liberally sprinkled with references to his catering for the education of nephews and cousins at Trinity College, Dublin, or the Inns of Court, providing or supplementing dowries of nieces and cousins, enabling promising relatives to improve themselves in their occupations or as tenants and paying the hopeless cases to keep their distance.[24] Cork was understandably very much in demand as a godfather to the children of his relatives both in Ireland and England. Such christenings were seemingly of importance to him since he recorded them in his diary. Furthermore, he followed the careers of his godchildren more closely than those of their siblings, frequently negotiated marriages for them and was invariably more generous to them. Thus, for example, Cork provided a dowry of £3,000 to his niece and godchild Barbara Boyle when he arranged for her to marry the son and heir of Sir Thomas Brown, while he arranged a far less attractive match for her sister Mary to whom he assigned a mere £400.[25] Another godchild, his nephew Boyle Smith, was sent by Cork to accompany his son Lewis on his continental tour because he thought it fit that Lewis should have one of his own kindred to be near and at hand.

The births, marriages and deaths of remote as well as close relatives were also dutifully recorded in Cork's diary, and anybody who could establish a blood relationship was assured of preference for any patronage that was in Cork's dispensation.[26] However, not all members of the newly established kinship group were anxious to settle in Ireland, since no matter how generously he provided for them they were destined to remain poor relations. Thus, for

example, the clergyman Thomas Burt who was assured of a
Munster living when he married Cork's niece Dorothy Smith was
reluctant to accept the offer 'especially in that place in the midst
of my wife's friends, among whom we must of necessity live (at
least in comparison to them) beggars, or leave a posterity of
beggars'.[27]

Despite Cork's efforts to draw as many as possible of his
relatives to Munster, he must have been conscious that they
formed a rather shabby kinship group. It may have been this
consciousness of the lack of social distinction in the Boyle family
itself which explains why Cork married two of his daughters into
the ranks of the long-established Irish nobility, and why he treated
his sons-in-law by these alliances differently from any others. The
matches in question, those concerning the marriage of Alice Boyle
to David, Viscount Barrymore, and of Joan Boyle to George, Earl
of Kildare, were arranged while the prospective husbands were
still in wardship. The fact that they were minors may explain the
patriarchal attitude which Cork assumed towards the unfortunate
husbands, but as they advanced in years Cork still refused to forgo
his oversight of their affairs; he treated the husbands themselves
as junior or even superfluous partners in the arrangements, while
their wives resorted to their father's residences in either Dublin or
Munster for the birth of most of their children, and, seemingly,
assumed full responsibility for the children's upbringing.

Cultural and religious considerations undoubtedly influenced
Cork's apparent desire to wean his sons-in-law from their Old
English connections, and to establish a monopoly on the relationship for the Boyles. That Old English matches would involve such
strains and difficulties must have been apparent to Cork from the
outset of the negotiations, but nevertheless he proceeded with two
such alliances at a time when he could have forged excellent connections by marrying his daughters in England or with the sons of
New English settlers in Ireland.[28] The only satisfactory explanation of why, on these occasions, Cork valued the Old English
alliances over other apparently more advantageous possibilities
was that he intended that the heirs of these long-established
dynasties should lend the lustre of their antiquity to the newly

established Cork line. The only means of ensuring that the graft would produce the desired result was to cut back the older growth to insignificance so that only the new branch would flourish but draw its sustenance from the long-established roots. The metaphor is certainly an apt one since Cork himself was an avid horticulturalist, and in developing his orchards was concerned that his apple trees should be grafted with the first such planted by an Englishman in Munster, that of Walter Ralegh in Lisfynny.[29] Cork's efforts at dynastic grafting were more complex and certainly painful for the growth that was being reduced to insignificance. In each instance, however, despite initial resistance the experiment proved so satisfactory that Cork, satisfied that he had improved his stock in Ireland, was better able to seek prestigious alliances elsewhere for the remainder of his children.

The first graft that Cork sought to make with an Old English family was that with the Barry's Viscount Barrymore; an alliance that was all the more desirable from Cork's point of view because it provided him with an opportunity to advance the material no less than the social interests of his family. By offering in 1617 to redeem mortgages on the Barrymore estate, up to the value of £3,000, in return for the 'breeding' of the minor Lord David with his eldest daughter Alice, Cork made known his designs on the Barry estates which were situated strategically close to his own.[30] The fact that a connection with the long-established Barrymore family would enhance his prestige in Munster cannot, however, have been lost to Cork, and this consideration seems to have come eventually to dominate his thinking on that particular marriage. From the outset incompatibility between the two families was evident, even though Cork took the precaution of sending his young ward to Eton for two years' education. However, within months of their marriage in July 1621 Cork complained bitterly that Barrymore had introduced dice-playing on Sunday into his household.[31] On the other side, as was mentioned by Alice, the Barrys unjustly held 'her living after the English fashion' responsible for the persistent insolvency of her husband,[32] and the Barrys seem also to have resented the fact that Barrymore's continual indebtedness placed him at the mercy of his

monied father-in-law. The Barrys were clearly correct in their
conjecture, since if Barrymore was to salvage anything of his estate
from his creditors he had no option but to call on the resources of
Cork. Barrymore repeatedly received financial assistance from
Cork which enabled him to free his estates from mortgage, to
exchange his title of viscount for that of earl and to rebuild the
family seat at Castlelyons.[33] In return for these advances Barrymore was obliged to transfer a considerable part of his property as
security to Cork, and to concede the subservience of his family to
the Boyle interest.[34] There is evidence that the young nobleman
resisted at first, but Cork's diary and correspondence bear witness
to the gradual and then total compliance of Barrymore with his
father-in-law's wishes.[35] The Barrymore children were closely
supervised by their maternal grandfather, Barrymore's son and
heir attended at Cork's free school at Youghal,[36] Barrymore
himself was advised by Cork in 1634 on how to prepare himself
for parliament, and he let his client-status be known publicly by
accompanying his father-in-law to Dublin and residing at Cork's
house throughout the duration of parliament.[37] Barrymore also
depended on Cork's English connection to obtain favours there,
and in 1638 he and his wife travelled to London in the Boyle
entourage.[38] Finally, Barrymore indicated his identification with
English concerns when he volunteered to raise an Irish regiment
to assist the king in the Scots war, and he proved totally committed to the planter interest in Munster when his allegiance was
put to the test in 1642 with the spread of rebellion to that province.
The soldier's funeral which Barrymore was accorded when he was
buried in Boyle's chapel at Youghal in September 1642 served
both as a reward for his services and as a symbol of the subservience of the Barrymore to the Cork dynasty. To ensure that this
relationship would continue to future generations Barrymore's
widow and family were removed to London where, in the household of their exiled aunt Lady Ranelagh, the children were
instructed by John Milton who was employed as their tutor.[39]

That improvement of the Boyle stock and the acquisition of
well-established Irish roots were of crucial importance to Cork
when seeking Old English alliances is more clearly evident from

his dealings with George, Earl of Kildare. That young earl's estates were situated principally in Leinster, and even the small portion of land which he held in Munster was not, like that of Barrymore, contiguous to the main bulk of the Boyle estates. Since no advantage other than that of a social nature was to be gained through the Kildare marriage alliance, this represents a much more clear-cut case of Cork purchasing prestige for his family through the marriage of his daughter Joan into Ireland's oldest noble dynasty. The marriage was negotiated in 1629 when Cork, being at the height of his influence, might have arranged for his daughter to marry an English peer. Despite the fact that he was aware that the Kildare estate was severely encumbered, and that the young noble led a dissolute life, Cork was still ready to pay £6,600 to the Duchess of Lennox for the wardship of Kildare.[40]

From the outset, Cork made his purpose clear. In October 1629 he wrote to Kildare in England to inform him that his 'friends' in Ireland were happy with the arrangement that had been made regarding his future, and that he himself would undertake to manage his 'disjointed' estate which had 'more than need of such a steward'.[41] Shortly thereafter, Cork took to advising young Kildare on educational and spiritual matters, while insisting that the management of Kildare's 'encumbered and decayed estate' should rest entirely in Cork's own hands. What Cork had in mind was that all the Kildare rental should be employed towards the redemption of those lands held in mortgage and towards 're-edifying' his 'decayed house' and furnishing it 'with plate hangings and utensils' of which it was 'utterly destitute'. The Earl of Cork clearly thought that such would be essential when his daughter became Countess Kildare, and he further sought to secure her dominance within the alliance when he implored young Kildare to give 'no ear nor entertainment' to his 'Irish kinsmen and followers'. If he followed this advice Cork promised him that he would become 'the greatest earl of Kildare for revenue that ever was in Ireland'. This prospect must undoubtedly have been attractive to the young earl, but certainly not the means recommended for its attainment. It would have been difficult for any noble to accept that he was 'not to hearken to or entertain any of his...kindred or followers' lest they 'flatter and betray [his] judgement', but this directive was made totally unacceptable when it involved his acknowledging that 'there was never Earl of Kildare had such a steward as God [had] sent [him] nor such a guardian'. Rather than pay to the Boyles the honour and respect that was due to his own ancient kinship group Kildare turned his back on the advice of his over-bearing father-in-law. But then when he sought to manage his affairs as he saw fit he quickly learned that Cork had frustrated his purpose by obtaining agreement from Mr Richard Talbot of Malahide, 'the sole feoffee of trust', that he would perfect no lease or conveyance of the Kildare property without the prior consent of Cork.[42] This interference quite understandably provoked Kildare, who by this stage had reached his majority and was father of an heir, to express to Lord Deputy Wentworth 'much bitterness and intemperancy' against his father-in-law.[43] What followed was an estrangement between Cork and his son-in-law modulated by reconciliations on the frequent occasions when Kildare found himself in financial difficulties. Lady Kildare took her father's part in the disagreement, and the outcome for Kildare, who according to Cork led 'the most licentious, prodigal and profuse way of life that ever noble man did',[44] was that the management of his affairs came increasingly under Cork's control, and he himself was reduced to being an unwelcome appendage in his own household.

Following the birth of Kildare's son and heir in Cork House in Dublin the child was christened by Kildare's chaplain but the principal godfather was the Earl of Cork and the name chosen for the child was Richard.[45] Kildare displayed his pique at this slight by pawning the silver goblets which Cork had offered as a christening gift,[46] but this feeble effort at independence did not halt Kildare's inexorable path to anonymity. The chapel at Maynooth which had fallen into disrepair was renovated at Cork's expense in 1632;[47] it was Cork's chaplain who preached the 'first sermon made [there] by a protestant minister in any man's memory', and it was Cork rather than Kildare who attended the service.[48] Cork's financial support made possible the erection of a new residence at Maynooth and he assumed full responsibility for the supervision of the work.[49] The device over the entrance gate was chosen by Cork, and it bore the coat of arms of the earldom of Cork as well as that of Kildare.[50] When the house was finally complete Kildare was absent in England, and it was Cork with his daughter Lady Kildare who presided over the feast which marked the official opening of the new Kildare seat.[51]

Cork's expressions of anger, frustration and anguish at the extravagant and dissolute life of George Kildare may well have been sincere, but they were more likely evoked by pity for his daughter rather than concern for the man.[52] In reality Kildare served Cork's purposes perfectly because his persistent indebtedness presented Cork with the opportunity to achieve 'the preservation of the ancientest earldom in the kingdom'.[53] This ambition to preserve the Kildare house was motivated principally by his concern that the glory of its antiquity would reflect in the newly established Cork line. Thus it was no idle curiosity which drove Cork to trace the genealogies of the three great Irish noble houses of Desmond, Kildare and Ormond. On the contrary, he wished to demonstrate that the Kildare house was the longest established of the three, and that by association with it the house of Cork shared in the prestige of this antiquity. Thus, whatever Cork might have thought privately of his son-in-law he had every reason to praise him publicly as 'renowned Kildare, prime earl of this isle'.[54] The dual necessity of fabricating an Irish historical past and bolstering the reputation of what previously had been a shabby Boyle kinship group explains why Cork entered into Irish marriage arrangements which, in financial terms, fell considerably short of what he might have negotiated elsewhere. That these two marriages made good what Cork considered the deficiency in his kinship group is indicated by his curt dismissal of all other approaches made on behalf of Irish nobles for marriages with his daughters.[55] That sentimental factors influenced Cork in negotiating the terms of the Barrymore and Kildare matches is also suggested by the fact that the conditions agreed upon were far more generous on Cork's part than those conceded to the New English families into which three of his daughters were married.

The first of the new English alliances was that between Sarah Boyle and Thomas Moore, eldest son of Lord and Lady Moore of Mellifont. This was first negotiated in 1617, when Cork agreed to pay a dowry of £3,000 and expected a commensurate jointure. The contract was duly signed in 1620 but the marriage which took place in 1621 ended three years later with the death of Moore.[56] A second marriage treaty between the families was arranged in 1633 but this never materialised because of the death in 1637 of Margaret Boyle, the prospective bride.[57] The Moores appear to have then set their sights on the unruly Mary Boyle who defeated their purpose by marrying Charles Rich.[58]

The marriage between Dorothy Boyle and Arthur Loftus, son and heir of the prominent political figure Sir Adam Loftus of Rathfarnham, was seemingly negotiated as early as 1623, the terms were ratified in 1626 and the marriage finally took place in 1632. The terms agreed upon in 1626 were that Cork should make an immediate advance payment of a dowry of £3,000 plus an interest free loan of £2,000 for two years. To this Cork added in 1632 a further payment of £100 to enable Lady Loftus to furnish Dorothy for the wedding.[59] These terms were on par with those agreed upon in 1630 when Catherine married Arthur Jones, son and heir to Lord Ranelagh. The initial dowry on that occasion was £3,000 but following further negotiation Cork raised this by £1,000 in 1634.[60]

In negotiating these three alliances Cork was dealing with heads of households who were no more securely established in Ireland than his own father-in-law had been. Thus whatever political benefit Cork hoped to reap from the connections was likely to be reciprocated. The similarity of the final terms indicates that these were probably the product of hard bargaining between social equals, and emotional or sentimental factors probably counted for little. That they did enter into it was, however, made clear by Cork himself in reference to the several Moore advances. He was, he acknowledged, deeply indebted to both Lord and Lady Moore, since 'under God' Moore's father was the one who 'first invited' him to Ireland. Furthermore, Lady Moore was Cork's 'gossip', and Cork considered himself 'much bound' in his first fortunes to Lady Katharine Cowly who was Lady Moore's mother.[61] While these considerations might have weighed with Cork in favour of accepting a marriage alliance with the Moores, they are not likely to have exerted any consequential impact on the financial terms which were slightly less generous than those offered to the more influential Loftus and Jones families. The money that Cork invested in the Ranelagh match was well spent since both father and son stood by Cork in his contest with Wentworth.[62] Not so Adam Loftus who steered such an independent line that he became the only prominent New English official whose career was actively promoted by Wentworth.[63] That this match did not produce the dividend that Cork had hoped for is suggested by the infrequency with which reference was subsequently made in Cork's diary to his daughter Dorothy. What mention there was, besides a cursory note of the birth of some of Dorothy's children, included reference to 'a very unpleasing passage' which took place in 1635 between Cork and his son-in-law 'touching a slight unkindness' which Loftus claims to have suffered from his wife. To Cork's 'great discontent' Arthur Loftus appeared 'heady and untractable' therein.

Thus, apart from consolidating the Ranelagh support, these New English alliances contributed little to the Boyle finances, influence or prestige, and the judgement passed on them in 1640, that they 'had not proved fortunate', was probably justified. Nevertheless they had the merit of being both relatively inexpensive and socially acceptable, and when combined these advantages made it possible for Cork to expend extravagant amounts in arranging marriage alliances for the remainder of the children into English noble or courtly families.[64]

The need to establish marriage alliances with England's aristocracy was for Cork a matter of the greatest urgency because he, who had only recently gained admission to the ranks of the Irish nobility, was anxious to achieve social acceptance and to advance himself socially in England. This sentimental factor explains why Cork was much less concerned with the financial aspect of these arrangements than was usual with men of his rank. A study of these marriages suggests in fact that Cork was so far from the mercenary Wentworth claimed him to be, that one could almost describe him as prodigal. Cork's enormous wealth explains why he could afford to settle for less than what to others would have appeared as the best bargain, but his own lowly origin meant also that the prestige and connections that came with noble marriages were more valuable to him than to other nobles. Consequently Cork was ready to pay the price for prestigious family links and convenient court connections by providing his daughters with extravagant dowries for impecunious but well-connected husbands, and by considering as wives for his well-provided sons some daughters of England's noble houses who were but modestly endowed. In general, Cork hoped to secure for his sons prestigious family connections which would add lustre to their lineage, but in arranging English marriages for his daughters he was happy to settle for court connections which would be of immediate short-term benefit to himself and his sons.

On Cork's own admission, 'the well-disposing' of Richard, Viscount Dungarvan, his eldest surviving son, was his 'principal concern' because on this depended both the 'happiness or ruin' of his heir and 'the establishing or overthrow' of the 'house which [he had] raised with a great deal of honest study, labour and industry'. Cork was 'ever determined' that the bride should be from the ranks of England's nobility and he seems to have decided also on having for his daughter-in-law an heiress whose property in England would complement the Irish estates of his son. Within these constraints Dungarvan was left free, from 1631 onwards, to choose his own bride.[65]

Several propositions were considered and some were almost completed before Dungarvan finally settled for Elizabeth Clifford. The first terms agreed upon seem to have been associated with wardship arrangements for Dungarvan in the event of his father's death before he had attained his majority. This arrangement involved a double marriage between Dungarvan and a daughter of Sir Edward Villiers, then president of Munster, and between Villiers' eldest son, subsequently Lord Grandison, and Joan Boyle.[66] The obvious advantage to Cork in such an arrangement, apart from the security of his estates in the event of death, was that it gave him access to the power and patronage of the great Duke of Buckingham then at the pinnacle of power.[67] Cork, however, had second thoughts on the advantages to be gained by this double match, and in 1626, despite having paid £5,000 which he recovered with difficulty, it was amicably agreed between himself and Villiers to dissolve the contract, principally because 'the weakness of his [Villiers'] estate' meant 'he could not perform the conditions'.[68]

The next possible match for Dungarvan ironically concerned Robert Carr, Earl of Somerset, the former royal favourite who had been displaced by Buckingham. Cork maintained that Somerset and his countess had 'a purpose to go and live in Ireland', and in 1629 twice bid for the marriage of their only daughter and heiress, Ann Carr, with Dungarvan. The supposed terms of £40,000 at marriage, a further £40,000 a year later and all the Somerset inheritance at the earl's death constituted, if true, a tempting offer, and it is likely to have been some reluctance on the part of Somerset rather than Cork's disregard for fallen favourites which explains why it was not proceeded with.[69] The next possible match for Dungarvan was to a daughter of the Earl of Bedford, but Cork, in 1631, released Bedford from obligations when he learned that his countess was 'not willing to adventure a daughter upon an Irish fortune'.[70]

From 1631 onwards when Dungarvan, having completed a brief education at Oxford,[71] was in attendance at court, suitable marriage partners were being sought out with some urgency. Dungarvan's interests at court were being looked after by Sir Thomas Stafford and Lord Goring,[72] and Cork was happy that their efforts were exciting interest in the proper quarters since he boasted that 'several noble families' had 'made motions' for a match with Dungarvan.[73] Goring was less sanguine and complained that many potential alliances had aborted because Dungarvan's estates were held exclusively in Ireland.[74] Goring may have had in mind a match with a daughter of the Earl of Leicester, which was being negotiated throughout 1630 and early in 1631,[75] but Goring's efforts proved fruitful when in 1631 another prospective Villiers bride, this time Lady Ann Fielding, niece to the dead favourite and daughter to the Earl of Denbigh, was found for Dungarvan.[76] It was seemingly accepted at court, and even at Lismore, that this match was all but finalised, when Wentworth complicated the proceedings by offering, through Lord Ranelagh, his niece Elizabeth Clifford as a wife for Dungarvan.[77] She was also an heiress so the financial terms of this alliance were far superior to anything previously offered, other than those with Ann Carr of which Cork still boasted.[78] Furthermore, the match had the seeming advantage to Cork of ensuring him the support of Wentworth who had just then been nominated to the lord deputyship of Ireland. Therefore, once the delicate matter had been overcome of receiving the consent of the king, who had strongly supported the Denbigh match, to this new alliance, nothing seemed to stand in the way of bringing the Clifford heiress into the Boyle fold.[79] Subsequently, and seemingly on the advice of Wentworth who had second thoughts on the advantages of the match, the Cliffords altered their terms. Cork considered that he and his son were 'much undervalued' by this unilateral alteration of conditions, and Dungarvan's pride was so hurt that his father had to remind him 'that marriages are not to be made merchandizes' and that 'the noble descent' and 'virtues' of the prospective bride should be preferred by him, being 'a new man', before 'any marriage portion'.[80] Thus, while Cork's enemies claimed that he desired the Clifford match merely to gain control over Wentworth, the fact that Elizabeth Clifford was a prospective English heiress and that she was a grand-daughter of the first Earl of Salisbury, for whom Cork had particular reverence, seem to have been the crucial factors. Indeed these weighed so heavily in her favour that Cork even countenanced the humiliation of a unilateral change in the terms of a marriage contract.[81]

Cork's three remaining sons of marriageable age, Lewis, Viscount Kinalmeaky, Roger, Baron Broghill, and Francis Boyle were married at court in quick succession between October 1639 and June 1641. Their father was then present himself[82] to look after his own and their interests, but once again he placed court connection and the lineage factor above financial considerations. The first to be married was Francis, the youngest of the three, and since he was then a fourth son who, by Boyle standards, was but moderately provided for, he did well to find a bride among the queen's maids of honour. She was Elizabeth Killegrewe, daughter of Thomas Stafford's wife by her first husband Sir Robert Killegrewe. The match was first negotiated between Cork and Lady Stafford but the formal proposal on Elizabeth's part was made by the king and queen. The couple were, consequently, married in the king's chapel, and at the reception provided by the royal couple Cork with his son and three daughters sat at the royal table 'amongst all the great lords and ladies'. The couple were then ritually bedded by the king and queen but, on Cork's insistence, the sixteen-year-old Francis, who was considered too young for the physical strains of marriage, was quickly separated from his wife and sent to travel in France with Robert his younger brother. In return for the public display of royal favour and social recognition Cork had to satisfy himself with Elizabeth's dowry of £2,000, which was subsequently exchanged with Sir Thomas Stafford for a manor and rectory in Devon.[83] By English standards this was a reasonable dowry for a bride to a fourth son, but by comparison with the portions that Cork was then offering with his remaining marriageable daughters it was derisory. Indeed, £2,000 was precisely the sum that Cork had provided for his granddaughters by Countess Barrymore.[84] This marriage therefore provides further support for the contention that Cork, more than well-established aristocrats, placed such a high premium on socially approved connections that he was ready to suffer considerable financial loss in pursuit of these connections.

Cork's second son Kinalmeaky was married within two months of Francis Boyle to Lady Elizabeth Fielding, daughter to the Earl of Denbigh and sister to Lady Ann Fielding, who had recently been spurned by Dungarvan. Here at last was the frequently contemplated Villiers connection which still carried the stamp of royal approval even if no longer the political weight of the Duke of Buckingham. No mention was made in Cork's diary of the size of the dowry, which suggests that it was shamefully small. The queen's gift to the bride of a diamond necklace, valued by Cork at £1,500, compensated in some way for the probably poor financial terms of the match, but it seems that Cork was so anxious for a second chance at the Denbigh connection that he hardly waited to bargain. That the unfortunate Kinalmeaky was rushed headlong by his father into this marriage is indicated by Cork's diary entry that Kinalmeaky 'was not in good order for a bridegroom' because, with the shortness of notice, he had to make do with the ill-fitting clothes used two months previously by his brother Francis, who was four years his junior.[85] This experience again suggests that the prospect of further royal favour and a second wedding at court within two months of the first far outweighed financial considerations in Cork's scale of values.

While these two sons were being advised by their father, the third, Roger, was competing with a young courtier for the favour of another royal maid-in-waiting, one Mrs Harrison. The young lady's contacts did not match her beauty, and Cork failed to comprehend why Broghill and Thomas Howard, son of the Earl of Berkshire, should fight a duel for her favours. After Broghill had prevailed in this ordeal it appeared that she was destined to be his bride but the match was 'unhandsomely (on her side) broken off, when they were so near being married as the clothes were to be made'.[86] Thereafter Broghill put his trust in his father's judgement and early in 1641 he was married to Margaret Howard, daughter to the recently deceased Theophilus, Earl of Suffolk. The dowry of £5,000 had been left to the bride on her father's death, but the Howards, like the Russells before them, had reservations about investing money in Ireland. Thus a further condition of this marriage was that Cork should match the dowry with a further £5,000, the total to be used 'upon some purchase in England for the use of the couple'.[87] Shortly afterwards the manor of Marstone Bigot in Somerset was acquired for Broghill and his lady.[88] The purchase was particularly fortunate since within months the Boyle estates in Ireland were overrun by rebellion. Nobody could have foreseen this at the time of the negotiations, so this example again illustrates the point that Cork placed such a high premium on connections with long-established, even if impecunious, English noble houses that he permitted them to state their terms.

It is evident from the foregoing that Cork, in arranging for his sons' marriages, was willing to accept dowries which were smaller than might be had on the marriage market, provided that the prospective brides were from long-established noble houses or brought court connections with them. This is proof that he conceded that title alone did not make a man noble, and that he was seeking to make good through marriage the social deficiency in his own circumstances. Even then, as was noted, Cork encountered considerable difficulty in finding brides with the appropriate background and connection. The fact that he was able to find them at all is partly explained by his previous success in winning social respectability through the marriages of five daughters in Ireland, and in acquiring a valuable court connection through one English match. In pursuit of this contact Cork endured much abuse and several rebuffs and finally achieved his end through the outlay of a dowry of £10,000 which was extraordinarily large by the standards of that time.[89] Even then he obviously wished further to consolidate his position at court since he also offered extravagant dowries with his two remaining daughters. All of this is a measure of the importance which Cork attached to such contacts, and of the social inadequacy which he considered was the result of the lack of contacts at court.

This is not to suggest that Cork was previously unknown at court, but the support which he did enjoy there – although sufficient to influence ecclesiastical appointments and to obtain new patents for his estate, as well as Irish titles for himself, three sons and one son-in-law – was support of the type that was available to every man who could pay the price of court favour for a particular occasion. Support of this nature was quite sufficient for anybody who was reconciled to a provincial existence, but Cork was obviously intent on launching his family to the top of the social pyramid. What Cork really required was a supporter or a group of supporters at court who would be constant in their endeavours to advance his interest and to protect him against attack.

During his early career Cork enjoyed the support at court of George Carew, Earl of Totnes, and of Sir Thomas Stafford, Carew's natural son.[90] Neither of these had any great influence at court, and the best they could do for Cork was to keep him informed of power shifts at court and to advise him on the court activity of his enemies.[91] If he was to achieve his social ambition, Cork had to forge a connection with one of the few great courtiers who alone were capable of promoting the careers of those who were accepted as their followers.[92] Marriage was the only means that Cork saw to forging such an alliance, and he used his well-dowried daughters as bait for covetous courtiers who might advance his career.

The first court contact that Cork sought was, logically enough, with the Duke of Buckingham who virtually monopolised patronage in the years prior to his assassination in 1628. The first step in this direction was the abortive double match with Sir Edward Villiers, already mentioned. After Cork had paid 'great sums' the match was cancelled at the request of the Villiers family, and Cork acknowledged that he was frustrated in his purpose 'to procure the duke's favour'.[93] Following upon this debacle Cork dabbled from 1621 to 1628 in an alliance proposed by Buckingham between his kinsman Sir Thomas Beaumont, heir to Viscount Beaumont,[94] and Catherine Boyle. Since the Fentons claimed descent from the Beaumonts this proposed alliance was particularly attractive to Lady Cork, and the earl contended that it was his wife 'with her kindred and friendship' who had persuaded him 'to yield to that unfortunate match'.[95] This remark was made in 1628 after Cork had been swindled and snubbed, but the entry of Beaumont's name beside that of Catherine in the 1623 edition of the 'True Remembrances' suggests that Cork then looked more favourably on the proposed alliance.[96] The terms agreed on in the contract of 1622 were that Cork should pay a dowry of £4,000, of which £3,522 was paid forthwith, to Beaumont to 'disengage his encumbered estate'.[97] Then in 1624 Cork was 'persuaded' to send Catherine to the Beaumont residence in England 'to be bred there', where she resided until 1628 by which time, according to Cork's exaggerated report, she had 'lost the foundations of religion and civility wherein she was first educated'.[98] More to the point, Lord Beaumont, who had negotiated the match, had died and when the time came to conclude the match his widow refused to proceed with it unless the dowry was supplemented by a further

£2,000. Cork refused to comply with this demand and immediately recovered his daughter from the Beaumont household.[99] Retrieving the money proved to be more difficult, because Lady Beaumont produced what Cork claimed was a fraudulent deed and clung tenaciously to the dowry for a further seven years. Even then she returned only £2,200 and Cork was also the poorer for the interest on the original £3,522.[100] One aspect not mentioned by Cork in his doleful narration of misuse was that during his visit to England in 1628 he was entertained lavishly by Buckingham and the Beaumonts, and it is probable that he would have been persuaded, for a price, to discharge the extra £2,000 had not the assassination of Buckingham removed the object of even the initial investment. The rapidity with which the wind-up of this long drawn out affair followed upon the assassination of Buckingham certainly suggests that the events were not unconnected.[101]

Even if this were true, the fact remains that in his pursuit of court connection, Cork was being treated by Buckingham and the impecunious Beaumonts with a disdain which they would never have dared to display towards an English noble. That this instance was not isolated is suggested by the difficulty Cork had in finding any appropriate English connection for his daughters. A match proposed in 1624 between Lettice Boyle and Lucius Cary, Lord Deputy Falkland's heir, also proved still-born,[102] and a match arranged in 1625 for the same Lettice with Lord Audley, son and heir to Mervyn Touchet, Earl of Castlehaven, was dissolved by Cork two years later because Audley was 'not conformable in religion'.[103] Indeed the only success that was recorded in these years was the marriage in 1626 of Sarah, the widow of Sir Thomas Moore, to Lord Robert Digby, Baron of Geashill, nephew to the Earl of Bristol.[104] This was to be a short-term marriage since Sarah died in 1633 in childbirth. By then, however, she had borne her husband a son and daughter, and Cork had become so attached to that particular son-in-law that, subsequent to the death of Sarah, he continued to favour him with financial support.[105] Politically, however, Cork regarded this alliance as, at best, a minor victory, since the Earl of Bristol was chiefly noted as a critic of the court and was in no position to exert the influence that Cork sought. The only political value that Cork placed on the Digby match was that the Earl of Bristol enjoyed considerable prestige in the west country, and the connection thus enhanced Cork's own position in that part of England with which he had most sustained contact. Nonetheless his calls on Bristol for advice even on local matters were so infrequent that, in 1637, Bristol complained that if Cork 'would not make use of him he could not help it', and Cork's own servant Thomas Cross remarked on the same occasion that he wished his master 'had about the court such a real and constant friend as the Earl of Bristol is in the country'.[106]

That such a comment could be made by a Cork confidant in 1637 is an indication of how disillusioned Cork had become with the one court connection which he had succeeded in making; that which resulted from the marriage, in 1629, of the frequently proffered Lettice Boyle to George Goring, son and heir to Lord George Goring, subsequently Earl of Norwich.

The Goring match was negotiated by Cork himself during his 1628–9 visit to England. It was then pursued by him with particular intensity because, following the assassination of Buckingham in August 1628 and the death on 29 April 1629 of his old friend the Earl of Totnes, he was worse off for court contacts than ever before. Lord Goring, who after the death of Buckingham was one of the chief advisors to Charles I, seems first to have entered Cork's life as the crown agent in negotiating a loan of £15,000 for the king, in return for which Cork was conceded yet another comprehensive patent for his estates and was nominated joint lord justice of Ireland. During the course of these negotiations the insolvent Goring came to appreciate that Cork, who previously was unknown to him, had 'abundance' and was 'a monied man' and that a contract of marriage for his spendthrift and dissolute son George with Lettice Boyle 'was the means to redeem and uphold the honour of his house and family'.[107] The happy coincidence of needs – Goring's for money and Cork's for social and political advancement – explains how Cork finally succeeded in clinching the type of alliance that had so long eluded him. The astronomical dowry of £10,000 which Cork proffered with Lettice was sufficient to overcome any misgivings which Goring may have had about accepting the daughter of such a controversial if not disreputable man as wife for his heir.

Now that he had invested £10,000 in the Goring alliance, Cork had every reason to expect a smoother passage at court for his various petitions and projects. In this he was to be sadly disappointed, and a study of the relationship which developed between Cork and Goring is particularly instructive because it illustrates the stakes for which Cork was really playing, and the hazards of the game in which he was involved. According to the formal terms of the marriage agreement Goring had undertaken to convey a handsome jointure to the couple for his own lifetime, and to settle all of his estates on his son at his death. Besides that, Goring had 'contracted' to procure for his son the office of lieutenant of pensioners and the secretaryship of Wales.[108]

Goring's failure to comply with the last condition was, according to Cork, the reason why the portion provided for the couple was insufficient to meet the extravagant demands of the young husband.[109] The couple fell hopelessly into debt and they persistently resorted to Cork for further financial assistance. It was only Cork's continued munificence in the form of loans, and eventually the purchase of a commission for young Goring in one of Lord Tilbury's regiments in the Netherlands, which saved them from total ruin.[110] Cork therefore had much reason to be angry at the outcome of this match, and since Goring had not fulfilled all the terms of the agreement it was possible for Cork to hold him responsible for the continued misfortune of the marriage. Cork's 'remedy' for the couple's financial difficulties merely exacerbated a difficult situation because it provided young Goring, who had from the outset treated his wife and father-in-law with contempt, with the opportunity to offer the final humiliation by deserting his wife in England while he went to serve in the Netherlands.[111]

What the reason was for marital breakdown in this case is anybody's guess. Some alleged that the infertility of the marriage, for which Lettice was held responsible, was the nub of the problem, but it appears from the sources that young Goring had taken to deserting his wife before infertility was accepted as final.

On one occasion Wentworth mentioned, with counterfeit concern at the humiliation of Cork's daughter, how Lettice had gone to Bath to prepare herself for conception only to find that 'the principal guest' was absent on one of his philandering exploits.[112] The real problem seems to have been that the dashing, spendthrift young gallant looked down on his wife and her family, and even Cork seems to have had nagging doubts that he had over-reached himself socially. In the series of letters to his erring son-in-law, Cork alternated pleading with hectoring tones, but he always sounded pathetically helpless in a situation which he could neither comprehend nor control. For example, in one letter he rehearsed the services he had rendered the Goring family, he complained of the disgrace which had befallen the Boyle family because of young Goring's treatment of his wife when 'her descent, breeding, deportment and portion deserve far better usage and respects', and he finally expressed his incomprehension at why young Goring should neglect his wife 'except some strange loves (not so worthy)' had 'bewitched' him, or unless he wished 'to have her fall into deep melancholy. . . or to run mad as it was ever reported in court she was'.[113]

Colonel Goring turned a deaf ear to his father-in-law's clamour except when he hoped for additional finance. Lord Goring, however, sought to defend himself against the barrage of complaints which were directed at him, and he retaliated by claiming he was 'an unlucky man' ever to have entered into the arrangement with Cork. If Lettice Boyle had not been so virtuous, averred Goring, her dowry of £10,000 would have been dearly purchased because ever since then Cork had never left him 'a free hour from travail'.[114] The reference here was to the agreement that the dowry was to be paid from the £15,000 which Cork had been obliged to give on loan to the king, and which Goring had undertaken to recover when the term of the loan fell due.[115] In other words, Cork had discovered an ingenious way to recover a loan which the king might easily have come to regard as permanent. Cork had also saddled Goring with responsibility for recovering the misplaced Beaumont dowry, and Goring was also 'enthralled for his service' in treating with the Duchess of Lennox for the

Kildare wardship, and investigating that young earl's debts.[116] Despite being thus treated as Cork's man-of-all-work at court, Goring sought to placate the disappointed Earl of Cork. A reconciliation was not achieved, however, until Goring procured the governorship of Portsmouth for his spendthrift son – a position, as Cork boasted, which had never hitherto been held by anybody of lower rank than an earl[117] – and until, during his visit to England of 1639–41, Cork was accorded the honours which, he suggested, Goring had undertaken to arrange for him when the marriage alliance was first engaged upon. These were, as he mentioned casually to Sir Thomas Stafford, that in return for the apparently excessive dowry he 'should be made a privy councillor or have the addition of a title of honour in England'.[118]

Once the first of these ambitions was within Cork's grasp, relations between himself and Lord Goring underwent a complete transformation. Cork expressed satisfaction at every indication of improvement in Goring's position in the king's favour, and he was particularly gratified when in September 1639 he and Goring, with four of Cork's sons, were given a hundred-gun salute as they approached the gates of Portsmouth, having ridden together from Cork's residence at Stalbridge in Dorsetshire. Here at last was evidence that he was accepted by Goring as an equal, and that their alliance was being publicly acknowledged by both Goring and his son, now governor of Portsmouth.[119]

However, the fact that Cork thought it necessary to win his way on to the English privy council or to obtain an English title is proof that he considered his previous worldly achievement to be somehow inadequate. This inadequacy, which he was reluctant to acknowledge publicly, derived from the fact that his estates, his title and the future of his dynasty were laid in Ireland. His frequently deprecating remarks on Ireland[120] indicate that he had little regard for anything which derived from that source. This does not mean, however, that he regretted having moved there, nor that he did not think others should do likewise. Far from it, whenever he departed from his eschatological view of his career Cork acknowledged that by moving to Ireland he had sidestepped the barriers to social advancement which existed in

England. Nevertheless he, like many other planters, measured worldly success in English terms, and valued achievement in Ireland only in so far as it progressed towards social advancement in England.

A close study of the surviving evidence reveals that from quite early in his career in Ireland Boyle intended to transfer at least some of his assets to England. Furthermore it would seem that the hero whom he wished to emulate was George Carew who, having laid the foundations to his fortune in Ireland, quietly transferred himself to England and used his wealth to obtain an English peerage and an office under the crown.[121] Carew's achievement was so highly regarded by Boyle that *Pacata Hibernia*, which was largely concerned with Carew's career in Ireland, became his most cherished secular discourse,[122] and even the 'True Remembrances' would appear to have been modelled on Carew's account of his own career which was preserved among Boyle's papers.[123]

That Boyle originally intended, after Carew's example, to employ his Irish profits to procure an office in England is suggested by his possession of 'a book of fees of all the king's offices in England' which he acquired in 1617,[124] just after he had become baron but before he had purchased an Irish earldom. Such documents were usually consulted by those who intended to purchase office,[125] and more tangible proof that Boyle then contemplated such a purchase emerges from a furtive letter sent in early 1618 from Boyle's cousin Christopher Browne at Deptford to Boyle's brother-in-law, Sir William Fenton, at Youghal. In this, Browne revealed that he had approached Sir Humphrey May, chancellor of the duchy, with a view to acquiring an office for 'a friend... who was desirous to deal for the same'. The office was allegedly valued by May at £700 per annum to the holder, and it reputedly carried with it 'the countenance of a privy councillor's place which is incident thereunto'. The only condition attached was that the holder should be 'both an experienced soldier and of a degree fitting the place of a privy councillor'.[126] The prospective customer can only have been Boyle and he would undoubtedly have considered himself suited to these requirements. However, since at the stated asking price of £1,000 the office was clearly a bargain, it is difficult to understand why Boyle did not push his suit, or why, if his bid was unsuccessful on that occasion, he did not canvass for other positions as they fell vacant.

That Boyle was, in these years, fairly intent on transferring himself to England is made clear by his then seeking information of Mr Ludloe's manor of Fareham in Hampshire 'that I am to purchase'.[127] No further mention was made of this property, but the Vaughan and Boyle cousins in Gloucestershire, like the Brownes in Kent, must have been primed to keep Richard Boyle informed of possible purchases since in 1612 and again in 1613 they let him know of land for sale in Gloucestershire, the county whence his 'ancestors came'.[128] One manor, that of Standish in Gloucestershire, was particularly recommended by his cousin Richard Boyle of Maistmore, and Boyle proceeded so far that he had a survey taken and, as he subsequently claimed, had paid £5,000 of the agreed price of £14,000. When the proprietor, one Mr Winston, and Sir Ralph Dutton's father defeated his purpose Boyle supposedly complained to King James who reputedly ordered the return to Boyle of his £5,000, together with £500 for breach of contract. Otherwise, claimed Boyle, the king was 'not willing [he] should make any purchase in England to divert [him] from Ireland'.[129]

This, like most other mention of royal intervention in Boyle's career, might be fanciful, but it does seem that at that point Boyle suddenly dismissed from his mind the idea of moving to England and instead, from 1618 to 1630, concentrated on pursuing his career in Ireland. After 1618, Cork involved himself in Irish politics which he had hitherto avoided, and he invested further money in Irish property.[130] By doing so, Cork acted contrary to the advice of supporters and potential allies. One of Cork's subordinates in Munster predicted in 1623 that his departure to Dublin and his 'continuance there' would bring about his 'ruin' and the decline of his fortune which had already 'ended her rising course'; a prognostication which the author believed to be so self-evident that 'none but the witless, misunderstanding the time, would expect the contrary'.[131] With regard to the continued purchase of Irish land, Cork acted in such complete defiance of all English advisors that when in 1621 he was negotiating a marriage alliance

with Sir Edward Villiers he had first to persuade him that he was
finally 'resolved' to follow his counsel 'and purchase no more land
in Ireland'.[132] Even then Cork did not honour his resolution, and
in 1630 Goring had to warn him sternly that if he wished to
match Dungarvan in England he should 'leave purchasing in
Ireland and plant here [in England], for me thinks all in an Irish
bottom with such pilots as have been and may be again when we
are dead and gone I cannot allow of'.[133] Nevertheless, Cork
succeeded in matching Dungarvan with Elizabeth Clifford, and
had it not been for his bitter experience with Wentworth, Cork
would seemingly never have recognised the wisdom or necessity of
diversifying his investment.

From 1634 onwards Cork, after a hiatus of sixteen years, was
again investigating the possibility of purchases in the English west
country or in his native Kent.[134] By 1636 he had opted for the
west country, because of its proximity to his Munster estates, and
he was then resolved 'to have a retiring place' in England where
he could 'spend the small remainder of the time allotted' to him in
the service of God 'and in the neighbourhood and society of good
friends'.[135] Shortly afterwards, Cork purchased from Lord Castlehaven for £5,000 the manor of Stalbridge in Dorsetshire which
became his English seat, and in 1637 he laid out a further £20,000
for Temple Coombe, another manor conveniently close to Stalbridge which he intended to be 'the last and only purchase' which
he would 'make in England'. This final resolution was broken
only at the insistence of the Howards who, as we saw, forced him
to invest a further £5,000 in English land.[136]

It is difficult to account for this pattern of behaviour, but one
possible explanation is that, having in 1617 encountered difficulty
in obtaining office in England, Cork set his sights on office in
Ireland which he hoped would finally win him social recognition
and acceptance in England. It was, after all, through tenure of
the lord deputyship of Ireland that Sir Arthur Chichester had
come to the attention of the government in England, and was
nominated to the English privy council as the final reward for his
services.[137] Cork had great admiration for Chichester,[138] and
obviously liked to consider that his social success established a

precedent, because Cork's involvement in Irish politics was obviously aimed at securing the lord deputyship. This barely eluded him in 1629 when he was forced to share the governorship of Ireland with Adam Loftus, but he then settled for the honorary office of lord treasurer in Ireland and waited for a future opportunity to improve upon this position. When he paid £200 to Sir William Beecher, clerk of the council in England, to solicit the treasurership for him, he pleaded that his approach remain secret, for he would 'rather lose it than any man should know' he had paid for the position. What he wished men to think was that 'it was bestowed freely... as a mark of his Majesties grace'.[139] But since he had convinced himself that favour could be purchased it was reasonable that Cork should expect eventually to be suggested for deputy. It took the assault launched against him by Wentworth to disillusion Cork. This final realisation may explain why Cork again looked to England for purchases, since if he was now obliged to seek social advancement in England itself he had to comply with the dictates of the arbiters of fashion there. Even then, however, he expected that his past service to the crown in Ireland would give him some claim to advancement. Furthermore, he never abandoned hope of succeeding to the lord deputyship which suggests that, having spent his career in Ireland, he had come to accept that advancement there was a worthy end in itself provided that it was complemented by some mark of recognition in England.

That Cork, towards the end of his career, was inclined to remain permanently in Ireland might be explained by the discomfort which he obviously experienced in associating with the upper echelons of English society. In matters of behaviour and comportment, Cork recognised that he lacked many of the graces, accomplishments and even vices of the true noble. His inadequacy in these matters was hardly noticeable in Ireland prior to Wentworth's arrival, where nobles and officials were either of Gaelic and Old English origin or were, like Cork himself, New English who had recently been elevated to eminent positions. Whenever Cork went to England, however, and even in Ireland subsequent to the arrival of Wentworth, he was made to feel socially inadequate as appears from his efforts to assume the mores of those with whom he would associate as equals.

'I am no courtier', wrote Cork to Goring, 'and therefore I pray expect no compliments from me, but a plain prosecution of my business.'[140] This display of bravado sounds unconvincing, and Cork's general discomfiture in associating with people of high station is suggested by his seeking out the company of provincial gentry rather than courtly nobles whenever he had leisure time available to him in England. Cork never forgot his 'own native inviolate soil of Kent upon which the conqueror did never set his foot',[141] and after his elevation to the Irish peerage he established contact with the local notables of Canterbury and Faversham. In 1633, when Dungarvan was returning from his continental tour, he was instructed by his father to travel through Canterbury where he should visit Sir Peter Hayman, Sir Christopher Man and Dean Bargrave before viewing the church and school at Faversham, where Cork had had most of his 'breeding', and the church at Preston where Dungarvan's grandparents were buried.[142] During his own visits to England Cork took time from the round of social calls on important political figures to visit relatives and acquaintances in Kent. When, in 1636, Cork contemplated the purchase of St Leger property at St Steven near Canterbury he deferred for advice to Sir Christopher Man and Dean Bargrave.[143] His Kent origin also served as an introduction to Sir Henry Wotton, Provost of Eton, who acted as his principal advisor on the upbringing and education of his sons.[144] Cork also rejoiced in the success of fellow Kentishmen, as for example the elevation of his countryman Sir John Finch of Canterbury to the position of lord chief justice of England. None of this means that Cork was, in his youth, acquainted with these men, and his cultivation of them may have been partly intended to convey the impression that he himself was of gentle origin. Nevertheless, the relative openness of his letters to them, compared with his deferential communications to courtiers, suggests that he sought them out because he could more readily relate to them as equals.

Cork's relationship with George Carew and Thomas Stafford was, as is evident from the correspondence, also open and warm.

In his later years in England one of the attractions of spending time at Stalbridge was its close proximity to Sherborne, the Earl of Bristol's residence, where Cork was always at his ease and mixed freely with the nobility and gentry of the west country;[145] pleasant relaxation, no doubt, after the stilted atmosphere at court where Cork was never comfortable but where he nevertheless felt compelled to attend in pursuit of his ambition.

It was to his English provincial friends that Cork confided his sense of inadequacy, and it was from these also that he sought advice. Thus in soliciting counsel from Sir Henry Wotton on how to organise a continental tour for his sons he was able without difficulty to acknowledge himself 'altogether ignorant' of such matters 'having never travelled out of England and Ireland'.[146] While making such self-effacing confessions to those he could trust and with whom he could most easily relate, Cork resolved to improve himself, and he was absolutely determined that his sons would never have to struggle with the consciousness of social inadequacy that he himself was plagued with. This explains his obsession with providing 'a religious learned and noble breeding' for his sons, to which by comparison all other worldly concerns were 'far inferior'.[147] At an early stage he was resolved to have them 'bred in England and abroad in the world, and not to have their youth infected with the leaven of Ireland'.[148]

As to Cork's concern with self-improvement, he constantly studied how to compensate for the absence of a gentlemanly upbringing and his lack of social grace. Even then Cork occasionally displayed some uncertainty, as when in 1639 he thanked his London agent, William Perkins, for having reminded him to send a New Year's gift to the king 'which I did never conceive was used by any of the lords of Ireland'.[149] His caution on that occasion may be explained by his excessive liberality with gifts in earlier years when he suffered the embarrassment of having some returned to him.[150] In the matter of dress, particularly for formal occasions, Cork was so uncertain of himself that he carried correctness to the point of fastidiousness. One of the functions of William Perkins was to keep Cork informed on changes of fashion in London, and to supply him and his family with suitable attire and furnishings for public occasions.¹⁵¹ Parliament robes were a matter of particular concern to Cork, and he became such an authority on parliamentary decorum that he was able to advise his sons and son-in-law, Barrymore, on how to prepare themselves for the occasion.¹⁵² House furnishings for Lismore castle and Cork House in Dublin were also acquired in London, and the current fashion in London determined the choice.

At Lismore also Cork sought to reshape the surrounding landscape in imitation of the surrounds of an English lordly mansion. The importance which this assumed for Cork can be gauged from the fact that the development and stocking of a deer park, the selection and grafting of fruit trees, the making of fish ponds, the development of a stud, the erection of eyries, the construction of a rabbit warren and the breeding of English cattle and sheep all assume as much importance in Cork's correspondence as the clearing of forests, the building of castles, towns and fortifications or the development of iron smelting or the erection of religious and educational foundations: they all contributed equally, in Cork's mind, to shaping the countryside – especially that adjacent to Lismore – after the English fashion.¹⁵³ Indeed Cork was so confident of his achievement in this direction that he assured Lord and Lady Clifford that when they visited him they would find life at Lismore little different from what they were accustomed to in Yorkshire, with 'frequent and good sermons and music in my chapel' for Lady Clifford, 'and to my Lord hawks and hounds'. Even in the construction of castles Cork always sought to imitate rather than to surpass what was accepted as good taste. Thus, in planning Carrigaline castle for his son Francis, Cork wished for nothing better than a direct replica of the St Leger castle at Doneraile.¹⁵⁴

Imitation also characterised Cork's personal comportment and behaviour. During his last visit to England, when he finally succeeded in winning acceptance at court, he reconciled himself to living after the extravagant manner of the court nobility. He kept 'so plentiful a house' at the Savoy that many years later his son Robert commented on the staggering cost. Mary Boyle also remembered her father at that time 'living extraordinarily high', and she herself having been in his house 'almost in constant crowds of company'. That their life style was a pose which he consciously adopted to suit present purposes is made clear from his decision prior to his departure from Ireland in 1638, as in 1628, to clear himself of all debts, thus making it possible for him to indulge in an orgy of extravagance which he seemed to believe was expected of a noble. Even then he tried to operate within an allowance, and was so perturbed to discover that his daughter Barrymore and daughter-in-law Dungarvan had overspent the household budget at Stalbridge by £700 that it was only consideration 'for the preservation of their credits and mine in the country' that persuaded him to meet the charge.[155] The brave show of extravagance and ostentation must really have convinced nobody who knew his tight-fisted nature, and while circumstances compelled him to affect extravagance as a public virtue he continued to regard it as a private vice.

Some of the noble pastimes which had not formed part of his early life, but which his elevation and his continued ambition forced him to pursue, seem to have been considered by him as bothersome distractions from the real concerns of life. Thus when, during his visit to Lismore, Lord Clifford was entertained by his 'old brother [-in-law] in his old suit' to more than a week's hunting, the expedition quickly descended to a practical level since, as Clifford put it, Cork would have had him 'survey all the land he hath in Ireland if I had the vanity to follow him, or the faith to believe him in his narrative legends concerning the provident purchases of them'.[156]

The most arresting instance of Cork seeking to win social acceptance through conformity was his involvement in games of chance and his placing of wagers during the period of Wentworth's residence in Dublin. Since gambling, even for small wagers, involved betting on chance, it was logical enough that it should have been strictly excluded from the household of one who attributed all chance or unexpected happenings to providence. Then suddenly, from 1634 onwards, regular entries appear in Cork's diary that refer to his losses at gambling. On first reading this suggests that Cork had cast all his earlier prudence to the wind, but then just as dramatically, in August 1637, all mention of gambling ceases and reappears only when he visits England. When on closer scrutiny it appears that most of the gambling incidents are associated with Wentworth and his followers, and that the seeming termination coincided with Cork's final departure from Wentworth's company, one is forced to conclude that Cork, in his anxiety to win acceptance among the new ruling group in Dublin, began to compromise on his earlier principles.

The first reference is to the loss of £6 at dice to Wentworth himself in January 1634; this was followed in April 1634 by the loss of a beaver hat in a wager with a gentleman of the lord deputy on a horse-race at the Curragh of Kildare. A lull seems to have followed these early forays, but there was reference in March 1635 to the loss of a gelding to Sir James Erskine for having incorrectly forecast the sex of the child which Cork's daughter, Lady Kildare, had then delivered. In June 1635 Cork wagered a pair of silk stockings with Lady Parsons on whether or not the Earl of Westmeath had returned from foreign travel.[157] In January 1636 Cork made mention of a loss of six pieces at play in the lord deputy's house, and in the same month he referred to a financial arrangement into which he had entered with his daughter-in-law Lady Dungarvan (Wentworth's niece) to assist her in recovering some of the £40 which she had lost at play over the Christmas period.[158] This record of what, by Cork's previous standards, can only be described as an orgy of speculation is a measure of the distance which Cork was prepared to travel in order to win acceptance, even in the social group that formed in Dublin around Wentworth and his clients. The fact that only losses are mentioned might mean that the diary entries were another dimension to his meticulous accounting system, but it is more likely that Cork was distinctly uncomfortable with this newly acquired vice and hoped to salve his conscience over these moral lapses by entering them in his diary.[159]

The fact that Cork never fully accommodated himself to the life style which was commensurate with the rank and social position to which he aspired, or never fully succeeded in suppressing habits and traits from his earlier life, is revealed in many other instances besides those related to gambling. Even in the matter of seeking patrons at court Cork could never bring himself to trust any man and failed dismally in his effort to conceal his mistrust of even those he sought to cultivate. Buckingham and the Villiers family may have, in several respects, treated Cork disgracefully but they did, for a price, assist him in several matters, most especially in obtaining titles for himself, his sons and Lord Barrymore. These favours were clearly of importance to Boyle at the time, but his failure to acknowledge them and his persistence in complaining that he had always been ill-used by the Villiers family gave King Charles reason to remind Cork that 'upon his knowledge', Buckingham 'was the truest friend' he 'had in England'.[160] Similarly, when Cork enlisted Goring as his solicitor at court he gave him every reason to complain of 'vexation and mistrust in every step' that Goring took on his behalf.[161]

All of this serves to illustrate the point that while Cork eventually attained most of his social ambitions, he himself was so conscious of his inability to assume the life style of those at court that he never got beyond the stage of role playing. What is important, however, is that he sought to play the role, and even if his awkwardness and self-consciousness gave him away on occasions he succeeded in playing the part with sufficient conviction to meet the requirements of those from whom he sought favour and with whose families he would intermarry. This was still a considerable distance from being accepted as an equal and it would appear that Cork had reconciled himself to never attaining this ambition, and he aimed instead to have his sons succeed where he himself had failed. Much of the training that he designed for them was intended to serve this purpose and the young Boyles so surpassed themselves in being schooled as aristocrats that Cork himself felt uneasy in their company.[162] There can be no doubt, however, that he rejoiced in this particular discomfiture, and the most welcome letter that he ever received may well have been that from Pembroke and Salisbury, in March 1638, which assured him that he had no need to proceed to England with undue haste because his son Dungarvan was 'a good courtier' with many 'friends and allies'.[163]

When Cork did travel to court he found that such was the alteration in political circumstances since his previous visit that it was now possible for him to revive his claim for further social advancement. The king and his advisors who had long since decided that Cork deserved no further elevation were not in a position to spurn support from any quarter, and therefore conceded to his request for appointment as an English privy councillor. Who proposed Cork for this particular elevation remains a mystery but one court observer was convinced that 'besides the late great alliance he hath contracted by the marriages of his children [Cork] hath paid both vows and oblations at some altar or other, before he could be admitted to the honour of the board'. This judgement seemed all the more valid because, in the light of recent events, Cork's 'exaltation' seemed to imply Strafford's 'diminution' and it was reported that Strafford himself feared 'that through the prospect of this promotion the earl looketh upon succeeding of him in the government of that kingdom'. This ambition, as was mentioned in the third chapter, was also fostered by Cork's confidants, and the fact that that particular appointment was denied him, as was the English peerage which Cork so dearly coveted, indicates that there were still some limits to what could be bought. Nonetheless, with the admission of Richard Boyle to the privy council it was being admitted that lowly birth and doubtful reputation were no bars to social advancement at the court of Charles I.[164]

It is tempting to speculate that the extension of this mark of social acceptance to the Earl of Cork further contributed to the erosion of respect in England for the king and his associates. There can be no doubt that many resented this final social elevation enjoyed by Cork but the most prominent among them would have been those like Wentworth whose attachment to the monarchy was unshakeable. As for those who were pitted against the king, they would, if anything, have noted Cork's elevation with approval because he was widely recognised as the principal victim of what was being described as Wentworth's tyranny in Ireland. Thus it would seem that this final elevation of the most remarkable parvenu in Stuart England possibly helped to prop up a monarchy on the point of collapse, and in no way contributed to an erosion of respect for either the court or the aristocracy.

5

The family life of Richard Boyle

It was noted in the second chapter that Wentworth took particular delight in casting aspersions on the Earl of Cork's domestic arrangements, and apart from their entertainment value Wentworth's remarks should be appreciated by historians because they served the unintended purpose of compelling Richard Boyle to reveal more than he would otherwise have done of the more intimate aspects of his career. Further scattered comments on his private life were unwittingly dropped by Cork in his business diary and in the course of his correspondence: comments that all are the more valuable to the historian because they were casual and hence unguarded. Such comments are thus very different from the detailed statements on the upbringing and education of his sons which the Earl of Cork compiled for the direction of their tutors. Even these measured statements have a unique value as a source for family history during the early-modern period because the extent to which the father followed his own counsel and the response that his training programme evoked from his children can be gauged from the mature reflections on their childhood years composed by two of the Boyle children: the youngest son Robert Boyle, and the youngest surviving daughter, Mary, Countess of Warwick.[1]

This almost unique range of material relating to his private affairs in itself renders the family life of Richard Boyle a suitable subject to study. The Boyle family experience also commands our attention because it was possibly the most remarkable family ever to be raised in Ireland. The only product of Richard Boyle's first marriage was a still-born son, but his second wife Catherine Fenton

TABLE 1. *The vital statistics of Richard Boyle's family*

No.	Name	Date of Birth	Interval between (months)
1.	Still-born son	14 December 1599	49 (from marriage)
2.	Roger	1 August 1606	36 (from marriage)
3.	Alice	20 March 1608	$19\frac{1}{2}$
4.	Sarah	29 March 1609	12
5.	Lettice	25 April 1610	13
6.	Joan	14 June 1611	14
7.	Richard	20 October 1612	16
8.	Catherine	22 March 1615	29
9.	Geoffrey	10 April 1616	$12\frac{1}{2}$
10.	Dorothy	30 December 1617	20
11.	Lewis	23 May 1619	17
12.	Roger	25 April 1621	23
13.	Francis	25 June 1623	26
14.	Mary	11 November 1625	29
15.	Robert	20 January 1627	14
16.	Margaret	30 April 1629	27

Richard Boyle (born 3 October 1566, died 1643) married on 6 November 1595 to Joan Apsley (died in childbirth 14 December 1599), and married on 25 July 1603 to Catherine Fenton (born c. 1588, died 16 February 1630).

bore a total of fifteen children of whom eleven survived to adulthood. Even more remarkable than the size of the family was the array of talent that was included within it, ranging from a political figure-cum-playwright[2] of the stature of Roger (Baron Broghill, and later Earl of Orrery), to a scientist-cum-philosopher of the eminence of Robert Boyle,[3] to Catherine, Lady Ranelagh, the most renowed female intellectual of her generation[4] and to an equally illustrious woman, Mary, Countess of Warwick, who, by her personal example, demonstrated how, through the cultivation of private devotion, a woman could achieve complete independence from the oppressive dominance of men.[5] Besides these luminaries, whose names are remembered even today, the family included Richard, Viscount Dungarvan and eventually second Earl of Cork, who became the great social success of the family when he was elevated to the English peerage first as Baron Clifford and later as Earl of Burlington; Lewis, Viscount Kinalmeaky (killed in battle, 1642), on whom the discerning father had pinned his highest hopes and whose military prowess impressed even the Gaelic poets of the seventeenth century;[6] Francis, Viscount Shannon, who achieved recognition in Restoration England as a moralist and social counsellor;[7] and the remaining daughters Joan, Dorothy, Sarah, Alice and Lettice, who, if not remembered by posterity, nonetheless contributed to their family's greatness by engaging upon the marriages that were negotiated for them.

Because the Boyle family was an intrinsically interesting one the study of it requires no apology, but the domestic life of Richard Boyle is rendered more attractive to historians because his life experience – moving upwards from lowly status to enormous wealth, and migrating from England to an overseas settlement – suggests that his family arrangements might serve as an appropriate test case for recent theses on the changing character of the English family during the early-modern period. Therefore as an aid to understanding the historical significance of the family life of Richard Boyle it will be necessary to look briefly at recent writing on the early-modern family with a view to considering this particular case study in its historical context.

The history, like the sociology, of the family as an institution first gained academic recognition in the present century, possibly because people were seeking reassurance that the apparent breakdown of family life which was associated with divorce would not lead to a complete collapse of the social order. If people were in fact seeking such reassurance, they must have been satisfied with much of what was written by sociologists and historians since this suggested that, in the past, the family had been a multi-purpose institution which was assigned with responsibility for the nurture, education, discipline and socialisation of children as well as care for the elderly but that, as one moved forward in time, many of these responsibilities were assumed by public institutions.[8] This suggestion indicated that where, in earlier periods, the family had indeed been an essential bulwark of the social order it was less essential to that end in more recent times, and therefore that more frequent divorce did not presage the social chaos that the prophets of doom were predicting. Associated with this idea, which was assumed rather than proven, was the notion that the structure of the family had also become simplified as one moved forward in time, as a shift occurred from an extended three-generational family that was supposed to have existed everywhere in the pre-industrial period to the simple nuclear family of parents and children that was evidently the norm in modern industrialised societies.[9]

In so far as historical evidence was provided for this supposed family transformation it was of a literary nature, and these assumptions found almost universal acceptance until they were shown to be seriously inadequate by the findings of the Cambridge Group for the History of Population and Social Structure. This group focused its attention on English parish records for the seventeenth century and demonstrated through its re-constitution of families in pre-industrial England that the nuclear family had been the norm in England long before the industrial revolution, and that whatever social upheavals might be attributed to that event one should not include among them any basic alteration in the composition of families.[10] Peter Laslett, the great populariser of that group's endeavours, has pressed home the point that the nuclear family as we know it today has been the great social constant in the modern history of the western world. Furthermore, Laslett has suggested that the experience of growing up in a family has changed little over time when he argues that divorce (which the sociologists and moralists believed to have created completely novel problems) merely played the part that premature death had previously done in bringing about the early dissolution of marriage – and with it the assignment of children to the care of a single parent, or a parent and step-parent, or to other relatives.[11]

The extent to which the evidence presented by the Cambridge Group for the early existence of the nuclear family has won acceptance among historians can be ascertained from the fact that those scholars who have since encountered the extended family in places and times not allowed for by the orthodoxy of the Group have usually sought to explain its occurrence as a deviation from the norm occasioned by a major demographic or economic disaster.[12] Acceptance of the orthodoxy has clearly deflected historians from engaging upon further family reconstitution studies, and family history as such might have ceased to be written were it not for the provocation caused by Laslett's second proposition: that the experience of growing up in a family did not change significantly over time. Since this proposition can be tested only against literary evidence, the principal long-term impact of the Cambridge Group's findings on the activity of other historians has been to divert them away from demographic data, on which their now generally accepted master-fact was based,[13] towards the investigation of literary material which, it was hoped, would cast light on how interaction between members of the nuclear family organism have responded to cultural and economic alterations in the society at large. That historians should consider the investigation of such family interactions to be worthy of attention derives, of course, from the general acceptance of the belief of psychologists that if one is to comprehend the behaviour of an individual in adult life one must have some knowledge of his socialisation in childhood.

The most notable contributions in the English language of this new type of family history have understandably come from the United States, where a knowledge of behavioural science has for long been considered an essential tool in the historian's kit. For the early-modern period Lawrence Stone, firstly in *The Crisis of the Aristocracy, 1558–1641* and more recently in *The Family, Sex and Marriage in England, 1500–1800*, has been most successful in shaping our understanding of how and why familial relationships underwent change.[14] Professor Stone, who draws principally on the English experience, argues that relationships within the nuclear family responded so readily to external pressures that one can speak of a sequence of dominant family types during the years 1500–1800, each sequential type being a product of a shift in values that had taken place in the macro-society. Indeed, that author is so convinced of the susceptibility of familial relationships to manipulation by outside forces, that he accounts for overlap between his designated family types by referring to variations in the pace at which the changing cultural values were dispersed throughout the different regions of England and through the several strata of English society.[15]

Thus, Stone argues that the three sequential dominant family types which he describes correspond to a sequence of three dominant value systems that prevailed in England during the early-modern period. The first family type – the Open Lineage Family – is thought to have flourished when England was dominated by a lineage culture which required the individual to focus his loyalty on the wider kinship group rather than on his immediate family, or even his father.[16] This family type gave way, claims Stone, to the Restricted Patriarchal Nuclear Family which was characterised by the father being the focus of loyalty within the nuclear family; a transformation that occurred when people throughout Europe came to attach supreme importance to personal rule as the only guarantee of social order.[17] This in turn, it is averred, was displaced by the Closed Domesticated Nuclear Family, a type that was characterised by affective individualism. This dimension to domestic relationships, which Professor Stone contrasts with the austerity that typified interactions between members of the Restricted Patriarchal Nuclear Family, is alleged to have resulted principally from the increased importance that came to be associated with individual effort in the thriving competitive society of eighteenth-century England.[18]

Another historian, working with literary evidence, who also argues in favour of three dominant family types during the early-modern period is Professor Philip Greven who presents his case for the family experience in colonial North America in a book entitled *The Protestant Temperament: Patterns of Child-Rearing, Religious Experience and the Self in Early America*.[19] Greven comes close to Professor Stone's position when he suggests that the principal factor that determines the formation of family types is the extent to which the loyalty of the family members is focused on the father as head of the household, and he is in complete agreement with Stone in thinking that the principal moral support for paternal authority is intense religious fervour. Where Greven diverges from Stone, however, is in seeking an explanation for the incidence of religious fervour during the early-modern period.

For Professor Stone this was something that people resorted to when they believed their social order was endangered, and which faded again when people had become confident that they controlled their environment. Professor Greven's reading of the colonial American material has, however, suggested to him that variations were evident in the intensity of religious fervour that obtained at any one time, and that these variations tended to coincide with levels of affluence: poor migrant families being closely identified with intense religious fervour and affluent sedentary families being less inclined to undergo the privations required by a fundamentalist religion.[20] This leads Professor Greven to the conclusion that the underpinnings of paternal authority were normally weaker in affluent than in poor households, and that the indulging of children (an essential aspect of Professor Stone's affective individualism) was something that was exclusive to wealthier households.[21] An even more fundamental difference between the two historians relates to the question of change over time. Philip Greven finds no evidence in the colonial material of a sequence of family types, and since each of the three types identified by him is associated with a particular level of affluence he sees no reason why, without a major alteration in the social and economic order, one should expect any one family type to displace the other two. Furthermore, Greven insists, throughout his book, that colonial North America was in some respects merely a segment of a society, and while making a case for the existence of three recognisable family types there he allows for the possibility that an even more extensive range of family types might exist in other places; the range being determined by the spectrum of wealth and the gradations of rank that existed in any given society.[22]

This brief historiographical account has sought to isolate the principal points of disagreement between the two leading historians who have addressed themselves to the problem of how general social change affected familial relationships in the English-speaking world during the early-modern period. However, the fact that disagreement exists points to the need for testing the general pattern as perceived by these two historians against the life-experience of individuals. The number of individuals who lend themselves to close analysis is extremely limited because of the dearth of source material that relates to people's private lives. For this reason alone, as was mentioned, the family life of Richard Boyle is particularly apposite for the purpose in hand, but it is also appropriate as a test-case for Lawrence Stone's argument for the following reasons: firstly because Richard Boyle's career, 1566–1643, coincides with the time-span that is allotted by Stone to the dominance of the Restricted Patriarchal Nuclear Family; secondly because Boyle was the most upwardly mobile Englishman of his generation and should, if one is to be guided by Professor Stone's contention that change in familial relationships first manifested itself in upwardly mobile families,[23] fit precisely with Stone's model; and thirdly because Lawrence Stone, himself, seems to have detected that the Boyle experience should support his general propositions, as is suggested by the frequency with which he cites the example of Boyle or his children to support various points in his argument.[24] Equally well, the Boyle family experience is suited to the purpose of testing the validity of Philip Greven's conclusions. In the first instance Boyle, like the subjects of Greven's analysis, was an unsettled migrant for much of his life, so that one would expect to find him gravitating towards a fundamentalist Protestantism which in turn would persuade him to adopt an extremely patriarchal attitude towards his children. Then again, Professor Greven's conclusions would lead one to expect that as Boyle's fortunes improved, his religious intensity, and with it his severe attitude towards his wife and children, should have become more moderate.

Both historians can derive consolation from the fact that the initial impression one derives from the sources is that Richard Boyle carried patriarchalism to an extreme level. This impression is conveyed firstly by outsiders, most especially Thomas Wentworth who remarked that Cork behaved in such an authoritarian manner towards his children that they had reason to fear and distrust him, and he further professed to be amazed that the Boyle children were so dutiful towards their father that they failed to appreciate that they were being abused by him.[25] Apart from such emotive reportage, there is plenty of evidence from Cork's own perspective which reveals that he saw himself as a patriarch and expected his wife and children to concede unquestioning obedience to him in all matters, even in those which bore upon their personal happiness more than his. This patriarchalism can be witnessed firstly in Cork's attitude towards his wife, his daughters and women in general and secondly in his attitude towards his sons.

The qualities which Cork admired in his own wife were that she was 'most religious, virtuous, loving and obedient',[26] but this last was seldom put to the test since Cork seems to have entrusted her with little of consequence. Housekeeping accounts were closely supervised by Cork,[27] the ordering and selection of gowns and jewels for important occasions were done by the earl himself,[28] and would-be creditors were instructed not to extend money on loan to his wife.[29] Decisions relating to the education of their sons or the marriages of their daughters would appear to have been taken by Cork with little consideration for his wife's views, and on one occasion when he acknowledged that her opinion had decided him on agreeing to a marriage he regretted that he had allowed himself to be influenced by the subjective considerations which she had introduced.[30]

The general impression conveyed by the sources is that Cork considered women to be unreliable because they were guided by emotion rather than reason. His belief in their unreliability was carried to such an extreme that he considered women could not even be depended upon to calculate correctly the number of days between the conception and delivery of their children. Two of his daughters, Catherine, Lady Ranelagh, and Sarah, Lady Digby, caused Cork acute embarrassment by their miscalculations, and Cork reported ruefully, after Lady Ranelagh had presented him with a fully formed infant which according to her own reckoning was ten weeks premature, that his daughter would 'never be one of his Majesties auditors'.[31] It may well be Cork's lack of confidence in women to deal with the one crucial function of which they could not be deprived which explains his curiosity over matters relating to female sexuality. Cork seems to have had some crude notion of a relationship between conception and the menstrual cycle,[32] and he certainly was aware of 'the unnatural and unchristian-like' practice of purging during the early stages of pregnancy which was liable to provoke abortion, and which therefore should be studiously avoided by those of 'religious breeding and disposition' when they found themselves in that condition.[33] Despite his knowledge in such matters, Cork appears to have been more concerned to determine the onset of pregnancy so that he could enforce precautionary measures against possible miscarriage[34] rather than to establish the date on which the birth was due. This latter appears in fact to have been a matter of some indifference to him, other than when it upset his travel arrangements, and there is no evidence that he assisted or was present at the birth of any of his many children. Since Cork was frequently absent from home when his wife's time of delivery was due, and since on one occasion he returned six days after the birth to find his wife 'at the point of death', we must suppose that he considered this to be an aspect over which he could exert no direct influence and which therefore did not require his presence.[35]

Even in the matter of grief, Cork was convinced that women were more emotional and hence less capable of restraining themselves than men. Since it was expected of the true Christian that he resign himself to the acceptance of losses and reverses as part of God's design, Cork was therefore implying that women were like children in being less capable than men of concentrating their minds on God. For example, after the death in 1623 of his son-in-law Thomas Moore, Cork conceded that he had permitted sorrow to make 'an over dear impression' on himself before he finally became resigned to God's will, but, as he put it, his grief was 'the greater' because his 'mother[-in-law] and wife with all the children' could neither 'be drawn' by Cork's 'persuasions in reason nor by religious inducements to give any end or pause to their lamentations'.[36] Cork's assumption that women were more emotional and hence weaker than men suggests that he also thought them incapable of intellectual concentration. This attitude is ironic in the father of Catherine, Lady Ranelagh, but from what can be gleaned from the sources it would seem that Cork provided no formal education for his daughters beyond that which they obtained from his chaplains who doubled as tutors. If one is to take Lettice Goring as a typical product of this instruction, she had, by the time of her marriage, hardly proceeded beyond a minimal level of literacy and one might suppose that she had never been exposed to any literature other than that of a spiritual nature.[37] This is an extreme example, and one must balance this evidence against Cork's gift of Philip Sidney's *Arcadia* to his daughter Mary when she was but ten years old.[38] What does distinguish between Cork's attitude towards sons and daughters is, however, the fact that he reveals in his diary and correspondence that he was constantly preoccupied with his sons' education while one gets the impression from the few scattered references to his daughters' upbringing that their formal education cost him little thought once he was satisfied that they were free from the corrupting influence of romantic literature.[39]

It might be argued that this contrast in attitudes towards the education of sons and daughters is as much a reflection of the role which was allotted by society to women of noble rank as it is of Cork's belief in women's incapacity for further education. Nevertheless, Cork emerges strikingly as a patriarch in the degree to which he appears to have regarded his daughters as a marketable commodity whose principal usefulness was to advance the political and social position of the parental family through their marriage connections. That this, rather than the future happiness of his daughters, was the prime consideration in Cork's mind also becomes clear when one compares the ages at which he set about negotiating marriages for his sons and daughters. The average age at which Cork entered into discussion relating to the marriages of those of his four sons who did marry was sixteen,[40] while offers for his daughters in marriage were entertained almost from the moment of birth, leading to the incredibly low average age of nine years for the commencement of negotiations.[41] Since many of the negotiations were inconclusive and since marriages were sometimes postponed for several years after the contracts had been concluded, the average ages of sons and daughters at first marriage

TABLE 2. *First marriage negotiations for sons and daughters*

Name	Date of Birth	Marriage first negotiated	Age
Sons			
Roger	1 August 1606	—	died 10 October 1615
Richard	20 October 1612	1624, possibly 1620	8 or 12
Geoffrey	10 April 1616	—	died 20 January 1617
Lewis	23 May 1619	1 November 1639	20½
Roger	25 April 1621	1639	18
Francis	25 June 1623	6 August 1639	16
Robert	20 January 1627	no negotiations pre 1643	

Average based on Richard, Lewis, Roger and Francis: 16
Mid-point of age range: 14, 15 or 16

Name	Date of Birth	Marriage first negotiated	Age
Daughters			
Alice	20 March 1608	5 December 1620	13
Sarah	29 March 1609	1617	8
Lettice	25 April 1610	January 1618	8
Joan	14 June 1611	4 August 1629	18
Catherine	22 March 1615	6 October 1621	6½
Dorothy	30 December 1617	6 March 1622	4½
Mary	11 November 1625	pre 12 August 1639	14
Margaret	30 April 1629	9 May 1630	1

Average age at which marriage was first negotiated: 9
Mid-point of age range at which marriage was first negotiated: 9

were not strikingly different, being nineteen and sixteen respectively.[42] Nevertheless, the remarkably young age at which Cork was ready to discuss his daughters' futures is the more important statistic because it indicates that much less consideration was given to his daughters, as opposed to his sons, exercising some degree of choice in the selection of marriage partners.

Even when it came to the point of co-habitation it appears that Cork showed greater concern for the health and well-being of his sons than his daughters. This certainly suggested when one compares Cork's response to the marriage of his sixteen-year-old son Francis to Elizabeth Killegrewe with his attitude to the marriage

TABLE 3. *Ages of the Boyle children at first marriage*

Name	Date of Birth	Date of Marriage	Age
Sons			
Roger	1 August 1606	—	died aged 9
Richard	20 October 1612	December 1633	21
Geoffrey	10 April 1616	—	died as an infant
Lewis	23 May 1619	26 December 1639	$20\frac{1}{2}$
Roger	25 April 1621	27 January 1641	20
Francis	25 June 1623	24 October 1639	$16\frac{1}{2}$
Robert	20 January 1627	Did not marry	

.Average age of sons at marriage based on Richard,
Lewis, Roger and Francis: $19\frac{1}{2}$
Mid-point of age range of sons at marriage: 19

Name	Date of Birth	Date of Marriage	Age
Daughters			
Alice	20 March 1608	29 July 1621	$13\frac{1}{2}$
Sarah	29 March 1609	29 July 1621	$12\frac{1}{2}$
Lettice	25 April 1610	25 July 1629	$19\frac{1}{2}$
Joan	14 June 1611	15 August 1630	19
Catherine	22 March 1615	April 1630	15
Dorothy	30 December 1617	13 February 1632	14
Mary	11 November 1625	July 1641	16
Margaret	30 April 1629	—	died aged 8

Average age of daughters at marriage: 16
Mid-point of age range of daughters at marriage: 16

of his twelve-year-old daughter Sarah to Sir Thomas Moore. The marriage of Francis Boyle has already been discussed in Chapter 4 when it was noted that Cork wished only for a contract in the short term and conceded to an immediate marriage only when it was insisted upon by the king and queen. Cork's desire for a postponement was motivated by fear for his son's health which he thought would be impaired by sexual intercourse at such a tender age. Eventually, while he permitted the wedding to take place, Cork nonetheless safeguarded his son's health by separating him from his bride within four nights of marriage and sending him, in the company of his younger brother Robert, on the Grand Tour.[43] By way of contrast, the twelve-year-old Sarah, following her marriage in 1621, was obliged to reside with her parents at Lismore for only two years when, still but fourteen and a half, she departed for her husband's home at Mellifont. There, co-habitation was obviously permitted to the couple since at Moore's death, which followed within two months, those at Mellifont thought it possible that the fourteen-year-old widow 'may be young with child'.[44] This contrast in attitudes may also be explained by cultural conditioning since it was widely believed, even in the twentieth century, that the loss of seminal fluid had a devastating effect on the constitution and could completely undermine the health of a growing youth.[45] The sudden expiry of the young Moore within eight weeks of his having commenced to engage in sexual relations with his wife may have convinced Cork of the validity of this assumption, which may explain his greater caution over the marriage of Francis Boyle. Even allowing for this experience it seems that Cork was more casual about the question of co-habitation where his daughters were concerned, and came to accept fourteen and a half or fifteen as the normal age for those of his own daughters who were married as children to take up residence with their husbands.[46]

Thus, the patriarchal attitude of Cork towards his daughters was made particularly manifest in the early age at which he sought to dispose of them through marriages which were primarily designed to enhance the political and social position of the earl and his sons. The apparent callousness of this is all the more striking when account is taken of Cork's seeming refusal to consider matches for his sons until they were much older, and of his admission in relation to his sons' marriages that there existed a connection between happiness in marriage and the exercise of personal choice in selecting a partner. It was specifically out of consideration for his eldest son's future happiness that Cork permitted Richard, Viscount Dungarvan, freedom to choose a wife; admittedly within the extremely limiting constraints that were discussed in the fourth chapter.[47]

The earl's younger sons were permitted greater scope, and the father had even reconciled himself to accepting as a daughter-in-law one Mrs Harrison of whom 'he heartily disapproved', but for whom his third surviving son Roger, Baron Broghill, expressed 'passionate love'. This potentially difficult situation was avoided when the controversial Mrs Harrison set her sights on a young English noble and withdrew her consent to the match.[48] Lest it be thought that the difference in Cork's attitude towards his sons' and his daughters' marriages is here being overstated, mention should be made of the fact that a daughter for whom a marriage was negotiated while she was still a child was theoretically free to veto the arrangement before the marriage was proceeded with. The frequently cited example of Mary Boyle proves that this veto could be exercised in practice, but it is equally important to note that, on mature reflection, Mary Boyle believed she had done wrong in defying her father's wishes.[49] In any event the right to veto a marriage is very different from enjoying the right to choose a partner, and an analysis of the careers of two other Boyle daughters, Catherine and Dorothy, indicates that, whatever the theory, they were never in a position to exercise any control over the marriages into which they had been contracted. Their utter helplessness derived from the fact, which did not operate in Mary Boyle's case, that soon after the treaties were finalised they were sent from home to be raised in the households of their future in-laws.

In the case of Dorothy Boyle, who was born on 30 December 1617, marriage was already being discussed before she was five years old and terms were finalised on 16 June 1626 for a match between herself and Arthur Loftus of Rathfarnham.[50] The marriage did not take place until 13 February 1632 but as early as 7 September 1626, when she was still in her ninth year, Dorothy Boyle was sent to reside at Rathfarnham.[51] The six years spent there prior to her marriage were not, as one might suspect, devoted to pre-nuptial dalliance since her future husband was spending that time in the company of Dorothy's eldest brother Richard, Viscount Dungarvan, firstly at Lismore and subsequently at Oxford.[52] The fact that she was, in effect, placed under the tutelage of her future parents-in-law must therefore have cancelled all possibility of Dorothy Boyle extricating herself from the match that had been finalised on her behalf by her father before she had attained her seventh year. The older Catherine Boyle, born 22 March 1615, seemingly was not the subject of marriage negotiations until she was six years old, but a year from then, in 1622, a contract was finalised for a marriage between herself and the son of Sir Thomas Beaumont.[53] Then, on 20 September 1624, in her tenth year, Catherine was sent to the Beaumont household in England where she remained until August 1628 when she was recovered in the circumstances of humiliating disgrace that have been discussed in Chapter 4.[54]

By bringing forward the age at which he would consider proposals for his daughters in marriage Cork was thus effectively denying them the element of choice which he seemed to think essential to happiness in marriage, and which he was careful to allow his sons when, approaching adulthood, marriages were being arranged for them. Furthermore, as has been suggested, the ease with which Cork could send his daughters as children to be raised in the households of their future in-laws, and the young age at which he would permit his daughters to co-habit with their husbands – a practice that he thought hazardous to the health of his own sons – combine to suggest that Cork's patriarchal attitude towards his daughters was carried to such extremes that, judged by twentieth-century standards, he would be condemned for having come to consider daughters an expendable commodity.

The fact that greater consideration for personal preferences in the selection of marriage partners was extended to the Boyle sons does not mean that they were exempt from patriarchal control. In a sense Cork had no option but to take account of his sons' preferences because they were almost fully grown men when their marriages were arranged, whereas the future of the daughters was decided while they were still children.[55] Besides that the earl did not need to be obvious in directing his sons' choice because the enormous resources at his disposal meant that he (on an altogether greater scale than the New England patriarchs described by Professor Greven)[56] held ultimate control over his sons through his freedom to dispose his property as he chose. Cork, like the New England patriarchs, made it clear that he intended to provide for all his sons but he deferred the final allocation of his property until his death, thus enabling him, again like the New England patri-archs, to use the threat of disinheritance to recall to obedience any son whose behaviour did not live up to his expectations. Thus, for example, in 1637 when Cork was reprimanding Lewis, Viscount Kinalmeaky, for his dissolute behaviour he threatened to withdraw the 'livelihood and estate' he intended for him.[57] This means that the choice in the selection of marriage partners conceded by Cork to his sons should not be taken as evidence that they were free from his control. Indeed, if he had not granted some choice to them he would, by implication, have been denying the efficacy of the entire educational programme that he had designed to form his sons' character.

Since, as has been established, Richard Boyle fits the description of a patriarch it should follow, if the models outlined by Professors Stone and Greven are valid, that he would have seen to it that his children were raised under close paternal supervision within a household that included none besides the nuclear family and their servants. One purpose of this upbringing would have been to focus the children's loyalty on their father as head of the family and to divert their attention from any external lineage or communal group. In seeking this obedience the father would normally strive to break the will of the child or bend it to his wishes by the imposition of harsh disciplinary measures that frequently included corporal punishment.[58]

A close study of the Boyle domestic situation and of the early careers of the Boyle children makes it clear that these characteristics did not prevail. The household itself conformed to neither Stone's nor Greven's requirements because it included a grandparent, in the person of Lady Alice Fenton, who appears to have enjoyed a prominent role in fostering a spiritual atmosphere within the household.[59] Then in Cork's later life, but while the last-born children were still very young, his household was frequently occupied for lengthy periods of time with older married sons and daughters together with their children and servants.[60]

To this extent the Boyle family can be considered extended rather than nuclear and was therefore completely at variance with what Professors Stone and Greven have led us to expect. Furthermore, it deviates from the patriarchal family types that they have portrayed because the Earl of Cork himself did not devote direct attention to the raising of his children. Whenever Cork was in residence at Lismore the claims on his time made by the regular stream of officials and landowners who came to visit him could only have diverted him from the personal oversight of any of his children who might have been residing with him.[61] Even without that, we know that he could not have given personal attention to the raising of his children because a close study of his movements, prior to 1628, shows that he was regularly absent from Lismore for extended periods of time, and subsequent to that date, after he had become active in politics at a national level, he usually lived in Dublin rather than Lismore, and none of his own young children seem to have lived with him in Cork House, his Dublin residence.[62] We do learn that a few of his younger children were then left at Lismore in the care of a tutor but the fate of these children was not very different from that of their siblings because the striking feature of the Boyle family, which sets it completely apart from what we have been led to expect by Lawrence Stone and Philip Greven, is that until they had almost achieved adulthood the children were as a matter of policy normally raised away from their parents in the care of a succession of individuals who sometimes bore no relationship to the family. This feature comes to our attention only when the early careers of the Boyle children are subjected to close scrutiny.

The sources reveal nothing of the earliest years of Cork's first-born, Roger Boyle, but we can assume in his case as in the others, for reasons that will be stated later, that his infant years were spent away from home in the house of a wet-nurse. Then in May 1613, before he was fully seven years old, Roger was sent to England for upbringing in the household of his uncle, John Boyle, at Deptford in Kent, where on 10 October 1615 he died.[63] Roger's early death, which came as a great blow to his father, may explain why of all the Boyle children only the second-born son Richard, who in 1615 became the principal heir, was, for the most part, raised in the parental household. Born on 20 October 1612, Richard Boyle's early upbringing and education remain obscure but if he was a victim of the usual wet- and dry-nursing regime in his earliest years he resided thereafter with his parents in Munster. Then, on

12 March 1629, when Richard was in his seventeenth year, he was summoned by his father to join him in London from where on 5 June 1629 he was sent to study at Oxford.[64] Previous to this we can assume that Richard was instructed by clergymen or French tutors at home but Cork's diary comments only on the notable events in his career. Thus we learn that Richard was knighted at Youghal on 30 August 1623; that he was a party to the ill-starred double Villiers match which in 1626 was dissolved; that during the summer of 1626 he went in company from Lismore 'to be merry' at Dungarvan, the town after which he was named, and that in May 1627 he and Arthur Loftus rode to Cork to be present at Lord Barry's horse-race.[65] The sojourn at Oxford which followed these years was short-lived; Richard was back in Ireland between September 1630 and June 1632 when, almost twenty, he was sent to England and then to the continent by a father who probably wished him, like his brother, free from 'the leaven of Ireland'.[66] Nevertheless, his son's marriage was also in Cork's mind, and Dungarvan's continental tour was ended abruptly, on his father's instruction, in September 1633; three months later at the age of twenty-one he was married to Elizabeth Clifford. Even following his marriage Richard and his wife normally lived with Cork either in Dublin or Lismore, although in February 1637 Cork contemplated the purchase of the house and seignory of Mallow from Lord President St Leger as a residence for Dungarvan and wife during Cork's own lifetime and as an inheritance for Robert Boyle thereafter.[67]

The sheltered upbringing of Richard, Viscount Dungarvan, was totally exceptional probably for the reason stated, and Cork's next two sons Lewis, Viscount Kinalmeaky, and Roger, Baron Broghill, were, like their deceased brother Roger, separated from home at an early age and seldom saw their father thereafter. After some years of out-nursing which we can assume,[68] Lewis and Roger (who were born respectively in 1619 and 1621) were probably together subjected to a tutor at Lismore. In any event on 5 May 1630, when they were eleven and nine respectively, Lewis and Roger were sent to study at Trinity College, Dublin. It is likely that contact with their father from then until 1634 was confined to vacation periods, if even then, and Lewis was totally removed from direct parental contact when in 1633–4 he partook of a practical education in navigation and mathematics aboard one of the king's ships.[69] In December 1634 these two sons were part of the Boyle company that then transferred residence from Dublin to Lismore, and from then until 13 February 1636 they, together with their two younger brothers Francis and Robert, were in the care of a tutor at Lismore.[70] The return to Lismore did not mean a return to direct parental supervision because their mother was long-since dead and Cork himself was present at Lismore for only four months of that time. By thus confining his sons to Lismore rather than to his Dublin residence Cork would appear to have been arranging to have them at a remove from himself, and they were certainly at a safe distance from their father from February 1636 to March 1639 when the two were engaged upon the Grand Tour, under the direction of a Genevan Calvinist tutor, M. Marcombes.[71] Thereafter they saw much more of their father, but the point that is being underlined here is that from the ages of eleven and nine until they were twenty and eighteen respectively Lewis and Roger Boyle spent little time in the household of their father, and, if we can judge from the experience of their younger brothers, it is likely that they also saw little of their father in their earlier years.

Much more information is available to us on the upbringing and education of Richard Boyle's two youngest sons Francis and Robert because they were reared together from December 1634 onwards, and considerable detail is thus available for both in Robert Boyle's autobiography.[72] Cork was absent from home when Francis was born on 25 June 1623, and did not return for the christening that followed soon after the birth.[73] It is likely that Francis was then farmed out to nurses for some years, but, since we know him to have been present at Lismore in April 1628,[74] it is probable that he had returned home before that date and was being taught there by a clergyman or French tutor. Apart from intermittent visits to Dublin, Lord Cork was usually resident at Lismore in the years immediately previous to 1628, but this is no guarantee that he or his countess involved themselves with their son's education. In any event, when the Boyles were preparing for their visit to England in 1628 the parents entrusted the five-year-old Francis to the care of the wife of Sir Laurence Parsons.[75] Francis probably remained at the Parsons' home until September 1634 when he, like Robert, would have been required in Dublin to welcome Dungarvan who was then expected to arrive with his lady. Francis was certainly a participant in the grand return of the Boyle family to Lismore in December 1634, and between then and September 1635 he, with Lewis, Roger and Robert, was assigned to a tutor at Lismore. This prepared Francis for his entry to Eton in September 1635 where he was accompanied by his younger brother Robert Boyle, who for the next few years became his constant companion.[76]

Prior to 1635 Robert, like Francis, had spent hardly any time under his parents' roof and the two were to become virtual strangers to their family from 1635 onward. Robert was born at Lismore on 20 January 1627 and christened there on 8 February 1627.[77] Then, 'as soon as he was able without danger to support the incommodities of a remove', Robert was 'sent away from home. . .to the care of a country nurse, who by early inuring him by slow degrees to a coarse but cleanly diet, and to the usual passions of the air' helped him to develop 'so vigorous a complexion, that both hardships were made easy to him by custom, and the delights of conveniences and ease were endeared to him by their rarity'.[78] This is the only clear reference that we have, apart from a similar mention in relation to a grandchild,[79] to one of the Boyle children being fostered to a wet-nurse, but Robert suggests that it was the normal procedure favoured by his father, and his recollection of the Spartan regime implies that it was prolonged well after he had been weaned. The relatively short intervals between the births of the Boyle children also indicates that lactation was not practised by Lady Cork, which again suggests that the infants were normally sent to a wet-nurse. Just how long Robert resided with his nurse is uncertain, but his autobiography suggests that he had not returned in February 1630, and indeed until he had attained an age which 'made him capable of admitting instruction'.[80] Then he was certainly brought back to the parental home where 'his father by a Frenchman, and by one of his chaplains, had him taught both to write a fair hand and to speak French and Latin'.[81] Robert Boyle had mastered these skills before he was eight years old and his progress was such that it 'endeared him very much unto his father, who was likewise impressed with Robert's 'veracity, of which. . . he would often give him testimony that he never found him in a lie in all his lifetime'.[82] The earl's favourable impression of his youngest son must, how- ever, have been based more on the reports of his tutors than on personal observation because from 21 April 1628 until 1 July 1635 Cork was absent from Lismore for all but four months.[83] That Robert spent this time in Munster while his father was away in England and Dublin is evident from his reference to the summons to Dublin which he received from his father in 1634 to await the arrival there of his eldest brother Dungarvan with his bride Elizabeth Clifford.[84] It was at this point that the careers of Robert and Francis Boyle coalesced, since as was mentioned, the two were tutored at Lismore until 9 September 1635 when together the twelve-year-old Francis and the eight-year-old Robert were committed to the custody of Sir Henry Wotton at Eton.[85] From then until August 1638, when Cork visited England, Robert and Francis Boyle were separated from the other members of their family except for a few visits, during the long vacations, to their sister Lettice Goring in Sussex, and one expedition to London in 1637 to see their eldest brother Dungarvan.[86]

Robert testifies that the reunion with his father in 1638 for 'some weeks enjoyment of the summer diversions at Stalbridge' was a happy one, but again in October 1638, when Cork was on his way to London, the two sons were restored to their former tutelage at Eton until 23 November 1638 when, on his return to Stalbridge, Cork took them 'absolutely away' from Eton.[87] Return to Stalbridge did not involve a return for the two to the bosom of their family because their father 'assigned the care of teaching' them 'to one Mr W. Douche, then parson of that place, and one of his [Cork's] chaplains'. The two were obliged by their father to 'lodge and diet' in the Douche household 'though it were not distant' from Cork's own residence 'above twice a musket shot'.

The 'old divine' was engaged until March 1639 in instructing the two in Latin prose and poetry, as well as in providing them with 'some skill in the music both of voice and hand'.[88] Francis Boyle, being taken ill at the Rev. Mr Douche's house, spent most of the summer of 1639 'lying sick at a doctor's house' to which he had been removed. As a consequence, both he and Robert were denied the opportunity to join their three older brothers in the king's expedition against the Scots.[89] Robert was, in the meantime, recalled to the parental residence and committed to the care of M. Marcombes, the tutor who had just returned with Lewis and Roger from the Grand Tour, and spent his time with Marcombes 'reading and interpreting the Universal History written in Latin, and partly in familiar kind of conversation in French'.[90] Then and for the only time in Robert Boyle's career, Cork involved himself directly in his son's upbringing when 'to oblige him to be temperate' he gave 'him the opportunity to be otherwise' by trusting him with 'the keys of all his gardens and orchards'.[91] This six-month stay with his father at Stalbridge was remembered by Robert Boyle as a 'pleasing time' but even this was accidental since it had been intended that both he and Francis engage themselves in the Scots war.

During this summer Cork had arranged for the marriage of Francis Boyle to Elizabeth Killegrew, which took place in London in October 1639 as soon as Francis's health was restored. Then, on 28 October 1639, four days after the wedding, Robert and Francis Boyle each with 'differing resentments of their father's commands' left England in the company of M. Marcombes on their Grand Tour.[92] Robert Boyle, who did not return to England until 1644, was never again to see his father alive, and Francis subsequently encountered his father only because he returned early from his continental perambulations, having permitted his desire for his wife to gain ascendancy over his obedience to his father.[93]

The precise details of the upbringing of Robert Boyle have established that, previous to his father's death in 1643 when Robert was aged sixteen, the total amount of time spent by him under the same roof as his father can be calculated in months rather than years, and that the only occasion when his father involved himself directly in his education, during the summer of 1639, happened by accident rather than design. The same holds true of the career of Francis Boyle from 1628 onward, and Lewis and Roger seem also to have had little direct contact with their father before they attained adulthood. Even more significant is the fact, stressed repeatedly by Robert Boyle in his memoir, that his father had consciously sought to have his sons raised at a remove from himself, and this was carried to its most extreme degree when Cork arranged for Francis and Robert to reside at Stalbridge with the Rev. Mr Douche rather than in his own house. These case-histories demonstrate, therefore, that formal education for the Boyle sons, like marriage contracts for the Boyle daughters, meant an early separation from the parental home; a development which Cork considered desirable and sought to arrange. Furthermore, what Robert Boyle had to say of his earliest years suggests that his father – like English noblemen generally at that time[94] – was strongly in favour of farming out his children to nurses for the first few years of life, so we can assume that others if not all of the Boyle children suffered the same experience.

This information suggests that the only years in which the Boyle children might, with any confidence, expect to spend with their parents were those between the ages of about three and nine, and even these might be interrupted, as they were in the case of Francis Boyle, by some years spent with foster-parents. We learn from the experience of Cork's two youngest daughters, Mary and Margaret, for which a detailed account is available in Mary Boyle's 'Autobiography',[95] that daughters were also liable to be fostered at an early age, and that planned absence from the parental home was also the normal mode of living for them. The sources are silent on the early career of Mary Boyle, who was probably born in November 1625,[96] but on 10 April 1628, shortly before her parents' departure for England, she was 'fetched from Lismore' to Mallow by Lady Ann Cleyton, the wife of an English planter Sir Randal Cleyton, and she continued to reside there until 1638 by which time she was thirteen years old. She was then recalled because Cork proposed to finalise the wedding arrangements which he had, without her knowledge, previously negotiated on her behalf with Lord Clandeboye.[97] The youngest of the Boyle children, Margaret, was born in London on 30 April 1629 but we know nothing of her early years prior to 25 May 1634 when the Earl of Cork, then a widower, sent Margaret to join her sister Mary at Lady Cleyton's house.[98] It is probable that Margaret never again saw her father because she died at Mallow on 28 June 1637 when he was conducting business in Dublin.[99]

The explanation offered by Mary Boyle for her father's choice of Lady Cleyton as foster-mother for herself and Margaret was that Lady Cleyton was childless, and Mary testified that she treated her as a natural child 'and took great care to have [her] soberly educated'.[100] This testimony is a tribute to Cork's prudence in the selection of a foster-mother, but we learn further from a casual entry in Cork's diary that Lady Cleyton had acted as early as 1615 as foster-mother to Alice Boyle, Cork's eldest daughter.[101] This information, added to the knowledge we have that Francis Boyle was fostered to Lady Parsons, suggests that fosterage was a more normal part of the upbringing of the Boyle children than the sources reveal. Such an arrangement was, of course, not required for Dorothy and Catherine Boyle because, as was mentioned, they were sent to be raised by their intended parents-in-law at the respective ages of nine and ten years.

The diary and correspondence of the Earl of Cork enable us to establish the precise date when each of the Boyle children departed formally from home, and therefore make it possible to calculate the average and mean ages of sons and daughters at the time of their final departure.[102] The insights into the upbringing of the Boyle children that the four case-studies, based on two autobiographies, have yielded tend, however, to suggest that these statistics have little meaning because the Boyle children spent as little time under the parental roof before their eleventh year as they did afterwards. Therefore, the final departure from home, before they entered into marriage or a formal education, can hardly be elevated to the status of a *rite de passage*. Cork's attempt to treat it as such is obviously a conceit, as is clear from his affected response to Catherine Boyle's departure in 1631 to take up residence with her husband Arthur Jones (the future Viscount Ranelagh) in London. He and those who knew Catherine were, he professed, 'full of sorrow for our unspeakable and unrecoverable loss' at her departure;[103] a profession that would be touching and even convincing if we were not previously aware that Catherine had, in effect, only come to reside with her father after August 1628 when the Beaumont alliance had been dissolved.

Thus, it would seem that the normal process of child-rearing as practised by Richard Boyle conformed to the following pattern. The new-born infant usually spent some weeks or months in the parental home before it was farmed out to a country nurse who reared the child to the age of three or four. Then the child spent some years in the care of a tutor at Lismore, or at the house of a carefully chosen foster-mother, but in either event was removed from direct parental supervision. At or before the eleventh year the sons were sent to attend an educational institution in Ireland or England, and their stint there was followed by some years touring the continent. By the eleventh year the daughters would either have been sent for upbringing to the households of their future in-laws, or would have remained with their foster-parents until, at the age of fourteen or fifteen, each went to live with whatever husband had been chosen for her. Finally, after the daughters had borne children, and when the sons had completed their formal education, the young Boyles, by now adults, were permitted to enjoy the company of their father in a relaxed or familiar environment. Most of them readily took advantage of this opportunity and were encouraged to do so by their father, and collectively the Boyle children accepted and upheld the authority of their ageing father as patriarch until 1643 when, at the age of seventy-seven, the 'good old earl' parted this life.[104]

It is suggested by the evidence that Cork intended and designed this pattern of upbringing for all of his children except Richard, his principal heir. The death of Roger, the first-born son, has been advanced as the probable explanation for the exceptional treatment accorded Richard, previous to his departure for Oxford. Apart from Richard, the only children whose careers deviated from this pattern and who spent a considerable number of years

TABLE 4. *Ages of the Boyle children at final
departure from home: sons and daughters*

Name	Date of Birth	Date of departure	Age
Sons			
Roger	1 August 1606	1613	7
Richard	20 October 1612	12 March 1629	16½
Geoffrey	10 April 1616	—	died as an infant
Lewis	23 May 1619	5 May 1630	11
Roger	25 April 1621	5 May 1630	9
Francis	25 June 1623	5 September 1635	12
Robert	20 January 1627	9 September 1635	9
Average age of sons at departure: 11			
Mid-point of age range of sons at departure: 12			
Daughters			
Alice	20 March 1608	29 July 1621	13½
Sarah	29 March 1609	1 October 1623	14½
Lettice	25 April 1610	21 April 1628	18
Joan	14 June 1611	21 April 1628	17
Catherine	22 March 1615	20 September 1624	9½
Dorothy	30 December 1617	7 September 1626	9
Mary	11 November 1625	1638	13
Margaret	30 April 1629	—	died aged 8
Average age of daughters at departure: 13½			
Mid-point of age range of daughters at departure: 13½			

in the parental home were Lettice and Joan, who suffered rejection in the many marriages which their father sought to negotiate on their behalf,[105] and Sarah who resumed residence at Lismore in the interval between the death of her first husband in December 1623 and her marriage in 1626 to Lord Digby.[106] These exceptions merely serve to underline the rule that, far from wishing to have his children socialise together under the paternal roof, the Earl of Cork strove to have them raised outside the family home, and in the company of not more than one other member of the family.

This dispersal of the Boyle children, far from being a hindrance to their being brought up to accept patriarchal authority, was, on the contrary, quite suited to that purpose, and Cork would seem to have come to believe that loyalty to himself as patriarch could best be fostered in his children by tutors, or indirectly by himself through correspondence. The Boyle children were obviously reminded from an early age by their tutors and superiors of their duty both to parents and siblings and especially of their absolute obligation to obey their father. It appears from Cork's letters to his children and their tutors that these messages were constantly reinforced especially as the children approached adulthood.[107] On the few occasions when a son or daughter threatened to defy the patriarchal authority he was accused of having betrayed his family, was threatened with disinheritance, and sometimes in a face to face confrontation with a person nominated by his father was recalled to his duty. Finally and most effectively the entire family identified openly with the patriarch until they forced the erring member to bend to his wishes.

The most revealing example of how Cork asserted his authority over his children comes from his dealings with his son Lewis, Viscount Kinalmeaky, between 1637 and 1641. In a letter of January 1637[108] Cork enjoined Lewis, then engaged upon the Grand Tour with his younger brother Roger, Baron Broghill, to serve God and avoid sin, to be selective in choice of company and only to associate with those from whom 'some increase in learning and knowledge' might be obtained. He was further warned against wasting his time and his father's money by being satisfied with the mere view of 'places and the rarities in them, for', as Cork put it, that 'he might have done staying at home in a cart or a map'. Instead, Lewis was directed to study 'the manner and condition of the people, the order of the government. . .the form of administering justice, with the customs and duties expected from the subjects in every place. . .how the king's or duke's revenue is levied or brought in, and how expended, and what forts and forces are in every place, and how the charge of them is defrayed'. The enrichment of his 'knowledge and understanding' which it was expected would result from this close observation was intended the better to equip him on his return to Ireland, 'to serve the king our great master, and to be an ornament and pillar in this commonwealth where your estate is like to be beyond any second son in this kingdom, or England itself'.

Even from this, one can see that Cork considered that respect for God, the king and his father should be his son's guiding principle, but the dominance of the father in this trinity becomes evident from the next passage where Lewis was invoked 'to keep safely' all his father's letters, 'to endorse them with the day of the receipt' as he had been 'wont to do', and every week to read over all of them 'that they may leave impressions' of what his father desired for his good. Then he was directed to concentrate upon the attainment of these goals set him by his father 'be they never so contrary' to his own 'vain purposes and imaginations', for, as Cork put it, 'I know what is fitter for you to do than you yourself can'. Lewis and Roger were both reprimanded for the curtness of their previous letters to him, and as a guarantee against further neglect on their part they were directed 'to keep' and send their father 'from time to time a diary or journal' of their travels with their 'material observations of the places' visited. Finally Lewis was directed to obey his tutor, M. Marcombes, and 'carefully to husband [his] reputation and purse' so that 'the liberal allowance' which Cork had provided 'may not be wasted or ill spent'. Advice along these lines would, of course, have been given to Lewis even before he engaged upon the Grand Tour, and it was now repeated because Cork had learned from Marcombes that the son was proving himself a difficult charge.

Lewis Boyle was therefore reminded of his dependence on his father on each of the three occasions when Cork referred to the 'liberal allowance' with which he and Roger had been provided on their travels. The point was brought home to him even more emphatically on each of the three occasions during the course of the letter when he was threatened with the loss of his father's blessing if he did not comply with his wishes. An even more effective reminder of where his duty lay must have been the assurance that the longer his father lived, and the better he himself deserved, the greater would be his patrimony, and the obverse of this which was the threat that if he did not desist from his evil ways his father would alter his resolution concerning the 'livelihood and estate' which he intended for him. Thus Cork hoped by first cajoling and then by threatening to disinherit him to divert

Lewis from his addiction to alcohol, evil company and extravagance, but he also sought to reinforce in him the notion of
loyalty towards his father and family. Persistence with his present
evil ways, he was reminded, would 'breed' his 'body full of dis-
eases' and his 'honour and reputation full of spots and blemishes',
but this was as nothing, claimed his father, compared to the
dishonour which would reflect on the king who had ennobled him
and on the reputation of his father and of his brothers and sisters.
Indeed the hazards were so great, averred Cork, that he himself
'had much rather hear' of Lewis's death than hear he had been
drunk 'or so much as to delight in excess of drinking'.[109]

Even this failed to divert Lewis from his carefree life, and over
the next several years Cork continued to bewail his dissolute
character[110] but desisted from enforcing the ultimate penalty of
disinheritance. Instead he seems to have mobilised the entire
family to his point of view and hoped that ostracisation would
force the erring Lewis to conform to the mores of the group.
The most revealing insight to this treatment comes from John
Walley, Cork's steward at Lismore, who during the earl's absence
in England was responsible for his interests in Ireland. In 1641
Lewis, by then a married man aged twenty-two, returned to
Lismore, seemingly seriously in debt as a consequence of having
in England pursued an 'irreligious course' without 'regard of
God', his father's 'honour or credit, or his own salvation'. When
reprimanding Lewis for his misconduct and recalling him to his
duty, Walley, without noticing the irony, 'laid before him the
most imitable precedents' of his father's 'most sincere, just and
honourable dealings with all men...which did proceed from the
knowledge of God and his divine word'. The example of his older
brother Richard Viscount Dungarvan was likewise invoked, and
in encouraging Lewis to pursue 'a new reformed life' Walley was
seconded by Kinalmeaky's eldest sister Lady Barrymore 'with
tears and a free sisterlike admonition'.[111] The response of Kinalmeaky to the brow-beating is not recorded but since he was, some
months later, fully reconciled with his father[112] it is likely that the
collective voice of the patriarchal group had succeeded where the
moral authority of the patriarch alone had failed.

That Cork's position as patriarch was conceded to him by his sons and daughters even when they entered adulthood, and that they would act in concert to assist their father in forcing the submission of an erring child is also made manifest in the famous case of Mary Boyle's defiance of her father's wish in the choice of a marriage partner.[113] Cork in his diary made it clear that his personal choice of James Hamilton as husband for his fourteen-year-old daughter became the collective choice of the kinship group, that in repeatedly refusing to marry him Mary displayed 'a very high averseness and contradiction to our counsels and commands',[114] and that she thereby spurned the advice of her father, all her brothers and sisters, her brothers-in-law, Lord Barrymore and Arthur Jones, 'and all other her best friends who did most effectually entreat and persuade her thereupon'.[115] The deprivations and isolations to which Mary Boyle was then subjected enjoyed the co-operation of her closest kin which bears out the assertion that the patriarch's will was synonymous with that of the family.[116] When subsequently Mary strayed further into error by secretly engaging herself to Charles Rich, in the knowledge that his suit would not find favour with her father, she was again exposed to the collective wrath of the family more than to the individual anger of her father. Significantly, it was her older brothers Dungarvan and Broghill who were despatched to her country retreat to persuade her to desist from her rash intentions and to comply with her father's wishes.[117] When Mary remained intransigent and persisted with her intended course she was again ostracised by her family. Even subsequent to her marriage to Charles Rich and the reconciliation with her father, none of her family would accompany her to her new residence at Lees in Essex other than her sister Catherine, subsequently Lady Ranelagh, 'whose great goodness made her forgive'.[118]

The stratagems employed by Cork himself to win his daughter's compliance with his wishes are also revelatory because they show him as an offended majesty more than a disgruntled father. When Mary first broke the news of her passion for Rich he assumed 'a very frowning and displeasing look'; when Lord Goring sought to persuade him to accept the match Cork wept and professed

that 'he could not but still hope she would not give herself away
without his consent'. Finally when Mary remained adamant 'he
was extraordinarily displeased' and banished her from his presence,
to which resolution he clung for ten weeks until Lords Goring and
Warwick finally brought Mary to her father's presence where on
her knees she 'begged his pardon' and he, having 'with great
justice' severely reprimanded her, received her to grace and con-
sented to the marriage.[119] The most striking feature of this entire
episode is that the delinquent daughter was completely isolated
within the family group, and even she subsequently admitted that
at no period in her life did she 'feel a more sensible uneasiness
than when that business was transacting' since her duty and
reason had frequent combats with her passion, which 'was always
victorious'.[120] In retrospect Mary Boyle herself conceded that by
permitting herself to be guided by passion and by disregarding her
father's wishes she was also disobeying God's command 'in his
sacred oracles' that children should obey their fathers. Thus she
came around to Cork's own view that he had behaved with
commendable restraint and clemency in the face of extreme
provocation.

This mature judgement passed by Mary Boyle on the episode
proves that her father's method of seeking to exercise control from
a distance could produce the desired effect of evoking a sense of
guilt in the child. The fact that no mention is made anywhere
in Cork's voluminous papers of his having resorted to the physical
punishment of a child suggests also that he did not consider it
appropriate for a father to punish a child and the only reference
made by him to corporal punishment significantly registered his
outrage at the 'proud, insolent...sharp, cruel...tyrannical conduct of Mr Goodrich', the schoolmaster at the Lismore free school.
Goodrich had apparently lost half of his seventy pupils because he
had 'broken the teeth of some of them with his clenched fist' and
his wife had 'cut them short in meat and drink'.[121]

Cork's seeming conviction that children were more easily disciplined by remote psychological control than by proximate physical
control makes it tempting to explain his dispersal of his children
exclusively in these terms but this as we shall see was only one of

the important considerations that influenced his decision to have his children raised at a remove from himself. Another factor in explaining his behaviour was his desire to have his children raised in England, as is clear from his expressed concern to have his sons freed from 'the leaven of Ireland'. The earl gave voice to the same sentiment in relation to girls when he remarked that 'Ireland holds no comparison with England for the education of a young lady, here being neither means to breed her well nor marry her well'.[122] Despite these protestations, however, he followed his own advice in relation to only three of his sons – Roger, the first-born, and Francis and Robert the two youngest – and only one daughter, Catherine, and even she was not sent to England until after the Beaumont marriage had been arranged for her. Cork's stated preference for England as a place in which to educate his children cannot therefore have been any more a deciding factor in influencing the pattern of upbringing than was the death of his wife while many of the children were still young. On the earl's own admission, her death rendered his household more unsuitable than it would otherwise have been for the raising of the Earl of Kildare's sister,[123] but the routine of sending his own children away from home had been established long before his wife's death. Another possible explanation of Cork's behaviour, and one which would immediately occur to specialists in Irish history, is that the earl was seeking to emulate the indigenous Irish lords who had customarily sought to consolidate their position by fostering their children to would-be clients of a lower social status than themselves. There can be no doubt that some English landowners in Ireland sought by such means to consolidate their position,[124] and in Cork's experience the standing of the two fostering families that have been identified, the Cleytons of Mallow and the Parsons of Parsonstown, is consistent with this interpretation.[125] Opposed to the notion that it was the crucial factor is the knowledge we have that the two families in question were already firmly entrenched within the Boyle patronage network, and also the statement from Mary Boyle that Lady Ann Cleyton had been selected as foster-mother because of her upright moral standing and because she herself lacked children.[126]

All the considerations mentioned would appear to have exerted some influence on Cork's behaviour, but neither singly nor collectively are they sufficent to explain what was obviously a policy on the earl's part to have his children raised outside his own household and beyond his immediate control. The deciding factor, to which the others are merely supplementary, seems to have been that repeatedly advanced by Robert Boyle which was that the earl feared he would indulge his children if they remained close at hand; a fear that derived from the notion that all such affectionate attachments were a sign of weakness in himself and detrimental to the character formation of his children.

Robert Boyle explained his father's decision to have himself, and others of the family, raised from infancy by country nurses in terms of the 'perfect aversion' which his father had for the 'fondness' of those 'who used to breed their children so nice and tenderly, that a hot sun, or a good shower of rain as much endangers them, as if they were made of butter or of sugar'.[127] Subsequent to this period of exile from home, Robert, as was noted, was still kept at a remove from his father who preferred to supervise his education from a distance. His father's later decision to send himself and Francis to Eton was also attributed by Robert more to Cork's belief that 'breeding great men's children... up at home tempts them to nicety, to pride and idleness, and contributes more to give them a good opinion of themselves than to make them deserve it', than to the earl's concern to improve their 'early studiousness'.[128] Later again Cork's truly extraordinary decision to have Robert and Francis reside with the Rev. Mr Douche rather than with himself in Stalbridge was explained by Robert Boyle in terms of his father's concern that they should 'avoid the temptations to idleness that home might afford'.[129] These reasons cited by Robert Boyle to explain his father's decision to keep him away from the parental home during his childhood and adolescence were endorsed by his sister Mary Boyle who believed that her father's decision to foster her with Lady Cleyton stemmed from 'the tender care' of her 'indulgent father' that she 'might be carefully and piously educated':[130] an education which she obviously considered would otherwise have been obstructed by his indulgence.

What has been said firstly of Cork's patriarchal attitude towards his family, and secondly of the measures to which he resorted in order to avoid indulging his children makes it tempting to conclude that the only difference between the Earl of Cork's familial behaviour and the general description of patriarchal behaviour as outlined by Professors Greven and Stone was that Cork had become so conditioned by spiritual exhortation against the indulgence of children that he could banish them completely from his sight. Even to posit this conclusion would be dishonest because a substantial body of evidence exists which indicates beyond a doubt that, in spite of his being separated from his many children, the Earl of Cork recognised each one as an individual; became emotionally attached to them, even at a distance, and derived satisfaction from the fact that his emotional attachment was recognised and reciprocated by his children. Thus it will emerge that the Earl of Cork was fully alive to the possibility of developing affectionate attachments with individuals but because such attachments were associated in his mind with the indulgence of children they were deliberately and consciously suppressed. The means that he devised for their suppression was the dispersal of children that has just been discussed, but it will also be noted that affective relationships finally flourished in the Boyle household when the earl in his declining years relaxed his former rigidity and derived pleasure from the succession of married sons and daughters, together with their children, who took up residence with him.

Because these features of the Boyle family life might be thought controversial they call for some substantiation. Firstly on the question of new-born infants, it must be stressed that while Cork's attachment to infants was not as firm as that to older children there is nothing in the Boyle material to support Lawrence Stone's contention that parents were so conscious of high mortality levels among infants that they recoiled from emotional investment in them.[131] On the contrary, the sources reveal that despite this consciousness the Earl of Cork readily developed an attachment to new-born children. The fact that Cork was concerned to enter in his diary the star under which most of his children and grandchildren were born signifies that he believed each of them to be endowed with an individual aptitude and temperament which was fixed from the moment of birth.[132] This belief certainly was held by Cork's youngest son, Robert Boyle, who thought that 'men's native dispositions are clearliest perceived whilst they are children and when they are dying'.[133] That Cork respected this individuality and sought to preserve it is also suggested by the attention he devoted to the selection of names for his children. The Christian names chosen were, with a single exception, those of parents, grandparents or godparents,[134] but Cork was concerned that each child should have a name particular to himself. This concern was made manifest on the one occasion when Cork broke the unwritten rule by calling his fourth son Roger, as he had done his deceased first-born, after his own father. We can be certain that this was no casual decision and it is possible that the father was conscious of having done his new-born son something of an injustice because he saw fit to enter in the 'True Remembrances' that this was his second son of that name.[135] Further, it appears that Cork readily developed an affectionate attitude towards his children, even in infancy, as is suggested by his use of pet names, such as Hodge for Roger, Dick for Richard, and Kathy for Catherine, almost from the moment of birth. Affection was also extended to infant grandchildren, as is clear from Cork's gift in March 1632 of ewes to his 'pretty grandchild Katie Barry to begin a stock of sheep'.[136] Thus, whatever explanation might be advanced for Cork's sending his children as infants to be wet-nursed outside his home it clearly was not a case of his being indifferent to their individuality.

This individuality which Cork recognised in his children as infants continued to be appreciated by him as they matured in years. Thus, despite the fact that Cork's sons and daughters were subsequently exposed to a similar pattern of upbringing and education, it emerges from his correspondence with their tutors that he continued to recognise each child as an individual possessed of particular strengths and failings. For example, in 1635, in commenting on his sons Lewis and Roger, Cork acknowledged that the fifteen-year-old Lewis was 'an acute scholar for his time', while Roger, aged thirteen, was 'of greater growth and stature but not so good a scholar as his brother'. The earl accepted, however, that each had his individual merits, that each would benefit in his own way from the Grand Tour, and the common educational programme they had just completed at Trinity College, Dublin was now cited as a preparation for life designed to make them 'scholars and linguists..., sound in religion, and of honest and unspotted fame'.[137] This means that whatever else might be said of the comprehensive educational programme that Cork designed for his children from birth to adulthood, it was not intended to suppress individuality.

Further evidence of his appreciation of individuality is that Cork preferred some children over others. Robert Boyle, for example, was convinced that 'he ever continued very much his [father's] favourite', and the most plausible explanation that he provided for this was that he, more than any other child, bore a 'likeness...both to his father's body and his mind'.[138] That Cork became more attached to some children than others is also evident from a study of the various responses he made on the death of those of his children who predeceased him. He was for instance able to internalise the grief he suffered on the death of those of his children who died as infants, but in his diary he isolated 9 July 1633 as a tragic date to be remembered because on it occurred the death of his 'second and most dear daughter Lady Sarah Digby'.[139]

Furthermore, in defiance of the more manipulative aspect of Cork's character to which attention was drawn when he was being considered as a patriarch, there is also evidence that he could be a kind and even tender man. When, for instance, his wife's chambermaid was found to be pregnant by Sir John Crosby she was, admittedly, dismissed but her immediate needs were provided for by a parting gift of twenty shillings.[140] The more humane aspects of Cork's character are also revealed by the casual mention in his diary of such trivial matters as a gift of £5 in 1620 'to the children for their masque'; or the provision in 1626 of a fat buck to the town of Dungarvan on the occasion of the first visit there of Cork's principal heir Viscount Dungarvan; and, following his wife's death, the distribution of her gowns, jewels and keepsakes among his daughters with the instruction that they were to treasure these in her memory.[141] Even more touching is the entry of 25 August 1626 that Cork attended the sermon and funeral for his deceased servant, Thomas Farmer, and the note of the lease worth £8 per annum made to the old footman David Gibbons in lieu of '39 years' honest service'.[142]

In this context it is relevant to mention that his youngest daughter Mary Boyle, who had most occasion to resent his domineering attitude towards women, remembered him as 'one of the best and kindest fathers in the world'.[143] This observation is telling because all others of the Boyle children also remembered their father as a severe yet kind man, and indeed the only one in adult life who recalled him with any degree of bitterness was Roger, Baron Broghill and subsequently Earl of Orrery, who on one occasion implied that his father had not left him as well provided for as he might have done.[144] Even Lord Clifford who frequently indulged in acerbic comments at Cork's expense acknowledged that his daughter Bess who was married to Dungarvan was 'happy in a kind father-in-law'.[145]

The fact that such unqualified judgements could be consistently passed by those who best knew Cork suggests that it would be totally incorrect for the twentieth-century observer to describe him as malicious, uncaring or insensitive. That the Boyle children could accept that their father's actions towards them were designed to further their happiness does make it clear that their perception of happiness differed greatly from ours. Different as it was, however, it included, as we have seen, the idea that people should be appreciated for their individuality, and it will now be argued that Cork's concept of domestic happiness also included the notion of close relatives developing and cultivating companionate relationships with each other.

The acceptance of such an idea on Cork's part would, for example, explain why when he sent his children to be fostered or educated away from home he usually sent them in pairs rather than singly.[146] Consistent with this was his practice of writing a single letter to these separated couples in preference to writing privately to each.[147] While no explanation is provided by Cork for these behavioural habits it is at least possible that he was striving to protect his children from the sense of loneliness or abandonment that might otherwise have assailed them. Even more crucial to our understanding of his relationship with his children is the fact that despite being removed from his home they were seldom removed from his mind, which may mean that he considered the psychological element of a companionate relationship to be the crucial one. If this were indeed the case it would explain why Cork's diary is strewn with references to his sending gifts and tokens to his absent children, and receiving gifts in return.[148] Besides these, Cork's constant concern for his children's futures is also clear from dowry arrangements for daughters and inheritance provisions for sons. Thus, while Cork might stand condemned by twentieth-century standards for having consigned his infant son Robert to a wet-nurse, the apparent harshness of the act is somewhat tempered by the knowledge that as early as 26 August 1627, when Robert was merely nine months old, Cork was already purchasing manors which would serve as his future inheritance.[149]

It is more difficult to see how Cork could satisfy himself that he was acting in his daughters' best interests when he arranged early marriages for them, one of whose purposes was to bring himself the social and political connections that he so desperately needed. It is likely that Cork, like Lady Stafford – described by Mary Boyle as 'a cunning old woman...too much and too long versed in amours' – subscribed to the notion that in seeking to marry them to 'great fortunes' he behaved with 'great kindness' towards his daughters.[150] Moreover it could be argued that Cork's sending some of his daughters as children to be raised by their future parents-in-law was with a view to providing them with an opportunity for establishing companionate relationships in the households where they were destined to spend the remainder of their lives. Whatever of that, we can say with a greater degree of certainty that Cork sought to mitigate the possible emotional disasters, which he must have realised were likely to result from some of the child-contracts, by striving to achieve equality in age between the partners. Thus, for example, one stated reason for dissolving the double Villiers match was the discrepancy in age between the couples,[151] while one factor in favour of the Beaumont match was the fact that the couple had been born in the same year – a fact that Cork noted religiously in the first edition of the 'True Remembrances'.[152] In this context it is interesting to note that what was a concern of Cork became an obsession of the Boyles, and Francis Boyle, who in his later life took to composing manuals on love and marriage, cited as one of his golden rules that 'among all the great and extravagant follies that are used in the inequalities of marriages. . . there is none appears. . .more irrational and unnatural than an old man marrying a young woman, which. . . seems a match fitter to make sport for others than to raise joy for themselves'.[153]

While Cork was obviously seeking to offset the emotional risks attendant on childhood alliances by striving to achieve equality in age between the prospective marriage partners, he also derived some solace from his assumption that social convention, if not affection, would promote some minimal degree of companionship between husband and wife. Furthermore, Cork was satisfied that even in the event of his daughters encountering acute difficulty with their husbands they would still enjoy a considerable degree of autonomy within their households.

That Cork made these assumptions emerges from his correspondence with his erring sons-in-law, George, Earl of Kildare, and George Goring. Among the charges that Cork brought against these two profligates was that they disregarded the most basic conventions in treating with their wives. While Cork was able to overcome the consequences of Kildare's neglect by having Lady Kildare and her children reside with himself in Dublin, he was driven almost to despair by young Goring's high-handedness. The most outrageous of Goring's presumptions, averred Cork, was to abandon his wife in Sussex while he went to join his regiment in the Netherlands. This suggestion, raged the earl, transgressed the fundamental assumption that a wife's place was with her husband, and he warned Goring that the likely consequences of his action was that his wife would 'fall into deep melancholy', which his previous 'neglect [had already] made her too much subject unto, or to run mad as it was ever reported in court she was'. This possibility, Cork hastened to add, was no reflection on his daughter's constitution, but was such as could be expected from any woman to whom 'a solitary country life' without the presence of her husband would be 'a prison'. Lettice's case was, claimed Cork, further aggravated by Goring's contravention of yet another basic convention – the denial of her right to choose her own servants. As a remedy Cork insisted that Lettice have the company of servants of her own choosing and not 'to live solitary and alone in a country house'.[154]

These points serve to show that Cork was not being totally irresponsible in arranging for his daughters' marriages while they were still children, and that his concern for his daughters' happiness did not cease at the moment of marriage. Much the same factors may have served to convince Cork that he himself was not being cruel in the treatment which he meted to his wife. The fact that he seemingly permitted her freedom of action in the selection of servants and that her mother was a member of the household certainly absolved him from the charge that he was consigning her to solitary residence in a country house. Furthermore, despite what has been said of Cork's patriarchal attitude towards his wife, it is evident that she exercised some control in family affairs. The abortive Beaumont alliance was, as previously mentioned, attributed by Cork to his wife's insistence; she accompanied her husband in 1627 when he visited the Earl and Countess of Castlehaven to dissolve the match that had been arranged between their son and Lettice Boyle; and Lady Cork was also a partner to negotiating the marriage between Cork's niece, Barbara Boyle, and Thomas Browne.[155] That she was apparently excluded from discussions relating to the marriages of most of her children does strike us today as high-handed on her husband's part, but it is nonetheless an issue on which we must refrain from passing judgement until we have more information on the division of responsibility between husband and wife in the noble household of the seventeenth century.

Since the Boyle children were unanimous in their affection for their mother we can assume that her domestic role was not altogether a passive one. Robert Boyle, who knew of his mother only by reputation, considered it 'amongst the chiefest misfortunes of his life that he had never known her whose free and noble spirit...added to her kindness and sweet carriage' made her 'hugely regretted by her children'. The principal attribute that Robert associated with his mother was her 'virtue', and Mary Boyle, who also knew of her mother but by reputation, believed her to have been 'wise' and 'pious'.[156] These references suggest that the principal role assigned to Lady Cork was to cultivate a spiritual atmosphere within the household, and this impression is sustained by the comment passed on her at her death that, whenever the opportunity presented itself, she was concerned to see her children:

> Walk by that rule, by which her self was led,
> The Word of God; which frequently she read
> And had their wished attention: her desire
> Was not to have them, as these days require
> Phantasticke, or what's worse –

It was seemingly in recognition of her dutiful performance in that role, no less than for the valuable connection and the large family with which she provided him, that the Earl of Cork remembered his wife as the crown of all his blessings.[157]

While taking note of the fact that Lady Cork was conceded merely a passive role in the making of important decisions, one must also allow for the fact that in marrying Catherine Fenton in July 1603 Cork contravened one of the few inflexible rules that he subsequently adhered to in arranging marriages for his daughters, in that he married a girl who was considerably younger than himself. Cork was thirty-seven at the time of his second marriage and his bride was so strikingly younger than he that, within a generation, the myth had gained currency that Cork had become engaged to his wife in March 1603 while she was still an infant.[158] The impossibility of this story is made clear by the birth of the first child by that marriage in August 1606, by which time we can assume the mother to have been at least eighteen. The fact that Lady Cork was still producing children in 1629 indicates that she cannot then have been more than forty which suggests that

Catherine Fenton was closer to fifteen than eighteen when she married the seasoned and worldly-wise widower Richard Boyle.[159] This factor makes it easier to understand how Cork fell into the habit of making all principal decisions for his wife and depriving her of even the control in domestic affairs which would normally have been left to the female partner in a marriage. The presence of her mother, who must have been closer in age to Cork, may also have served to undermine the role that Lady Cork might have expected to play in the important decision making of the household.

Even allowing for these possibilities one cannot be certain that relations between Cork and his lady were quite as distant as the sources suggest. The birth of fifteen children in the twenty-seven years of Boyle's second marriage is, in itself, proof that sexual relations between the couple were on a regular basis. Cork's diary is unfortunately completely silent on the intimate details of their life together, as it is on the companionate aspect of their marriage. One is thus left with his outburst of grief at the loss of his 'dearest dear wife' in February 1630 as the only yardstick with which to measure his affection for her. Since Cork then appears to have been totally distraught, and since thereafter 'he annually dedicated the day of her death to solemn mourning for it' and also (although this is a dubious denial for a man of sixty-four) 'rejected all motions of any other match', we can assume that the emotional attachment between the couple cannot have been completely negligible.[160] All of this suggests that the sense of distance between husband and wife which is conveyed by the bulk of the evidence was more apparent than real, and what aloofness did exist is probably accounted for by the great discrepancy in age between the couple.

While it would not be permissible to argue on this basis that relationships among the Boyle family members were companionate, the evidence cited does make it clear that Richard Boyle was familiar with and attracted towards the concept of a companionate relationship as he was also attracted by the concept of individuality. That Cork found it necessary, because of religious pressures, to resist such attractions contradicts the notion upheld by both Professors Greven and Stone that affective individualism and the companionate marriage were inventions of the eighteenth century.[161] The Boyle experience suggests rather that these dimensions to normal human interaction appeared novel in the eighteenth century merely because people were persuaded to refrain from their enjoyment during the early decades of the seventeenth century when an intense religious fervour held sway among English Protestants at home and abroad.

Of equal interest to the historian of the family is the means resorted to by Richard Boyle to avoid these forbidden relationships: a means that resulted in the effective destruction of the Boyle family as a nuclear unit. This response is of interest because it suggests that Cork respected neither the theory nor the reality of the nuclear family, and the suspicion that he did not do so is confirmed by the evidence, cited in Chapter 4, which makes it clear that Cork had no scruples over seeking to have his daughters Alice and Joan, subsequent to their marriages to Lords Barrymore and Kildare, focus their loyalty on himself as head of a kinship group rather than on their husbands as heads of their respective households. When allowance is made for the absence of any such attachment to the concept of a nuclear family it becomes clear that Cork's sending his children away from home, which strikes the twentieth-century observer as an extreme manifestation of patriarchalism, cannot in fact be taken as evidence that he was uncaring towards his children. This means, of course, that due weight must be given to the evidence that a moderately warm relationship between father and children was sustained even when they were separated from each other. One manifestation of this which should earn the Earl of Cork the admiration of the twentieth-century reader, no less than it did the sympathy of his own contemporaries, was his pronouncement that 'all the cares that this world [could] lay upon' him were 'far inferior' to his 'study and endeavours' to provide his 'sons a religious, learned, and noble education'.[162]

From such statements we learn that despite Cork's belief that a man's aptitude and temperament were formed from birth he clearly thought that education determined the formation of character. It was, seemingly, in this belief that he set his mind to design an educational programme intended to equip each child to fulfil the social role that his own material success had made possible for them. That the children successively lived up to his expectation is clear from his ever-increasing zest for life as he proceeded well into old age and as death crept ominously nearer. That he was conscious of his approaching end is clear from the occasional mention, from his fifty-sixth birthday onward, of advancing years, from the regularity with which he updated his will and from his more regular comments on the deterioration of his health due to palsy and other maladies.[163] Yet his pride in his children's achievements, his satisfaction that he made the correct decisions relating to their education and his awareness that they, unlike himself, by virtue of their education could accommodate themselves to the noble life, combined to make him wish to cling to the last few threads of life, as is evident from his *cri de cœur*: 'as I do not fear death, so I do not wish it'.[164] Then also in his declining years he indulged and took pleasure in his grandchildren within his own household in a way that he never permitted himself to enjoy his own children.[165]

Besides seeking to rehabilitate the reputation of the Earl of Cork by drawing attention to the more humane aspects of his character, this analysis of his family life is also intended to serve as a contribution to the current debate on the history of the family. The evidence cited upholds the idea, on which all leading historians of the family are agreed, that the acute social upheavals and intense religious zeal that characterised the early-modern period did indeed exert a considerable influence on relationships between the father and other members of the family. What is surprising, however, is that in this particular case the response to the external pressure was so extreme that it led to the effective dissolution of the Boyle family as a nuclear unit. This deviation from what is accepted as the norm would lead one to treat the Boyle family experience as a complete aberration were it not for the fact that in other respects the Earl of Cork behaved in a very predictable fashion. In the matter of sending children to be wet-nursed away from home, the Earl of Cork adhered to what Lawrence Stone believes to have been the general practice among English ruling families,[166] although not for the reasons posited by Professor Stone. There is also corroborating evidence from other planter families in Ireland that they, like Boyle, clung so rigidly to this habit that they would send their children to Gaelic Irish homes for wet-nursing.[167] Then again Richard Boyle cannot be said to have been completely innovative in sending his children to be fostered outside the home both because that was a Gaelic custom that was, apparently, widely imitated by English planters[168] and because, as Professor Edmund Morgan has shown, certain fathers in puritan New England who faced a dilemma similar to that encountered by Richard Boyle also overcame it by assigning their children to foster-parents.[169]

On the basis of these findings it would be tempting to posit the conclusion that what we have witnessed exemplifies a family type that emerged among the New English planters in Ireland in response to the peculiar circumstances in which they found themselves. This would invite further research on Irish planter society, but it would also involve discarding Lawrence Stone's proposition for a transition over time from one dominant family type to another in favour of Philip Greven's idea of the co-existence of several distinct types of familial relationship; these types being determined by such variables as religious intensity and levels of affluence. To attempt such a generalisation would, however, be to defeat the purpose of this exegesis which has been to stress the need for further studies of particular family experiences before we seek to draw any final conclusions about general trends or patterns. That such studies, based on a close reading of all surviving sources, are required becomes clear when it is noted that if attention had been confined to printed material of the type on which the books of Professors Greven and Stone are principally based one would be unaware in the case of the Boyle family that wet-nursing was practised, that his children were frequently sent by Cork to be fostered by relatives or other planter families in Ireland and that the Boyle children spent most of their teens as well as their early years away from home; in other words without such a rich body of evidence one would easily arrive at the conclusion, now shown to be incorrect, that the Boyle children were raised in the family household.

Even while stressing the need for close attention to all surviving evidence relating to particular cases before advancing any general conclusions on family history, one must also stress the hazards involved in seeking in a body of evidence for information that it was never intended to yield. Cork's diary was designed primarily as a record of business transactions, and his correspondence was also preserved for official reference purposes. Therefore the comments relating to his private or family life that are to be found scattered through these collections come to us by accident, and if they do cast an occasional beam into the recesses of Cork's private life they cannot be trusted to provide full illumination where it was intended that darkness should prevail. That Cork wished his family concerns to remain shrouded in darkness is explained by the fact that he, like many others of extreme Protestant inclinations, believed that everything relating to the emotions – whether joy or sorrow – should be suppressed. He had, for example, so well mastered the art of internalising grief that his cousin Lawrence Parsons acknowledged that he had learned from Cork how 'to submit...to God's will lest his hand and visitation fall the heavier'.[170] What was true in the case of the Earl of Cork was equally true of his contemporaries, which fact should be sufficient to persuade us that, pending further detailed studies of particular families at different social levels, one must consider works such as those of Lawrence Stone and Philip Greven as but highly stimulating hypotheses on the character of familial relationships during the early-modern period. To consider them as such is not intended to diminish their importance since it is clear from what has been written that they have served to concentrate the mind on the key problems relating to family history, and they have indicated areas where further investigation might be profitable. In so far as they have been found deficient it is because, as with all such hypotheses, they are not sufficiently complex to accommodate the wealth of evidence that is available to us in the particular instance of the Boyle family.

6

Richard Boyle: Anglo-Irishman

In the course of a letter written in 1619 Henry Peers warned his patron Richard Boyle that 'the greatness of his estate and God's providence therein' had occasioned such 'wonderment' at his 'rise' that his enemies 'would dive into the mystery of it, how it came to pass'. The comprehensive investigation into the origins of Boyle's fortune and social elevation was delayed for a further fourteen years, and then Peers' further prediction that Boyle's enemies would find him sufficiently 'fenced in' to survive the investigation was also borne out by events.[1] Boyle's successful defence ironically explains why until now we have known so little of the outlook and purpose of Richard Boyle because instead of seeking to understand the man's personality historians have taken up where Wentworth left off and devoted their energies to revealing the means by which Boyle achieved his dramatic success. Terence Ranger's study of the career of Richard Boyle, completed in 1959, provided the first convincing explanation to the hitherto unsolved mystery and Ranger's service in disposing of that problem has made it possible to study Richard Boyle on his own terms and to seek to situate him in historical context.[2]

The previous chapters have suggested that the English social system was sufficiently elastic and Boyle's personality sufficiently adaptable to allow him eventual admission into the upper ranks of England's social hierarchy, but on being admitted Boyle was accepted as an Irish peer whose past achievements had been in Ireland, and whose expected future service to the crown would be in Ireland. Significantly, no member of the Boyle family was conceded an English title – the mark of a man being fully accepted by his English peers – until 1644, the year after Richard Boyle's death, when his eldest son Richard, Viscount Dungarvan, was created Baron Clifford.[3] It appears that the Earl of Cork himself recognised that his ultimate ambition was being denied him and came so fully to accept the terms on which he was being granted admission to England's privy council that he, who hitherto had despised his association with Ireland, came to take pride in the description 'Irishman'.[4]

This suggests that if we wish to place Richard Boyle in context we must consider him as an Englishman who made his career in Ireland. When Terence Ranger considered him as such, the most striking of his conclusions was that Boyle's actions in Ireland were characterised more by his perseverance and efficiency than by his originality. Thus, as Ranger demonstrated, the means by which Boyle laid the foundations of his fortune were commonplace among Elizabethan adventurers in Ireland, and he was outstanding only in the single-minded dedication with which he foraged for title to land.[5] Subsequent to the resumption of activity by speculative adventurers in Ireland during the early years of King James I, Boyle was again exceptional because, of the successful adventurers, only he failed to diversify his interests either by the acquisition of office in Ireland or by transference to England.[6] It was this single-minded devotion to the extension and development of his estates which explains how Boyle achieved an economic success far greater than anything achieved by his contemporaries. Nevertheless, Boyle showed that his ambitions were in line with those of his contemporaries when, once his fortune had been made, he relentlessly pursued the goal of social elevation.

That Boyle's various achievements can be attributed to the consistent pursuit of a single ambition at any one time should not blind us to the fact that he selected his goals only after he had considered the various possibilities. Thus, as was noted in Chapter 4, Boyle quite early in his career contemplated the employment of at least some of his Irish capital to acquire property and office in England, and he presumably then resisted the temptation either because the way to social advancement in England was not promising for one with such a sinister background as his, or because the lure of quick profits in Ireland was too tempting to be resisted.[7]

Boyle's disregard for the opinion of those who thought Ireland an 'unsafe bottom' cannot, however, be explained solely in terms of his greed or his caution. Equally important was the fact that with the passage of the years of peace, 1603–41, Cork began to feel increasingly secure in Ireland and increasingly convinced 'of the good affections of this people to their king and country'.[8] In this he was quite typical of the New English group generally and like many others of the group he became so relaxed that he permitted himself to be drawn towards Irish culture and dependent upon Irish people. Some of Cork's earliest accomplices in Ireland were of Gaelic origin[9] and both he and also his son Roger, Baron Broghill, continued to employ Irish servants of proven loyalty even when, subsequent to the broils of the mid-century, it was considered dangerous to do so.[10] Most of the principal tenants on the Boyle estates in Counties Cork, Limerick and Waterford were English, but Irish sub-tenants were everywhere welcome, and were even permitted within the model towns of Tallow and Bandon if they undertook to build after the English manner.[11] The Boyle lands in County Kerry were held almost entirely by Irish tenants, and the collection of rents there was mostly entrusted to one Dermot Moriarty who went by the name of Dermot Dingle.[12] Cork and his associates came to believe that Irishmen could be trusted with arms as when in 1639 Cork's son-in-law Barrymore sought to recruit Irishmen into the regiment that he had contracted to raise to fight for the king's cause in Scotland.[13] This growing dependence of the planters on the native population explains the logic of the leaders of the 1641 rebellion when they called upon those Irish who dwelt among the planters to forsake their masters, claiming that their desertion would undermine the planters' power and thus pave the way for an Irish victory.[14] In the event it was the English soldiers' 'hatred against those poor people that live peaceably and endeavour to pay their rents' rather than the enticements of the rebels that forced the Irish tenantry to abandon the lands on which Cork had 'planted them'.[15]

Cultural contacts between Boyle and his Gaelic neighbours

were so frequent that it is possible that some of the Boyle children were farmed out to Irish wet-nurses. Only this would make sense of the assertion made in 1610 by Sir Thomas Browne that it was likely that Roger, the eldest of the Boyle children, then four years old, had 'Irish sufficient to be his father's interpreter'.[16] If Cork did indeed send his children to be nursed in Irish-speaking households he was not exceptional as is clear from the numerous references in the depositions taken subsequent to the 1641 rebellion to the children of planters being in the custody of Gaelic families. While there is no direct evidence that Cork himself ever acquired a knowledge of the Irish language it is clear that he realised that such a knowledge would be of advantage to his sons. Only this would explain his hiring Robert Carew who had a knowledge of the language to serve as personal tutor to Cork's sons Francis and Robert Boyle while they attended at Eton. Carew who was obviously instructed to keep Cork abreast of their progress reported in relation to the Irish language that of the two 'only Mr Robert sometimes desires it and is a little entered in it' but for the most part he found that 'they practise the French and Latin but they affect not the Irish', this despite the 'many reasons' shown by him 'to bind their minds thereunto'. What these reasons were he did not reveal but it is likely that Cork, like his less successful contemporary Sir Matthew de Renzi, had come to appreciate that a landowner in Ireland was at a distinct disadvantage in dealing with his neighbours and tenants if he was not conversant in their language. We also know of Cork that he, like many other English planters, thought it absolutely essential that Protestant clergymen have a facility with the language if ever the Irish were to be drawn from error and superstition.[17] It is of interest that Piaras Feiritéir, one of the outstanding Gaelic Irish poets of the early seventeenth century, held his lands from Cork, and despite the fact that on Cork's orders Feiritéir's cattle were sometimes distrained in lieu of rent the poet nonetheless looked to the earl to protect him against the rapacity of Dermot Moriarty, Cork's rent collector in Kerry.[18] The earl in turn seems to have had regard for Feiritéir and his father since he resisted the various requests made to him by the Irish enemies of the Feiritéirs to have them deprived of their

tenancy.[19] The bond between Cork and Piaras Feiritéir was not
sufficiently strong to survive the wrench of the 1641 rebellion,
but Cork's steadfastness towards Feiritéir during the previous
calmer years earned for him a respectful mention in one of
Feiritéir's poems as *Iarla calma Chorcaigh*[20] (the brave Earl of
Cork).

Whether Cork ever learned of this or had any knowledge of
Feiritéir's poetry is uncertain but it is probable that he had some
appreciation of Gaelic culture since an Irish harp was kept at
Lismore castle.[21] There is no evidence that an Irish harper was
employed but the value of the instrument was certainly appreciated since it, or one similar, was considered an appropriate gift for
one of Cork's more influential supporters in England.[22] This gift
was clearly exceptional, but as his career advanced Cork made a
point of selecting distinctively Irish gifts such as Waterford frieze,
pickled scallops and Irish whiskey for his patrons at court.[23]
Runlets of whiskey were seemingly popular as a gift, and Cork
waxed eloquently on the merits of the spirit. He cited Richard
Stanyhurst's *Chronicle of Ireland* as the source of his opinion, but
it seems to have been based also on personal experience since he
mentioned that those forced to live in the 'moist climate' of
Ireland had discovered 'by observation that the drinking of two
or three spoonfulls of [whiskey] fasting in a winter's morning help
to digest all crudities and raw humours in the stomack, expels
wind, and keeps the inward parts all day after very warm without
offence'.[24]

Cork's conscious attachment to things Irish as well as his
concern to fabricate an Irish historical ancestry, which was noted
in Chapter 4, were characteristic concerns of those of the New
English elite who came to prominence in Ireland during the early
years of the seventeenth century, and who subsequently accepted
that their principal family seat would be in Ireland. Indeed, some
carried this to such extremes that they strove to emulate the work
of English Protestant apologists in arguing for the antiquity of the
established church there, by advancing the proposition that the
established church in Ireland was the same as that founded by
St Patrick.[25] Typical also of the New English outlook was Cork's

analysis and understanding of the benefits that had accrued to Ireland as a result of the Elizabethan conquest and of the reasons for the previously disturbed state of Ireland.

The diagnosis presented by Cork for what he described as Ireland's 'national disease' was that 'the greatest part of the main body of this nation' was reluctant to work. The idle ones that he and numerous observers of Gaelic Ireland resented and feared were those who saw war as a source of booty and who consequently encouraged and provoked disturbance.[26] Their activities had admittedly been considerably restrained as a result of the Elizabethan conquest, and Cork maintained that there had been some improvement since 'the idlers', although still 'of great numbers', were being maintained by 'the few of ability' and were thus 'kept from wandering'. Indeed, this system of relief had proved so efficient that Cork believed Ireland to be less 'infested' than England with 'vagabonds and sturdy beggars'. Nonetheless he was uneasy, firstly because he believed the relief system caused the impoverishment of the Irish lords and secondly because the 'very great numbers of younger brothers and inferior ranks of people' living 'utterly idle and unsettled' were, 'as a cloud of terror, ready to break into any wicked action if opportunity were offered'.[27] Cork obviously believed that such opportunity was not likely to occur in Munster, which had been settled largely by himself, and he clearly considered his investment to be much more secure there than in Ulster. As late as 1630, he referred to Ulster as 'a rude and remote part of the kingdom' and the 'first...likely to be wasted...if any trouble or insurrection should arise'.[28] Even allowing for the lingering doubt which is revealed by this far-sighted remark, Cork was generally optimistic that the future of the planter was secure. Furthermore, he believed that an environment favourable to advancing Ireland further towards civility would be created if an English army were continually maintained during peace-time, 'it being the error of England for 200 or 300 years last past to withdraw armies immediately upon quenching of rebellions'.[29]

This observation was very similar to one made by Sir John Davies in his *Discovery of the True Causes* in outlining his reform

programme and Cork would also have agreed with Davies in his
contention that a barbaric society first needed to be broken by
force before civility could be introduced.[30] There is no clear
evidence that Cork had read Davies, and he certainly never cited
him. It is not necessary to establish a connection, however, because
the belief that an environment conducive to the development of
civility could be created only by force, and that the people would
have to be initiated into the ways of civility before they were
introduced to true religion was a commonplace among the New
English in Ireland, and indeed among all English who partici-
pated in civilising missions during this period.[31] It was consistent
with this view that Cork should repeatedly recommend the extension of plantation schemes into Connacht and Ormond, which he
described as 'the only neglected part of this kingdom in which no
English (in effect) are yet planted'. Only such action, he believed,
would liberate the subjects from the thraldom under which they
suffered and would 'occasion the natives to forsake the following
of their Irish lords'. Only then, he believed, would they 'submit
to the course of English settlement, whereunto the prosperity of
the neighbouring plantations already made doth much encourage
them'.[32] Also consistent with this view was Cork's concern to see
the vigorous enforcement of the recusancy laws, because he
believed the Catholic clergy, and most especially seminary priests
from the continent, were serving, like the Irish lords, to distract
the subjects from their true allegiance.[33]

Such punitive measures which were being constantly recommended by Cork, as they were by most planters of the early
seventeenth century, were therefore directed against very specific
targets and not against the majority of the population who, it was
assumed, were naturally inclined towards good, and were sufficiently perceptive to recognise the superiority of the English social
and religious system. Already in 1630 Cork was convinced that
some Irish Papists were taking example from their Protestant
neighbours who were 'all employed in some calling or industry
and wholly disposed to peace', while 'very many of them' who
possessed land (which he asserted had recently increased in value
from 6d. an acre to 3s. or more) had settled 'into an honest and

fair course of life and doubtless [were] well affected to the English monarchy'.[34]

Those Papists who had thus taken advantage of the peaceful conditions which followed the cessation of hostilities in 1603 to advance themselves economically were obvious candidates in Cork's opinion to receive the Protestant message. He probably believed these compliant Papists to be most plentiful in that part of Munster which was controlled by himself, where the removal of native proprietors had been most complete and where the importation of English Protestant craftsmen – and thus the creation of a propitious conversion environment – had been on such a scale that one historian has likened it to a nascent Brandenburg.[35] Even where there was little evidence of civil living Cork was satisfied that the lords had become so attached to peace that the time was opportune to move against them since he believed they would go no further in resisting than 'to make brave outsides and flourishes so as to beget and nourish fear'.[36]

There were thus three distinct stages to the programme favoured by Cork for achieving the reform of Ireland. The first, the punitive stage, was intended to remove the obstacles to reform, the second concerned itself with the promotion of manufacturing and was intended to lure the population from their erstwhile idleness to an attachment of civil living and the third stage, the educational one, was intended to secure the support of a now civil population for true religion. The punitive stage, being the first, is that which historians have tended to associate with the New English almost to the exclusion of all others,[37] and Cork himself, who took such pride in the destruction of St Patrick's purgatory and the closure of secret friaries and nunneries in Dublin, has frequently been isolated as an exemplar of the intolerance and bigotry of the New English.[38] This judgement has been passed because historians have failed to recognise Cork's apparently modern concern for the promotion of crafts and manufacturing as part of a religious reform programme. In his endeavour to promote trade and manufacturing Cork, and subsequently his son Roger as Earl of Orrery, surpassed all others in Ireland, but their enterprise should not blind us to the fact that similar attempts were being made almost everywhere settled by the English in Ireland throughout the seventeenth century.[39] The educational dimension to the reform effort, being dependent on the prior success of the other two phases, was that less frequently witnessed in seventeenth-century Ireland, but most planters acknowledged its necessity, even if, before 1641, few planters had taken steps to implement it.[40] Therefore, by sponsoring schools which were open to Irish as well as planter children,[41] Cork excelled his contemporaries, but his recognition of this as but the final stage of a reform programme explains why he could describe the endowment of schools as 'commonwealth work' and also why he could take pride in it as 'a work not inferior to building of churches'.[42]

The strident opposition of the New English to Irish lordships, which were represented as an anachronistic carryover from a bygone age,[43] indicates that all who came to Ireland had previously been influenced by an English shift in the concept of honour from being something associated with faithfulness to lords and friends to being something identified as a reward for service to the common good.[44] Such a perception had obvious appeal to individuals such as Cork who had little claim through lineage to marks of honour and social distinction, but it also had a more immediate and pragmatic appeal to the New English who could argue that since only Protestants could contribute to the common good only they should enjoy official privilege and patronage.[45] It is the second consideration which explains why English planters took a special pride in the description 'servitor' since they saw this as giving them, as opposed to English courtiers, Scots favourites or Irish landowners, a special claim to reward for what they represented as services rendered to the government. Indeed the New English, with Cork frequently as their spokesman,[46] came to place such an emphasis on this aspect of the government's function that it appeared that, besides advancing a reform programme dictated by themselves, they considered the state to serve no purpose other than to dispense favour to them.

These considerations would lead one to expect that, in the interest of presenting the appearance of a harmonious society which always co-operated with the state, the New English would have sought always to sublimate their differences and to place the interest of the government before their private concerns. It comes, therefore, as something of a shock to discover that, almost from the moment of their arrival in Ireland in significant numbers, the New English were noted for those very traits which they reviled in the Irish: their factiousness, their readiness to enter into conflict or litigation with each other and their disregard for the state in Dublin.

As early as 1581 the English official Sir Henry Wallop, who was the bane of all adventurers in late Elizabethan Ireland, protested that 'the former English' who had settled in Ireland were 'generally' so factious that 'no two of them that dwell within twenty miles can agree together, had they nothing when they came hither they account themselves great personages...and each to make his profit without regard of service'.[47] The adventurers themselves might have denied some of these charges, but the more successful deliberately fostered and cultivated personal loyalties and they made it clear that they considered their subordinates to be more bound by the loyalty which they owed them as patrons than to the government in Dublin.

An analysis of the relationship between any Elizabethan adventurer and his followers, or between any seventeenth-century planter and his tenants, would support this case, but it is particularly well illustrated by the relationship between the Earl of Cork and his subordinates. For example, one Robert Paget in seeking a tenancy from Cork in 1634 addressed him in the language which he obviously thought would have appeal to his would-be master when he professed that his only wish was to have an opportunity 'to fight under your honour's banner'.[48] Another tenant who was well established in Munster sought to flatter his master by assuring him that not 'for five hundred pounds' would he 'willingly' lose his 'lord's love and respect' since he had 'not such a true faithful friend...not in Ireland'.[49] That such professions were appreciated by Cork can be judged from his outbursts when any of those indebted to him did not honour what he considered to be their obligations. Thus when one Peter Wyngrove, bailiff of Youghal, who had once served the Earl of Cork as coachman and butler, turned evidence against him in a case that concerned Sir William

Power, who was Cork's arch-enemy on the local scene, the earl's vituperative vocabulary became so exhausted that he was reduced to the lusciously inconsistent charge that Wyngrove was 'a puritanical rascal' whose 'wife by her familiarity and entertaining of Popish priests, hath helped to consume wastefully what he got wickedly'.[50] Similarly, when some of the clergy who had been nominated to their livings by Cork sided with Wentworth against him, his rage knew no bounds.[51] The most revealing evidence on the store that Cork placed on personal loyalties is the fact that the ultimate term of abuse known to Cork was 'perfidious servant', a description that he reserved for Richard Blacknall and Henry Wright, the former managers of Cork's iron works who he believed had cheated him of £7,000 before they joined with his enemies in presenting to the King 'a devilish book of articles...as full of falsehood as themselves'.[52]

The attention that Cork devoted to the achievement of what he believed to be the natural frontiers of his Munster estate is a measure of the seriousness with which he treated his role of protector of his tenants and the suspicion he fostered for his neighbouring lords. Some of these, such as the Condons and Fitzgeralds, were represented as inveterate enemies to all planters, but Cork was equally hostile to men such as Sir William Power, who had a proven record of loyalty to the crown, and Sir William St Leger who, besides being a planter, served as president of Munster. The fear, suspicion and even hostility which marked Cork's relationships with his neighbouring lords, whether planter or native, is evident from his very sharp reactions to even the smallest incursions upon his property or jurisdiction. When, for example, during Cork's absence in England 1638–41, Sir William St Leger sought, in his capacity as president of Munster, to have all fishing weirs on the rivers of the province broken down it was suggested to the earl by his advisers that he seek to have St Leger removed from office rather than countenance 'this intended fury...in a thing which hath been no prejudice to the commonwealth'.[53] This extreme response to a minor infringement on the earl's jurisdiction was typical of New English behaviour, and Cork's opponents reacted in much the same way whenever they were threatened by him. Rather than submit to an official investigation of his boundaries, which had been authorised at Cork's instigation, Sir William Power 'swared' he would 'bring all those to the star chamber that would tread his lands being in the county of Cork', and that he would 'spend a thousand pound to defend it by law'.[54] Cork himself was not quite so brash as his Old English opponent, but while he claimed to be by 'nature and disposition. . .inclinable to peace with all men', he too acknowledged that he was not 'ignorant how to prosecute a good suit'.[55]

Because of their competitiveness and their tendency to cultivate bonds of personal loyalty, the New English left themselves open to the charge that they had succumbed to Irish degeneracy. That they were oblivious to the image which they were presenting to the outside world can be partly explained, as has been argued elsewhere,[56] by the fact that so many of the New English were bent on profit and advancement that they had no opportunity to consider the inconsistency of their own position. The presence of a disproportionate number of military men among the New English also serves to explain their strong attachment to personal loyalties,[57] as does the shortage of manpower in Ireland. The phenomenon is, however, best explained in terms of the New English lack of confidence in the government and administration in Dublin. The state to which they had been innured to owe respect was the monarchy in England, and they so persisted in their professions of loyalty to the crown that they invariably represented their endeavours as being ultimately in the service of the crown. Where the government in Dublin was concerned, the planters regarded it with suspicion, and subsequent to the deputyship of Sir Arthur Chichester, who was himself a servitor and planter, the New English came to regard as interlopers any besides themselves who held office in Ireland. Thus Cork was not alone either in resenting the 'ill deserving servants' who had 'long deluded that state with lies and falsities', or in deploring how 'private ends and profit [were] by some [in the Dublin government] too greedily pursued'.[58] This tendency of the New English planters to monopolise the description 'servitor' for themselves, also explains what Cork had in mind when he expressed the hope that the govern-

ment of Ireland would never be entrusted to 'any unknowing
covetous person...sent to repair or raise a decayed fortune out
of the ruins of this poor kingdom'.[59]

Because they lacked confidence in the Dublin government, the
New English planters also lacked a universally accepted focus of
loyalty in Ireland. In the absence of such focus each proprietor,
while still regarding the crown as the fount of honour, became his
own arbiter of proper conduct in Ireland, and came to regard his
enemies as agents of the corruption that he believed to be everywhere present in that kingdom. Thus, every advance by the
government in Ireland towards desirable goals was interpreted by
each planter as a personal victory, and every public retreat from
these goals was considered a personal defeat. This personalisation
of political affairs in Ireland largely accounts for the striking
competitiveness that persisted as a feature of Anglo-Irish society
until the end of the eighteenth century.[60] The fact that in this
competitive atmosphere each planter was convinced that he
personally upheld the interests of the crown explains why he could
believe that his actions were also in co-operation with the purposes
of God. Richard Boyle's conviction that he was chosen to fulfil
God's purpose has already been analysed, but the point being
stressed here is that the conviction that individually and collectively they were specially chosen to fulfil God's purpose was widespread among the New English and helps explain both their
behaviour and their blindness to their own weaknesses and inconsistencies. The widespread nature of this belief was made particularly manifest in the years following the breakdown of social order
after the 1641 rebellion. The disturbance itself, according to one
author, was God's design, and while confident that the planters
would ultimately 'drive this rebellious crew headlong into the sea'
he believed this to be delayed because it was 'not God's will, his
work [being] not yet finished' and the planters 'not yet sufficiently
humbled'.[61] When victory did come as in the Battle of Liscarroll,
1642, this too was attributed to God as it was by Tristram
Whitcombe who believed 'it was the finger of God only that did
direct us, that his power and providence in his own cause might be
the more clearly discerned by us'.[62]

The Earl of Cork, who was still alive to enjoy the victory, would certainly have endorsed this opinion. This, and what has previously been said, suggests that Cork can be considered a representative of a New English attitude which was already becoming so distinctive that it deserves to be labelled Anglo-Irish. That his contemporaries saw him as a representative of their views and values is suggested by the popularity which his struggle with Wentworth enjoyed among the New English. Therefore Cork's ultimate victory over 'that strange man Strafford' was hailed by Sir William Parsons as a collective New English victory which would 'let the world see and our own consciences tell us, we are the same men to the king and his service'.[63]

'I cannot say I know Ireland,' wrote Cork in 1630 'for that is more, I think, than any statesman can say in this age, the body of the realm standing at such a distance through the enmity of popery...with the governor and statesmen being Protestant'.[64] This disclaimer, made when Cork was still in government, summarises the predicament in which he found himself, and accounts for what previous historians have thought to be inconsistencies in him and in the New English as a group. Despite his ignorance, and the despair which sometimes resulted from it, Cork was confident that he could eventually arrive at a full comprehension of the country in which he found himself, and proceed from there to draw it towards what he perceived as a model of civility. Stern measures against the Catholic clergy constituted an essential part of the strategy to the attainment of this goal, but the short-term repercussions that these measures provoked forced Cork to admit that the New English were an isolated group in an alien land. In writing to Sir Henry Wotton in 1636 he complained that he could not even find a doctor to treat his palsy since those of the 'physicians of Ireland' who were 'learned and experienced...are all of a contrary religion with me, and I have provoked them very highly when I had a prime hand in the government'.[65]

For the most part, however, Cork was satisfied that the intransigent ones in Ireland were a small group and he proposed to reach beyond them to the great bulk of the population by authorising further plantation, by sponsoring manufactures, by encouraging trade and by promoting an educational and religious drive. There can be no doubt that this programme elicited a ready response from the Irish in the decades prior to 1641, and evidence of anglicisation was becoming increasingly evident. On the other hand, the New English in their effort to relate to the Irish either for exploitation or reforming purposes were themselves being drawn towards Gaelic culture with the result that the planter society, of which Richard Boyle was one of the outstanding members, was becoming part of a larger hybrid Anglo-Irish society. This position has been described most graphically, if in exaggerated terms, by Sir John Temple, and it is only in this context that we can understand Richard Boyle and what he stood for:[66]

These people of late times were so much civilized by their cohabitation with the English as that the ancient animosities and hatred which the Irish had been ever observed to bear unto the English nation seemed now to be quite deposited and buried in a firm conglutination of their affection and national obligations passed between them. The two nations had now lived together forty years in peace with great security and comfort, which had in a manner consolidated them into one body, knit and compacted together with all those bonds and ligatures of friendship, alliance and consanguinity as might make up a constant and perpetual union betwixt them. Their inter-marriages were frequent, gossipred, fostering (relations of much dearness among the Irish) together with all others of tenancy, neighbourhood and service interchangeably passed amongst them. Nay they had made as it were a kind of mutual trans-migration into each others manners, many English being strangely degenerated into Irish affections and customs, and many Irish, especially of the better sort, having taken up the English language, apparel and decent manner of living in their private houses.

7

Conclusion: the Boyles, Ireland and the 'New Science'

Since several books on the career of Richard Boyle are readily available, it remains to highlight the contribution that it has been intended this book should make to historical knowledge. A straight biography of Richard Boyle would have been a less exacting assignment than seeking to come to grips with particular facets of his career and character, but the latter course has been chosen in the interest of demonstrating the direct relevance that Irish experience during the early-modern period has to contemporary events elsewhere in Europe.

Those who have treated of the question of upward mobility in English society during this time-span have seen little occasion to comment on what was occurring in Ireland.[1] What has been said of Richard Boyle in this respect demonstrates that social developments at the upper level of Irish society during the seventeenth century were so closely intertwined with those that were then taking place in England that it would be quite improper to study one without the other. The analysis of the upward movement of this one individual will, it is hoped, encourage other scholars to subject other Irish noble families – whether rising or falling in the social scale – to similar scrutiny. Then when a sufficiently wide range of such studies becomes available it should be possible to speak of the problem of self-perception that confronted the emerging social elite in Ireland, and how their solution to this problem compared with that devised by other elites that were then in the process of formation in other European overseas settlements.[2]

The unique possibilities that the experience of Richard Boyle offered for a case-study in family history were mentioned at the beginning of Chapter 5, but it is important to bear in mind that other noble and gentry families in Ireland have left manuscript material which, if properly analysed, would shed light on problems that bedevil the history of elite families everywhere during the early-modern period.[3] Equally well, the 1641 depositions provide information on almost every facet of social life among the English colonists in Ireland from all social levels. When this unwieldy mass of data has been examined in the systematic fashion that was adumbrated by Professor Aidan Clarke in his presidential address to the Irish Historical Society for 1978,[4] it is possible that we will have more precise information on some facets of the social and economic life of this group of colonists than on any other people in western Europe during the early-modern period.

Mention of social mobility and family history is prompted by the concerns of this book but it is important to recognise that the bulk of the Boyle material at Chatsworth and in the National Library of Ireland relates to the business activities of the Earl of Cork and to his political career in Ireland. That this material has not been exploited as it might have been for the purposes of the present study is a tribute to the excellent treatment of these matters in Terence Ranger's thesis whose work in these respects could hardly be improved upon.[5] Another factor in explaining why the estate material has been left to one side is that an analysis of it will be absorbed into a comprehensive statement on planter society in Ireland based on all relevant estate records and on the 1641 depositions. This statement will constitute a substantial part of the present writer's projected book on *Ireland in the English Colonial System, 1580–1650*.

By confining attention to the more personal element in the surviving Boyle manuscript collections the author is aware that this work might be taken as but a further contribution to the centuries-old debate on the morality of Richard Boyle's activities.[6] Lest there be any doubt on this score it must be stressed that moralising has found no place in this book. The purpose behind the chapter on the mental world of Richard Boyle, and elsewhere, has been to expose to view the mind-set of the most successful and the most voluble English planter in early-modern Ireland. How typical Boyle's outlook was will become apparent only when others of his kind have been dissected in similar fashion. Even in the absence of such dissections it should be possible to compare the political attitudes that have emerged from the present study with the political attitudes that have been revealed through the Gaelic poetry written during the same period. This study, it is hoped, will uphold the contention made by the present writer in 1977 that the range of literature that survives from the seventeenth century in Ireland provides material for 'a study of contrasting *mentalités* such as the experience of few if any other European country has produced'.[7]

These few paragraphs will hopefully persuade early-modern historians who know little of Ireland that, whatever its geographical location, the country's historical experience is of central importance in assisting our understanding of the issues that provoked turmoil in early-modern Europe, and how these issues were resolved. That such a claim can be made is explained by the fact that groups, representing almost every shade of religious and political opinion then known to Europe, competed for dominance in Ireland throughout the seventeenth century. Knowledge of this fact will, hopefully, stimulate others to join forces with the handful of dedicated scholars whose work, principally on political and military events and now conveniently summarised in the third volume of *A New History of Ireland*, has kept alive an interest in early-modern Ireland over the past forty years.[8]

While thus striving at one level to arouse new interest in early-modern Ireland, this book is also offered as a corrective to the writings of one group of scholars, treating of a problem of universal significance, who have assigned a position of special importance to Ireland (and more specifically to the Boyle family) in their scheme of thinking. The historians in question are those who seek to uphold the thesis, which has received its most elaborate formulation in Charles Webster, *The Great Instauration*, that the great scientific achievements of seventeenth-century England derived from the millenarian cast of mind that was such a striking feature of English life approaching, and throughout, the revolution of the mid-century.[9] Those who are credited with first harnessing millenarian expectation to the needs of practical scientific inquiry are a small group of Protestant refugees, principally from the Palatinate, Bohemia and the Netherlands, together with their English disciples who are known to historians as the Hartlib Circle. Ireland enters the picture with the onset of rebellion in 1641 which produced a major addition to the number of Protestant refugees in England. The more sensitive of these (the names most frequently mentioned being Catherine, Lady Ranelagh; her brothers Robert Boyle and Roger, Baron Broghill; Sir John Clotworthy and Archbishop James Ussher) are shown to have been so attracted by the concerns of the Hartlib Circle that they themselves began to engage in scientific enquiry of a similar kind. Charles Webster, who devotes close attention to chronological detail, recognises that the scientific interest of the Anglo-Irish group was aroused before their arrival in England and that the Invisible College which they formed was for a time an independent entity which was later subsumed into a larger formation that was dominated by the earlier Hartlib Circle. That writer provides no explanation how the Irish Protestant émigrés first came by their scientific ideas, which permits those following him to supply their own explanations. T. C. Barnard finds the explanation in the presence in Ireland in the years immediately preceding the Irish insurrection of a few scattered scientists, notably the Dutch brothers Arnold and Gerard Boate, who had studied medicine at Leyden; Nathaniel Carpenter, 'a determined opponent of scholasticism', and Benjamin Worsley who worked 'in some unspecified capacity in Strafford's household'. All of these are shown to have been closely associated with the Hartlib Circle and they are given credit for having aroused among Protestant planters 'sympathy for the projects and reforms of the Hartlib Circle'. The scientific interest that manifested itself among Anglo-Irish exiles in England, subsequent to 1641, is thus attributed by Dr Barnard to the previous activity of Hartlibean scientists in Ireland in the interval between 1636 and 1641. Previous to 1636 Barnard seems convinced that the Irish planters were principally preoccupied with 'rapacity', since he credits Archbishop James Ussher, when he sought to 'lure' scientists to Ireland, with having 'ensured that [Protestant]

Ireland did not become totally isolated from the European intellectual world'. Professor J. R. Jacob would also seem to have worked from the assumption that Irish Protestants lived in an intellectual backwater, and since he was seemingly unaware of Dr Barnard's work he was forced to provide his own explanation. By doing so, Jacob disregarded Charles Webster's caution in relation to dates and attributed the scientific formation of the Anglo-Irish group to contacts they established with the Hartlib group after they had emigrated to England. Thus, as he sees it, the Invisible College was merely an extended version of the Hartlib Circle, the formation of which occurred to Robert Boyle after he had come under the influence of the Hartlib Circle.[10]

Despite the prominence that is given to the part played by the Irish members in the later doings of the College – with Lady Ranelagh offering her London residence as a salon, and Robert Boyle as its most illustrious member – it is important to recognise that, in the circumstances of the 1640s, they are portrayed as but passive acceptors of the intellectual positions that had earlier been worked out by Samuel Hartlib and his associates rather than as contributors to any debate on what political or intellectual position to adopt towards the dramatic events that were then being enacted about them. The later philosophical and scientific writings of Robert Boyle are thus attributed to his mind having been moulded in England by the Hartlib Circle, and he is further credited with having transmitted to a later generation of English scientists – those who belonged to the Royal Society – the scientific outlook that derived from fundamentalist Protestantism, and with which he supposedly first became acquainted, after his return from the Grand Tour in 1644, in the household of his sister Lady Ranelagh.[11]

The Boyles are given credit for having performed yet a further service to the scientific movement in England when they mobilised their far-flung Irish connection to procure the appointment of some of their more prominent scientific acquaintances in the Cromwellian army that undertook the reconquest of Ireland, and with it the recovery of the Boyle estates. These scientists, it is argued, were seeking an opportunity to give practical application to the theories they had worked out in England, and they are represented as looking to Ireland for such an opportunity because they had become disillusioned with the course the Revolution had taken in England itself. Thus, it is contended, Cromwellian Ireland became the resort of scientists of the Hartlib stamp because only Ireland, which was reduced to ruins first by the rebels and then by the Cromwellian army, offered an opportunity for the creation of a completely new society based on scientific principles: these being the principles that had been formulated in England by the Hartlib Circle in the decade preceding the revolution there. Then also it becomes clear to those who subscribe to this thesis in all its aspects that the Dublin Philosophical Society of the Restoration period (which included among its members some of the English scientists who migrated to Ireland during the Cromwellian years) was, like the Royal Society in England, a direct descendant of the Hartlib Circle.[12]

The evidence presented in the present book impinges only marginally on this elaborate and intricate thesis on the origin and nature of scientific thought in seventeenth-century England, but despite being marginal it does compel one to question the claims that are being made for the Hartlib Circle as the *exclusive* formers of scientific and social opinion. In questioning this exclusivity reference will be made firstly to the response of the Cromwellian 'scientists' to Irish social conditions, and secondly to the influences that shaped Robert Boyle's mind. Then it is intended to conclude this work by drawing attention to a hitherto unacknowledged influence that contributed to the formation of attitudes in seventeenth-century England.

The key role that is assigned to Ireland and the Boyles in the advancement of English science would appear, on first sight, to be justified by the evidence, and no academic historian of Ireland would deny the contention that has received its finest formulation in T. C. Barnard's *Cromwellian Ireland* that many of those who accompanied Cromwell were guided by altruistic motives; the horrible consequences of this altruism notwithstanding. What proves difficult to accept for a historian who is intimately acquainted with the sources for the previous century of Irish history is the notion that the ambition of the Cromwellians to build in Ireland a completely new society, free both from the defects of that which had preceded it and of those of all previously known societies, stemmed exclusively from the theorising of the Hartlib Circle. This difficulty arises from the knowledge we have that all waves of English adventurers in Ireland during the previous century (those who accompanied Lord Deputy Sidney in 1565; those who went to plant Munster in 1585; those who accompanied Essex to Ireland and who remained on to settle the country after 1603 when peace ensued and finally those who accompanied Thomas Wentworth) articulated a similar ambition, and in terms almost identical to those employed by the Cromwellians, to treat Ireland as a *tabula rasa* on which might be imposed whatever print was thought fit;[18] this despite the fact that all but Wentworth and his associates pre-dated the formation of the Hartlib Circle, while Wentworth represented that culture to which Hartlib and his circle were most opposed. Thus, while conceding that the work of Hartlib and his circle did much to sharpen the perceptions of Petty and the other notables who accompanied Cromwell to Ireland, it cannot be said that it was anything more than one factor among many in forming their opinions. That it was no more than this can be confidently asserted because of the similarity of the response of succeeding waves of adventurers during the century 1560–1660 to Irish social conditions which were so different from anything in their previous experience that they could only visualise their total displacement, most especially when such an opportunity seemed readily at hand in the aftermath of war.

The most successful product of one such wave of adventurers was Richard Boyle, the subject of this book, and it is clear from what has been said of him that, in his early years, he, like the Cromwellians who were to follow him, saw no merit in the social order that confronted him in Ireland. Also like the Cromwellians, he decried the measures taken by those Englishmen who immediately preceded him in Ireland, and he set himself to construct – admittedly on a local level – a social order that he believed to be entirely innovative. Neither is it correct to suggest that the

Cromwellians were unaware of the achievements of Richard Boyle and his contemporaries in Ireland. The lord protector himself is reported to have remarked that if all planters in Ireland had followed the example of Richard Boyle in Munster then no rebellion would have been possible in Ireland.[14] Even if we discount this report on the grounds that its author Roger Boyle, Baron Broghill, was equal to his father in the art of fictional reconstruction,[15] account must be taken of the fact that Gerard Boate in his book *Ireland's Natural History*, which is accepted by historians as the classic exposition of the new science, devoted much attention to describing the exemplary measures taken by the pre-1641 planters to exploit Ireland's natural resources. Indeed, Boate recommended a fresh start in Ireland not because of any insufficiency in the earlier experimental projects, which he praised, but because these efforts had not been sufficiently numerous or on a sufficiently large scale, and because these achievements had been cancelled by the rebels whom he repeatedly portrayed as destroying in symbolic fashion everything that reminded them of the English presence in the country.[16]

This short exposition makes it clear that recent champions of the Hartlib Circle have stretched their thesis further than the evidence will permit both in asserting that the Cromwellians in Ireland were conscious that their intended measures for Ireland were without precedent, and in citing the concerns of the Hartlib Circle as the exclusive source of inspiration for the positive intentions of the Cromwellians in Ireland. The same criticism can be levelleled against the attempt to view Robert Boyle and his sister Catherine, Lady Ranelagh, as creatures of the Hartlib Circle. The most recent historian to indulge in this exercise of tracing intellectual origins is J. R. Jacob in his book *Robert Boyle and the English Revolution.*[17] The structure of the mind of Robert Boyle as outlined in that book is quite convincing because it accords with the evidence, and because it closely resembles the mind of his father that has been uncovered in the present study. Where the book fails to convince, however, is in tracing the formative influences on the mind of Robert Boyle. This failure is explained firstly by the curt dismissal of all possible sources of 'scientific' influence on him other than that which was supposedly exerted by the Hartlib Circle. Thus, for example, Lucius Cary, Viscount Falkland, is mentioned as a possible influence on Boyle's opinions merely to be dismissed; a curt dispatch that appears somewhat rash when allowance is made for the long-standing political association between Cary's father and Richard Boyle, when account is taken of the fact that Cary himself once almost came to the point of marrying Lettice Boyle and when one notes that when marriage was in prospect Cary spent a considerable time at Lismore castle after which he remained a close friend of the family.[18]

The curt dismissal of the possibility of Lucius Cary having had some influence on the formation of Robert Boyle's opinions is mentioned because it arouses one's suspicion that Professor Jacob is engaged upon the exercise of writing mono-causal history and wishes to see no influence on Robert Boyle other than that of the Hartlib Circle. This suspicion is further aroused when we discover that those characteristics of Robert Boyle's mind which Professor Jacob avers, on very thin evidence, were due entirely to his contact with the Hartlib Circle are some of the most striking features of his father's outlook; a fact that is important because we *know* from evidence cited in earlier chapters that Richard Boyle had held himself before his sons as an example to be imitated. The principal points that are cited as evidence that Robert Boyle had come under the Hartlib influence are his belief that in pursuing practical goals he was fulfilling God's purpose; his belief that the pursuit of evangelical work among a primitive people was a futile exercise until such time as they had been incorporated into a disciplining social framework; and his belief in a broadly based Protestant church 'that would tread a middle course between the extremes of sectarianism and strict conformity'. These, as we have seen, were three firmly held convictions of Richard Boyle.[19] Neither do we have to look further than Richard Boyle to discover how one could reconcile an aristocratic with a practical work ethic; a problem that Professor Jacob seems to think was beyond the comprehension of Robert Boyle until such time as he suffered the loss of his estates through the rebellion in Ireland.[20] This is not

to suggest that Robert Boyle never developed intellectually beyond
the level attained by his father, nor that he was so fixed in his
views from an early age that his views underwent no change as a
result of his English experience. In fact, it is likely that his
enormous erudition gave Boyle the courage and confidence, as he
proceeded through life, to test the validity of beliefs and assumptions that he once held as closely as he held his religious convictions. Thus, it would seem that if one is to seek for the basic cast
of mind of the young Robert Boyle – which is what Professor
Jacob is concerned with – then one is closer to the truth in
accepting the mental outlook of his father, rather than that of the
Hartlib Circle, as the original die. That such was the original is
further confirmed when we take account of the striking similarity
in the outlook of the children that are best known to us – Robert,
Catherine, Roger and Mary – a similarity that cannot be
attributed to their all having come under the influence of the
Hartlib Circle.

It might seem plausible to argue that it was in being a scientist
that Robert Boyle was unique in his family and that it was in this
matter that he had been influenced by the Hartlib Circle. To
argue in this manner would be, however, to ignore the fact
that the principal characteristic of Hartlibean science was its
dedication to gaining control of the physical environment through
improvement in technology; a matter that was a constant preoccupation of Robert Boyle's father. Furthermore, Richard Boyle
recognised that he himself was deficient in the theoretical basis of
science, and he strove to ensure that those for whom he was
responsible would not be similarly handicapped by devising an
educational programme that laid particular stress on 'Philosophy
and the Mathematics' such as would 'value' them 'in all wise
men's judgements and opinions'.[21] Furthermore, despite the Earl
of Cork's belief in the direct involvement of God in human affairs,
he too, like his son Robert, reconciled this with the idea that God
had permitted man some scope to control his environment. Even
in medical matters Richard Boyle was no fatalist, as is clear from
the trust he placed in medical science, and even alchemy, in his
effort to stave off death and disease;[22] this despite the fact that

when a loved one died he resigned himself to God's will and sought to conduct his affairs as if nothing had occurred. In other words, it appears that Richard Boyle exemplified the scientific outlook that we have come to think of as characteristic of the Hartlib Circle, and he seems to have arrived at this outlook independently of that group.

When allowance is made for this fact it seems that Professor Jacob was treated unfairly when it was implied that he had offended against the historical canon by bending the facts to fit a preconceived model. Far more likely is the possibility that he, and other enthusiasts of the Hartlib Circle, have unwittingly fallen into the error of attributing the mental attitudes of certain Irish Protestant intellectuals to the influence of Samuel Hartlib simply because their views closely resembled those of Hartlib himself. When this is taken into consideration, it comes as no surprise that, when in exile in England, Irish Protestants should consort with the Hartlib Circle, and it is probable that they helped to shape the ideas of the Hartlib Circle while, in turn, their own attitudes were being reinforced or modified by what was to be learned in England.

Neither is it surprising to discover such a close affinity between the ideas and attitudes of the more sensitive Irish Protestants and the members of the Hartlib Circle that they should recognise each other as kindred spirits. The position of Protestants in seventeenth-century Ireland was, after all, not altogether dissimilar from that of their co-religionists in the Palatinate, Bohemia and the Netherlands who constituted such a significant element in the Hartlib Circle. Like them, the Irish Protestants had to live with the nagging misgiving that their position would be swept away by a sudden Counter-Reformation offensive, and life in Ireland was made tolerable for them only by having resort to millenarian expectation which convinced them that they were a chosen people, but which also gave rise to ideas similar to those cherished in England by the advocates of the 'New Science'. When this is taken into account it will become apparent that Ireland served as an intellectual forcing-ground for those Englishmen who had occasion to live there, with the result that these people's ideas appeared 'advanced' whenever they returned to England.

Evidence of this forced growth was not, of course, limited to the religious/scientific realm. Many years ago J. G. A. Pocock isolated Sir John Davies as the most advanced historical thinker of his generation, and Pocock attributed this precociousness to Davies' sophisticated notion of cultural change over time which he explained in terms of the direct contact with cultural diversity that Davies had experienced during his service in Ireland.[23] More recently, Brendan Bradshaw has demonstrated how the attempt to introduce the Reformation to Ireland compelled English officials and divines to address themselves for the first time to the problem raised by an evangelisation effort among a non-compliant population, thereby forcing them to recognise rifts and contradictions that had hitherto lain dormant within the English Reformation movement itself.[24] The present study of the social and intellectual life of Richard Boyle has also served to demonstrate how the series of problems that confronted him in Ireland obliged him to think these problems through to arrive at solutions that were so advanced for the England of his day that they have been mistaken by historians as products of the Revolutionary experience in England.

Of equal interest is the knowledge we have that those who influenced Richard Boyle[25] were principally Protestants like himself who had lived in Ireland and who were driven by their experiences there to arrive at what were, by contemporary English standards, advanced opinions. These opinions, developed in Ireland, eventually became as potent a force in shaping the attitudes of English intellectuals as were the opinions of the Hartlib Circle. This hitherto unacknowledged fact justifies the conclusion that England's association with Ireland in the seventeenth, as in the twentieth, century was in the long term an enriching experience for Englishmen because it compelled them to devise solutions for problems of universal import that they would never otherwise have encountered, not even during the course of their much-vaunted Revolution, in their sheltered, insular and disciplined existence.

Notes

I. THE ENIGMATIC CAREER OF RICHARD BOYLE, 1566–1643

1. See for example works as diverse as Henry Kamen, *The Iron Century: Social Change in Europe, 1550–1660* (London, pb. edition, 1971), p. 57; Charles Webster, *The Great Instauration: Science, Medicine, and Reform, 1626–1660* (London, 1975), pp. 62–6 *et passim*; Lawrence Stone, *The Family, Sex and Marriage in England, 1500–1800* (London, 1977), pp. 168, 187, 204; Lawrence Stone, *The Crisis of the Aristocracy, 1558–1641* (Oxford, 1965), pp. 113, 116, 140, 428 *et passim*.
2. See for example James Carty, 'The Early Life and Times of Richard Boyle', unpublished thesis presented for the Travelling Studentship of the National University of Ireland, 1928. (A copy is deposited in the Archives Department, University College, Dublin.) The comments on Boyle in H. F. Kearney, *Strafford in Ireland, 1633–41* (Manchester, 1959); the article by Terence Ranger, 'Richard Boyle and the Making of an Irish Fortune, 1588–1614', in *Irish Historical Studies* (*I.H.S.*), X, pp. 257–97, also places much stress on the dishonest means by which Boyle acquired wealth and social position, and in this respect reflects the hostile view of Boyle's contemporaries.
3. The bulk of the papers and personal correspondence of Richard Boyle is kept at Chatsworth House, Derbyshire, but some important material is also to be found among the Lismore Castle Papers in the National Library of Ireland. The relevant material at Chatsworth is made up of twenty-four volumes devoted to correspondence and business affairs, a further three volumes are devoted to Boyle's diary; two letter books covering Boyle's political career from 1629 to the early 1640s; and a 'Book of patents relating to the Lands of Richard Boyle, First Earl of Cork'. The material in Dublin is unpublished and will be referred to as

N.L.I., Lismore Castle Papers; references to original material at Chatsworth will be cited as Chatsworth, Lismore Papers, or Chatsworth, Cork Letter Books 1 & 2 or Chatsworth, Cork Patent Book. The diary was edited by A. B. Grosart and published privately in five volumes in 1886; this published edition will be referred to as Grosart, ed., *Lismore Papers*, 1st series with volume and page reference. Some selected material from among the twenty-four volumes at Chatsworth were also edited, frequently inaccurately, by Grosart, and these selections together with Grosart's biography of Boyle were published as a second series of five volumes. These are referred to as Grosart, ed., *Lismore Papers*, 2nd series with volume and page reference. Citation of Boyle material in the British Library will be in the usual way.

4. There are at least two surviving versions of the 'True Remembrances'; the earlier one prepared in 1623 but with some later additions is available in Grosart, ed., *Lismore Papers*, 1st series, II, pp. 100–17; the second edition prepared in 1632 is most readily available in the introduction to the first volume of Thomas Birch, ed., *The Works of Robert Boyle* (5 vols., London, 1774), pp. vii–xi.

5. See for example Eustace Budgell, *Memoirs of the Life and Character of the Late Earl of Orrery and the Family of the Boyles* (London, 1732); Charles Smith, *The Ancient and Present State of the County of Cork* (Dublin, 1750); Birch, ed., *The Works of Robert Boyle*; A. B. Grosart, ed., *Lismore Papers* (10 vols., London, 1886–8); and Dorothy Townshend, *The Life and Letters of the Great Earl of Cork* (London, 1904).

6. Referred to in n. 2 above.

7. T. M. Healy, *Stolen Waters: a Page in the Conquest of Ulster* (London, 1913), and *The Great Fraud of Ulster* (Dublin, 1917).

8. Healy, *The Great Fraud*, p. 88.

9. Healy, *Stolen Waters*, p. 3.

10. Hugh O'Grady, *Strafford and Ireland* (2 vols., Dublin, 1923).

11. C. V. Wedgwood, *Strafford* (London, 1930).

12. Edmund Curtin, *The History of Ireland* (London, 1936); Brian Fitzgerald, *The Anglo-Irish: Three Representative Types: Cork: Ormond: Swift, 1602–1775* (London, 1952).

13. It is worthy to note that English historians concerned with the diary as a historical source have been more alert to the importance of Cork's diary than have historians of seventeenth-century Ireland. See for example Alan Macfarlane, *The Family Life of Ralph Josselin, a Seventeenth-Century Clergyman: an Essay in Historical Anthropology* (Cambridge, 1970), pp. 3–11;

G. E. Aylmer, *The King's Servants: the Civil Service of Charles I* (2nd ed., London, 1974), p. 149.

14. W. Knowler, ed., *Letters and Dispatches of the Earl of Strafford* (2 vols., London, 1739).

15. Kearney, *Strafford in Ireland*, pp. 183–4; Terence O. Ranger, 'The Career of Richard Boyle, First Earl of Cork, in Ireland, 1588–1643' (unpublished D.Phil. thesis, Oxford University, 1959). The first section of this thesis, which has been summarised in the article by Ranger referred to in n. 2 above, treats of Richard Boyle's rise to wealth and influence down to 1614, and, since generally based on evidence hostile to Boyle, it does not present him in a very favourable light. Nonetheless, the author seeks to redress the bias in the evidence by making occasional mention, as on p. 170 of the thesis, to Boyle's 'vision – essentially self-centred but nonetheless remarkable – of a prosperous, anglicised, Munster dominated by his sons, virtually ruling the province from the great mansions he planned for them, each surrounded by its block of estates'. The Boyle perception and sense of mission emerges much more in the second section of Professor Ranger's thesis 'The Planter in Politics, 1614–43' which remains unpublished. Some of the material on which this section is based has been employed by Terence Ranger to a different purpose in his exhilarating article 'Strafford in Ireland: a Revaluation', in *Past & Present*, no. 19 (1961), pp. 26–45.

16. The approaches to the appraisal of historical evidence that the present author has found most suggestive for this work on Boyle have been those adopted in Keith Thomas, *Religion and the Decline of Magic* (Harmondsworth, pb. edition, 1971); and in the various works of Alan Macfarlane, but most especially in *Witchcraft in Tudor and Stuart England* (London, 1970), and in *The Family Life of Ralph Josselin*. The structure of the third chapter of this book was suggested by the essay by J. H. Elliott on 'The Mental World of Hernán Cortés', in *Transactions of the Royal Historical Society* (*T.R.H.S.*), XVI (1966), pp. 41–58. A special word of acknowledgement is also due to Lawrence Stone whose work has provided a focus for the fourth and fifth chapters of the present work; and the fact that the conclusions presented here are sometimes at variance with his should do nothing to diminish the extent to which the author is indebted to his work for the inspiration it has provided.

17. The basic facts as presented in the 'True Remembrances' have for instance been fully adopted by the author of the piece on Richard Boyle in *D.N.B.* This is supplemented by Scott Robertson, 'Preston Church, next Faversham', in *Archaeologia*

Cantiana, XXI (1895), pp. 131–2; and Carus Vale Collier, 'Coats of Arms in Kent Churches', in *Archaeologia Cantiana*, XXIII (1898), pp. 113–14. See also John Venn and J. A. Venn, ed., *Alumni Cantabrigiensis* (Cambridge, 1922), I, p. 196, under Boyle, John, Boyle, Richard, and Boyle, Richard (son of Michael, of London). I am grateful to Raymond Gillespie and Dr Peter Clark for assistance relating to tracing Boyle's Kentish background.

18. The charges brought against Boyle in 1599 together with his defence are to be found in B.L., Add. Ms. 19,831.

19. Detailed information on Boyle's rents is available only for the years he was absent in England, 1613, 1629 and 1637–42. Then a copy of his rental as well as much correspondence relating to defaults were forwarded to him for his inspection. It should be noted that the increase in income is a reflection of his purchases as well as of his improvements. The improvement in tenure and leases of the Boyle property is discussed in Ranger's article 'Richard Boyle and the Making of an Irish Fortune', and that author's work was rendered more difficult because he did not enjoy access to Boyle's patent book (Chatsworth, Cork Patent Book). Boyle's increase in rent has been discussed in Ranger, 'The Career of Richard Boyle', pp. 95–100, but see also the relevant documents: the 1613 rental (Chatsworth, Lismore Papers, IV, no. 100); the 1629 rental (N.L.I., Lismore Castle Papers, Ms. 6,232); half-year's rental ending Lady Day 1637 (N.L.I., Lismore Castle Papers, Ms. 6,239); general rentals 1639–42 (N.L.I., Lismore Castle Papers, Mss. 6,240–1, 6,246–7, 6,248–9).

20. Stone, *Crisis*, p. 140.

21. Cork was one of the few survivors of the sixteenth-century disturbances in Ireland who lived to witness the 1641 rebellion and its aftermath. On Cork's response to rebellion in 1641 and his confidence of ultimate victory see the entries for the years 1641–3 which are devoted almost exclusively to the rebellion in Grosart, ed., *Lismore Papers*, 2nd series, IV.

22. Webster, *The Great Instauration*, pp. 62–7, *et passim*.

23. Stone, *The Family, Sex and Marriage*, p. 187; Mary Boyle as Countess of Warwick is also rightly famous for her remarkable spiritual diary and her book of spiritual meditations (B.L. Add. Mss., 27,351–5 and 26,356).

2. THE HOSTILE WITNESS:
BOYLE'S CAREER THROUGH THE EYES OF HIS ENEMIES

1. Mountnorris to Wentworth, 23 Aug. 1632 (Sheffield City Library, Strafford Papers, Letter Book I, ff. 60–2).

2. Ironically Mountnorris was one of Boyle's principal propagandists as long as Boyle was satisfied to remain a planter: see copy of Francis Annesley to Sir Humphrey May, 1613 (Chatsworth, Lismore Papers, IV, no. 75(b)).

3. Cork to Sir William Beecher, 14 March 1631 (Chatsworth, Cork Letter Book I, ff. 274–6), where he speaks of the 'ill deserving servants' who 'when fully anatomized and their hidden actions brought to light will in due time receive the rewards of their iniquities'.

4. Mountnorris to Wentworth, 17 Sept. 1632 (Sheffield City Library, Strafford Papers, Letter Book I, f. 65ᵛ).

5. Mountnorris to Wentworth, 23 Aug. 1632 (Sheffield City Library, Strafford Papers, Letter Book I, ff. 60–2).

6. *Ibid.* Mountnorris concluded with the remark that 'it were no such extraordinary match for my Lord Clifford's daughter who …may be a wife for the best man's son in England'. On this point Lady Clifford was in agreement with Mountnorris but the more pragmatic father saw the financial advantage of the Boyle alliance since 'few good matches are now to be found in this kingdom, and upon how hard terms for me to compass them, having no great store of ready money', Clifford to Salisbury, 10 Jan. 1634 (Historical Manuscripts Commission, *Calendar of Salisbury Manuscripts*, XXII, *1612–88*, ed. G. Dyfnallt Owen (London, 1971), pp. 275–7).

7. Mountnorris to Wentworth, 21 Nov. 1632 (Sheffield City Library, Strafford Papers, Letter Book I, ff. 83–5); same to same, 17 Sept. 1632 (Sheffield City Library, Strafford Papers, Letter Book I, f. 65ᵛ).

8. Compare for instance Wentworth's comments on the match in Wentworth to Mountnorris 19 Aug. 1632 (Sheffield City Library, Strafford Papers, Letter Book I, f. 59), and in Wentworth to Mountnorris, 2 Sept. 1632 (Sheffield City Library, Strafford Papers, Letter Book I, f. 63). In the first Wentworth is assuring Mountnorris that his position will not be altered as a consequence of the marriage alliance, and in the second he is suggesting that the marriage might not take place. The second letter was written in reply to Mountnorris' scarifying attack on Boyle of 23 Aug. 1632. A year later Wentworth was firmly set against the match and sought to deflect Clifford from it, Wentworth to

Clifford, 7 Dec. 1633 (Sheffield City Library, Strafford Papers, Letter Book 8, pp. 58–60).

9. Wentworth to Lord Marshal, 19 Aug. 1633 (Sheffield City Library, Strafford Papers, Letter Book 8, f. 11); the English members of the 1622 commission did much to erode the credibility of New English planters and officials in Ireland. See for example the comments of Sir Dudley Norton on Charles Coote: 'about a little more than a year since from the provost marshal of Connacht which he yet holdeth, he proceeded to be raised so high as a baronet and a privy councillor. A stirring man fuller of wit than judgement, very pragmatical but his own ends so much in his eye as he is become an eye sore to the country who have grievously complained against him for extortion' (Sir Dudley Norton to Cranfield, 14 June 1622 (Kent Archives Office, Sackville Ms. U269, O.N. 8459); the tone of this condemnation is very much in tune with other complaints of New English planters and officials, see in the same collection Sir Dudley Norton to Cranfield, 10 Dec. 1621 (U269, O.N. 7508); same to same, 27 Dec. 1621 (U269, O.N. 7549); James Perrott to Cranfield (U269, O.N. 8445); Sir Dudley Digges to Cranfield, 18 Apr. 1622 (U269, O.N. 8442).

10. Wentworth to Lord Marshal as in n. 9; on Wentworth's break with Mountnorris see Kearney, *Strafford in Ireland*, pp. 70–2.

11. Wentworth to Lord Treasurer, 6 Dec. 1632 (Sheffield City Library, Strafford Papers, Letter Book 1, ff. 88–90); on Wentworth's dismissal of the New English as social equals see T. O. Ranger, 'Strafford in Ireland: a Revaluation', in *Past & Present*, no. 19 (1961), pp. 26–45.

12. Wentworth to Clifford, 17 Jan. 1638 (Sheffield City Library, Strafford Papers, Letter Book 10(a), ff. 96–7).

13. On this point see Ranger, 'Strafford in Ireland: a Revaluation'.

14. Windebanke to Wentworth, 22 Oct. 1635 (Sheffield City Library, Strafford Papers, Letter Book 9, ff. 307–8); Windebanke warned Wentworth against overstepping the mark with Cork since 'a person of his quality, now in the declination of his years and that heretofore had so eminent a part in the government of that kingdom' was certain to arouse sympathetic support at court.

15. Wentworth to Laud, 18 March 1634 (Sheffield City Library, Strafford Papers, Letter Book 6, ff. 34–5); Wentworth was here describing what he later referred to as Cork's pedigree which was depicted on the monument. Dr Weston was grandfather to Lady Cork and had served as Irish Lord Chancellor in the 1570s; Geoffrey Fenton was father to Lady Cork and had

served as Irish Secretary and Privy Councillor; Kinalmeaky was Cork's second son Lewis, Viscount Kinalmeaky, who was his father's favourite and generally believed to be the most forceful of the Boyle children.

16. Wentworth to Cottington, 31 Oct. 1635 (Sheffield City Library, Strafford Papers, Letter Book 3, f. 227); Clifford to Wentworth, 2 Apr. 1635 (Sheffield City Library, Strafford Papers, Letter Book 16(c), no. 181); on another occasion Wentworth described Cork as 'too great a fish to be held in that slender net', Wentworth to Windebanke, 14 Dec. 1635 (Sheffield City Library, Strafford Papers, Letter Book 9, ff. 128–30).

17. Wentworth to Clifford, 2 May 1635 (Sheffield City Library, Strafford Papers, Letter Book 8, ff. 230–2).

18. Wentworth to Laud, 18 March 1634 (Sheffield City Library, Strafford Papers, Letter Book 6, f. 34).

19. Wentworth to Clifford, 7 Dec. 1633 (Sheffield City Library, Strafford Papers, Letter Book 8, ff. 58–60); Wentworth to Laud, 11 March 1635 (Sheffield City Library, Strafford Papers, Letter Book 6, f. 34).

20. Wentworth to Clifford, 7 Dec. 1633 as in n. 19.

21. Wentworth to Laud, 29 Jan. 1634 (Sheffield City Library, Strafford Papers, Letter Book 6, ff. 9–16).

22. Same to same, 31 Oct. 1633 (Sheffield City Library, Strafford Papers, Letter Book 8, f. 44).

23. Stone *Crisis*, pp. 113, 116, 140, 428, 568, 571, 580, 697–8; on each of these occasions Professor Stone was citing Boyle in support of a general thesis; Christopher Hill, *Society & Puritanism in Pre-Revolutionary England* (London, 1964), p. 128 cites Boyle's attitude to work in support of a general theory. That the Boyle example has not been used more frequently may be explained by his adoption of a royalist position during the early years of the Civil War.

24. Wentworth to Clifford, 22 July 1635 (Sheffield City Library, Strafford Papers, Letter Book 8, f. 253); same to same, 2 May 1635 (Sheffield City Library, Strafford Papers, Letter Book 8, ff. 280–1).

25. Clifford to Wentworth, 15 July 1635 (Sheffield City Library, Strafford Papers, Letter Book 8, ff. 252–3); the character Sir Tristram True Stock who was known to Wentworth as well as Clifford must have been a stock figure in some play of the time. Not even Dr Christopher Hill has been able to identify him, but I thank him for his assistance.

26. Wentworth to Laud, 18 March 1634 (Sheffield City Library, Strafford Papers, Letter Book 6, ff. 34–6).

27. Wentworth to Cork, 25 Dec. 1632 (Sheffield City Library, Strafford Papers, Letter Book 1, f. 95ᵛ).
28. Wentworth to Goring, 19 Aug. 1633 (Sheffield City Library, Strafford Papers, Letter Book 8, ff. 8–11); the last charge was made because Cork justified his possession of Youghal College 'saying that he would turn the benefit thereof to his school house and almhouse' (Sheffield City Library, Strafford Papers, XXIV, XXV, nos 438, 439).
29. Clifford to Wentworth, 15 Dec. 1635 (Sheffield City Library, Strafford Papers, Letter Book 8, f. 339).
30. Wentworth to Clifford, 17 Jan. 1638 (Sheffield City Library, Strafford Papers, Letter Book 10(a), ff.96–7).
31. Wentworth to Clifford, 22 July 1635 (Sheffield City Library, Strafford Papers, Letter Book 8, f.253).
32. Wentworth to Clifford, 22 July 1635 (Sheffield City Library, Strafford Papers, Letter Book 8, f.253).
33. There is no evidence that Cork ever accused Wentworth of being a Papist other than Wentworth's own statement to that effect to Laud, 22 Oct. 1633 (Sheffield City Library, Strafford Papers, Letter Book 8, f.33). Wentworth introduced the cruel twist about St Patrick's purgatory, a traditional place of pilgrimage in County Donegal, because Cork took special credit for having brought about its destruction, Grosart, ed., *Lismore Papers*, 1st series, III, p. 159.
34. Wentworth to Laud, 31 Dec. 1633 (Sheffield City Library, Strafford Papers, Letter Book 6, ff.3–9). 'I persuade his Lordship [Cork] to take this physic [loss of church property] otherways believe me all the lectures (and two of these a week he hears all this while devoutly) and Perkins' *Cases of Conscience* to boot would never have been able to enforce it upon him.' I wish to thank Dr Christopher Hill for confirming that the *Cases of Conscience* were indeed part of the *opus* of the puritan William Perkins on whom he has written in *Puritanism and Revolution* (London, pb. edition 1968), pp. 212–34
35. Wentworth to Laud, 18 March 1634 (Sheffield City Library, Strafford Papers, Letter Book 6, f.36); Cork to Goring, 30 April 1634 (Sheffield City Library, Strafford Papers, Letter Book 8, f.120).
36. Wentworth to Goring, 1 Feb. 1634 (Sheffield City Library, Strafford Papers, Letter Book 8, ff.71–2); same to Clifford, 2 May 1635 (same letter book, ff.230–2); same to Clifford, 27 Nov. 1636 (H.M.C., *Cal. Salisbury Mss.*, XXII, pp. 282–3).
37. Wentworth to Laud, 31 Dec. 1633 (Sheffield City Library, Strafford Papers, Letter Book 6, ff.3–9); same to same, 22 Oct.

1633 (Sheffield City Library, Strafford Papers, Letter Book 8, ff.33–4).

38. Wentworth to Cottington, 22 Dec. 1635 (Sheffield City Library, Strafford Papers, Letter Book 3, f.235).

39. Wentworth to Laud, 9 March 1636 (Sheffield City Library, Strafford Papers, Letter Book 6, ff.330–1). On Atherton see Aidan Clarke, 'The Atherton File', in *Decies: Old Waterford Society*, no. 11 (1979), pp. 45–54.

40. Cork to Wentworth, 4 March 1632 (Sheffield City Library, Strafford Papers, Letter Book 1, f.34).

3. THE MENTAL WORLD OF RICHARD BOYLE

1. For references to the two versions see Chapter 1 n. 4.

2. In 1623 he mentioned that since his arrival in Ireland 'the blessing of God, (whose providence guided me hither), hath enriched my poor estate, and added no care, or burden of conscience thereunto', Grosart, ed., *Lismore Papers*, 1st series, II, p. 106.

3. It should be noted that Cork took Lady Ralegh's challenge seriously because Ralegh had by the 1630s assumed hero if not martyr status in England and there was the possibility that her plea, which had no basis in law, would become a popular one. On Ralegh's image see J. P. Kenyon, *Stuart England* (Harmondsworth, 1978), pp. 72–3. The Ralegh episode received no mention in the first edition of the 'True Remembrances', but Boyle made a lengthy reference to it in the 1632 edition where he mentioned George Carew, later Earl of Totnes, as the inspirer of the purchase and Sir Robert Cecil, later Earl of Salisbury, as the intermediary. 'True Remembrances', in Birch, ed., *The Works of Robert Boyle*, I, p. viii.

4. Cork to Carew Ralegh, 16 Jan. 1632 (Chatsworth, Cork Letter Book 1, ff.389–92); not all of the story was fictitious since it appears from Cork's diary that in 1617 when Ralegh was on his voyage to Guiana he did stop in Munster, received supplies from Boyle and was presented with gifts and money. Grosart, ed., *Lismore Papers*, 1st series, I, pp. 145, 157, 158, 160, 162, 163.

5. 'True Remembrances', in Birch, ed., *The Works of Robert Boyle*, I, p. vii.

6. Cork to Sir Philip Mannering, March 1640 (Chatsworth, Lismore Papers, Letter Book 2, f.418); same to Strafford, 16 March 1640 (Chatsworth, Cork Letter Book 2, f.424).

7. This was mentioned, in an inventory of Cork's papers and personal belongings taken on his death in 1643, as 'A parchment book containing the whole proceedings against the Earl

of Cork in the court of castle chamber...touching the custody of Youghal etc. left to posterity to testify the said earl's innocency, 1636' (Chatsworth, Lismore Papers, XXIV, no. 20).

8. Cork to Laud, 10 Dec. 1638 (Chatsworth, Cork Letter Book 2, ff.309–10); the other man referred to was Ralegh who first encroached upon most of the church property in question and which then passed to Boyle by purchase. Even Wentworth acknowledged Ralegh to be the true culprit when he professed Cork's control of the Lismore episcopal lands to be 'no more for the most part than a building up and finishing of the rotten sacriligeous foundation set by Sir Walter Rawley who first laid his unhallowed hands upon those church possessions', Wentworth to Laud, 29 Jan. 1634 (Sheffield City Library, Strafford Papers, Letter Book 6, ff.9–16).

9. Cork to Lord Chamberlain, 28 June 1635, and same to Salisbury, same date (Chatsworth, Cork Letter Book 2, ff.89–90).

10. See Cork to Sir Thomas Stafford, 9 Sept. 1635 (Chatsworth, Cork Letter Book 2, ff.103–4), and Cork to King Charles, draft, late 1629 (Chatsworth, Lismore Papers, XXIV, no. 97). In the second of these he claimed credit for having built 'more churches, market towns, castles and bridges, and more strong plantations of English protestants than ever was made by any native of England since the first conquest of Ireland'. All of these he would have described under the heading, as he did in writing to Stafford, 'good works for civilizing of this commonwealth'.

11. Thomas, Archbishop of Dublin to Northampton, 24 July 1613 (Chatsworth, Lismore Papers, IV, no. 74); same to Archbishop of Canterbury, 24 July 1613 (Chatsworth, Lismore Papers, IV, no. 75); Francis Annesley to Sir Humphrey May, July 1613, a copy (Chatsworth, Lismore Papers, IV, no. 75(b)).

12. The report of the 1622 commission (B.L., Add. Ms. 4,757, ff.95, 96, 97 for report on baronies of Inchiquin, Kinalmeaky and Carrigaline).

13. Cork to King Charles, draft, late 1629 (Chatsworth, Lismore Papers, XXIV, no. 97).

14. The two supposed encounters with Queen Elizabeth are described in the 'True Remembrances', in Birch, ed., *The Works of Robert Boyle*, pp. vii and viii; his meeting with King Charles I when Cork was appointed joint lord justice is described by Cork to Bedford, 15 Sept. 1630 (Chatsworth, Cork Letter Book 1, f.187); his royal visit in 1638 when he was received to favour after he had endured Wentworth's onslaught is described by

Cork to Walley, 30 Nov. 1638 (Chatsworth, Cork Letter Book 2, ff.301–2). Cork's sole meeting with King James is mentioned in Grosart, ed., *Lismore Papers*, 1st series, I, pp. 32–4.

15. 'True Remembrances', in Birch, ed., *The Works of Robert Boyle* I, p. vi; and in Grosart, ed., *Lismore Papers*, 1st series, II, p. 106.

16. 'True Remembrances', in Birch, ed., *The Works of Robert Boyle*, I, pp. vi and viii.

17. Cork to Laud, 10 Dec. 1638 (Chatsworth, Cork Letter Book 2, ff.309–10).

18. Grosart, ed., *Lismore Papers*, 1st series V, p. 170.

19. Grosart, ed., *Lismore Papers*, 1st series, V, p. 164.

20. Grosart, ed., *Lismore Papers*, 1st series, V, p. 164.

21. Walley to Cork, 21 July 1640 (N.L.I. Lismore Castle Papers, Ms. 13,237 (25); same to same, 28 Sept. 1640 (same collection).

22. Walley to Cork, 25 March 1641 (Chatsworth, Lismore Papers, XXII, no. 1).

23. Walley to Cork, 25 June 1641 (Chatsworth, Lismore Papers, XXII, no. 31).

24. Walley to Cork, 12 Dec. 1640 (Chatsworth, Lismore Papers, XXI, no. 75).

25. See for example Cork to Sir Thomas Stafford, 9 Sept. 1635 Chatsworth, Cork Letter Book 2, ff.103–4); Cork to Walley, 30 Nov. 1638 (Chatsworth, Cork Letter Book 2, ff.301–3).

26. Clifford to Wentworth, 2 Apr. 1635 (Sheffield City Library, Strafford Papers, XVI (c), no. 181); Wentworth to Clifford, 2 May 1635 (Sheffield City Library, Strafford Papers, Letter Book 8, ff.230–1).

27. Grosart, ed., *Lismore Papers*, 1st series, IV, pp. 179–185; this provides plentiful detail of Cork's reluctance to settle for a fine of £15,000 and the efforts of his principal heir Dungarvan to persuade him.

28. Nicholas Canny, *The Elizabethan Conquest of Ireland: a Pattern Established 1565–76* (Hassocks, 1976), pp. 117–36; Nicholas Canny, 'The Permissive Frontier', in K. R. Andrews, N. P. Canny and P. E. H. Hair, eds., *The Westward Enterprise: English Activity in Ireland, the Atlantic and America, 1480–1650* (Liverpool, 1979), pp. 17–44 esp. p. 18.

29. Wallop had for years relentlessly pursued those English in provincial Ireland whom he thought to be guilty of deviation from civilised norms. See for example Wallop to Walsingham, 1 March 1581 (P.R.O., S.P.63/81/2); same to same, 15 May 1582 (P.R.O., S.P.63/92/42); same to same, 25 June 1585

(P.R.O., S.P.63/114/47). For Boyle's explanation of Wallop's pursuit of himself see 'True Remembrances', in Birch, ed., *The Works of Robert Boyle*, I, p. vii.

30. See the letters of Wallop cited in n. 29, and Canny, 'The Permissive Frontier', in Andrews, Canny and Hair, eds., *The Westward Enterprise*, pp. 17–44.

31. This manuscript book which the present writer has been unable to locate was given on loan in February 1620 to Sir Dudley Norton, one of the commissioners for Ireland, Grosart, ed., *Lismore Papers*, 1st series, I, p. 242. Cork was more careful with his *Pacata Hibernia*, to which he made frequent reference, since his loan in 1633 of these two volumes to Chief Baron Lowther and Sir Adam Loftus was 'to be returned' which they obviously were since he gave them on loan to Sir Arthur Cayles in 1640 and they were later listed among Cork's belongings at his death. 'Holinshed's Chronicle in Large Folio' was also listed in 1643 among Cork's possessions, but he referred to it less frequently than to *Pacata Hibernia* during his life. See Grosart, ed., *Lismore Papers*, 1st series, III, p. 211, V, p. 148; List of Cork's possessions on his death (Chatsworth, Lismore Papers, XXIV, no. 20).

32. Cork to Lord Treasurer, 9 August 1630 (Chatsworth, Cork Letter Book 1, f.167); same to Sir William Beecher, 29 Oct. 1630 (Chatsworth, Cork Letter Book 1, f.203).

33. Cork, born in 1566, was already 22 before he first reached Ireland. He came from Kent where the Reformation was well advanced and where some pockets of puritans existed, and he had spent some time at Bene't College (now Corpus Christi College) Cambridge which was noted as a centre of puritanism. On Kent see Peter Clark, *English Provincial Society from the Reformation to the Revolution: Religion, Politics and Society in Kent, 1500–1640* (Hassocks, 1977), esp. pp. 149–84. I wish to thank Mr Alan Forde of St John's College, Cambridge, for the information on Bene't College.

34. An inventory of Cork's possessions at the time of his death (Chatsworth, Lismore Papers, XXIV, no. 20); Grosart, ed., *Lismore Papers*, 1st series, II, p. 284 where Boyle mentions a gift of his 'manuscript Bible' to his uncle Dr Weston for the library of Christ Church, Oxford; Grosart, ed., *Lismore Papers*, 1st series, IV, pp. 5, 200, V, p. 69; Wentworth to Laud, 31 Dec. 1633 (Sheffield City Library, Strafford Papers, Letter Book 6, ff.3–9). Wentworth appears to have been genuinely taken by 'all his piety' and he was particularly disturbed to find that the Archbishops of Dublin and Armagh were both happy 'to set

forth this earl as a chief patriarch of this church'. Wentworth to Laud, 18 March 1634 (Sheffield City Library, Strafford Papers, Letter Book 6, ff.34–6). The author is conscious that while this reading list can be regarded as being theologically left of centre this in itself is not proof that Cork was a puritan. One measure of his religious concern is that at the height of his power he maintained eighteen chaplains, Grosart, ed., *Lismore Papers*, 1st series, III, p. 122. On the witch trial reference see Dungarvan to Cork, 29 May 1634 (Chatsworth, Lismore Papers, XVIII, no. 12).

35. Keith Thomas, *Religion and the Decline of Magic*, pp. 90–132, esp. pp. 95, 125, 131; see also 'An Account of Philaretus [Robert Boyle] during his Minority', in Birch, ed., *The Works of Robert Boyle*, I, p. xvi, where Robert Boyle in listing his lucky escapes from misfortune mentions that he 'would not ascribe any of these rescues unto chance, but would be still industrious to perceive the hand of heaven in all these accidents; and indeed he would profess, that in the passage of his life, he had observed so gracious and so peculiar a conduct of providence, that he should be equally blind and ungrateful should he not both discern and acknowledge it'.

36. See for example in Grosart, ed., *Lismore Papers*, 1st series, I, Cork's reaction to the death of his brother, John, Bishop of Cork, resulting from a broken leg.

37. Grosart, ed., *Lismore Papers*, 1st series, I, p. 19, a loan of 'my Guyceiardyne being Sir Geoffrey Fenton's to Thomas Russell of Ballyea'. On the structure of Florentine political thought see Felix Gilbert, *Machiavelli & Guicciardini* (Princeton, 1965); and J. G. A. Pocock, *The Machiavellian Moment* (Princeton, 1975).

38. An example of the news from Europe that Cork invited is R.C. to Cork, 29 Nov. 1623 (N.L.I., Lismore Castle Papers, Ms. 13,237(4)); Cork revealed his attitude to Europe in his correspondence with sons on the Grand Tour, but he revealed his loyalties also by gifts to the exiled court of Bohemia, as for example Grosart, ed., *Lismore Papers*, 1st series, IV, p. 56, and his purchase of a commission in the Netherlands for his son-in-law Goring.

39. Grosart, ed., *Lismore Papers*, 1st series, III, pp. 13, 14, 106, 159. St Patrick's purgatory in County Donegal was, as it is to the present day, a place of popular pilgrimage.

40. Cork to Dorchester, 10 May 1631 (Chatsworth, Cork Letter Book 1, ff.312–13).

41. Cork to Dorchester, 10 May 1631 (Chatsworth, Cork Letter

Book 1, ff.312–13); his real objection was that the idle ones in Ireland were saved from taking up useful employment by the Irish lords who relieved them 'to their utter beggary, bearing their surcharge with so strong patience'.

42. See for example Grosart, ed., *Lismore Papers*, 1st series, II, p. 182 where on 22 Apr. 1626 Cork provided £500 for construction of bridges at Cappoquin and Fermoy, and described it as 'good common wealth's work'; and Grosart, ed., *Lismore Papers*, 1st series, IV, p. 224 where on 16 Feb. 1637 Cork provided £100 towards building a bridge near Clonmel 'it being a work of charity'.

43. Grosart, ed., *Lismore Papers*, 1st series, IV, p. 50 when Cork recorded a gift to Capt. Sholburg, who was destitute, at the request of his father John Sholburg, 'an ancient follower of my dear and worthy friend Sir Walter Ralegh'; another such example Grosart, ed., *Lismore Papers*, 1st series, III, p. 107.

44. Grosart, ed., *Lismore Papers*, 1st series, III, pp. 136, 161.

45. On Downham and Ussher see *D.N.B.* The writings of both prelates were significantly among Boyle's possessions, and Ussher played some part in the upbringing of the Boyle children. See for example T. C. Croker, ed., *Some Specialities in the Life of Mary Countess of Warwick* (London, 1848), p. 22 where Mary Boyle mentions that 'my Lord Primate of Ireland's preaching against plays' had 'resolved' her 'to leave seeing them'.

46. On Atherton see Laud to Wentworth, 23 Jan. 1636 (Sheffield City Library, Strafford Papers, Letter Book 6, f.319) and Wentworth to Laud, 9 March 1636 (*ibid.*, ff.330–1). On Boyle's efforts to situate his relatives in Munster livings see Grosart, ed., *Lismore Papers*, 1st series, I, pp. 44, 62, 167, 232, 253, III, p. 14.

47. Walley to Cork, 28 Sept. 1640 (N.L.I., Lismore Castle Papers, Ms. 13,237 (25)).

48. Walley to Cork, 7 Aug. 1639 (Chatsworth, Lismore Papers, XX, no. 94).

49. Walley to Cork, 21 July 1640 (N.L.I., Lismore Castle Papers, Ms. 13,237(23)); the charge against Atherton was 'sodomy with two youths that waited upon him, and his adulterious and adulterate attempts'. Walley further revealed that Atherton's wicked ways were so many that it had 'taken up 6 or 7 quires of paper' to detail them. These unfortunately have not survived.

50. Walley to Cork, 4 Sept. 1639 (Chatsworth, Lismore Papers, XX, no. 107). This letter was occasioned by a commission granted to Bishop Atherton and others 'to inquire of all hospitals, lazar and leper houses in Munster'. Walley believed the real aim of

the commissioners to be the recall to crown possession of the priory at Lismore and he reported to Cork: 'If I can hear of a leper in all these parts (whereof I am diligent to inquire) I will put him into one of the two houses that are now void, that the commissioners when they come may find a leper therein, and the place being so employed. I do think it may work some change in their proceedings.'

51. Laud to Wentworth, 29 Dec. 1638 (Sheffield City Library, Strafford Papers, Letter Book 7, f.157); same to same, 31 Jan. 1639 (*ibid.*, f.159).

52. As late as 1675 Mary Boyle, as Countess of Warwick, recalled in her diary how grateful she was for the choice of Lady Cleyton as foster-mother 'who nourished me as her own' (B.L., Collections out of Lady Warwick's papers, Add. Ms. 27,358). On Cork's painstaking search for a tutor see Cork to William Perkins, 20 June 1635 (Chatsworth, Cork Letter Book 2, ff.82–4).

53. Grosart, ed., *Lismore Papers*, 1st series, II, p. 33; Croker, ed., *Some Specialities in the Life of Mary Warwick*, p. 22, and p. 41, where she remarked that it was her sister-in-law Elizabeth Kilegrew (wife of Francis Boyle) who first introduced her 'to seeing and reading plays and romances, and in exquisite and curious dressing'; Cork to Lewis, Viscount Kinalmeaky, 6 Jan. 1637 (Chatsworth, Cork Letter Book 2, ff.142–3).

54. Corker, ed., *Some Specialities in the Life of Mary Warwick*, p. 21; her remark was as follows: 'I was so fond of the court, that I had taken a secret resolution that if my father died, and I was mistress of myself, I would become a courtier.'

55. This is discussed in Chapter 5, but see Dungarvan to Cork, 16 July 1632, in Grosart, ed., *Lismore Papers*, 2nd series, III, pp. 184–7.

56. Laud to Wentworth, 29 Dec. 1638 (Sheffield City Library, Strafford Papers, Letter Book 7, f.157); Cork to Strafford, 2 Jan. 1639 (Chatsworth, Cork Letter Book 2, ff.324–5) where he requested his adversary to 'take away your heavy hand from me, and receive me into your favour'; see also Cork to Laud, 10 Dec. 1638 (Chatsworth, Cork Letter Book 2, ff.309–10).

57. Grosart, ed., *Lismore Papers*, 1st series, V, p. 170; Cork's attitude to Wentworth is difficult to pin down. The entry in Cork's diary for 23 July 1633 (Grosart, ed., *Lismore Papers*, 1st series, III, p. 202) where Wentworth was described as 'a most cursed man to all Ireland, and to me in particular', would seem to be a decisive condemnation, but on 12 Jan. 1640 Cork entered in his diary (Grosart, ed., *Lismore Papers*, 1st series, V, p. 121) that 'the noble lord deputy' was created Earl of Strafford. The first

of these entries was obviously made long after 1633 and with the benefit of hind-sight.

58. Grosart, ed., *Lismore Papers*, 1st series, V, p. 183; Strafford's last recorded reference to Cork as 'old Richard [who] hath sworn against me gallantly' sounds somewhat affectionate, and Strafford then reserved his venom for Viscount Ranelagh, Cork's son-in-law (Strafford to Sir Adam Loftus, 4 Feb. 1641, Sheffield City Library, Strafford Papers, Letter Book 34).

59. Cork to Dungarvan, 21 Nov. 1642 (B.L., Egerton Ms. 80, ff.14–16) where he advised Dungarvan and Broghill, then seeking aid in England to quell the revolt in Munster, 'to be extreme careful how you carry yourselves and what company you keep, for the times are so full of danger that no honest man knows who to trust'.

60. Cork to Richard Parsons, 14 Jan. 1640 (Chatsworth, Cork Letter Book 2, ff.403–4).

61. Grosart, ed., *Lismore Papers*, 1st series, I, pp. 223, 243, II, p. 268; a note of Cork's personal belongings at his death (Chatsworth, Lismore Papers, XXIV, no. 20); accounts of the Earl of Cork, under appropriate dates (N.L.I., Lismore Castle Papers, Ms. 6,242).

62. Cork to Richard Parsons (as in n. 60); in this letter he encouraged young Parsons to visit England 'to observe the passages in the parliament' and Cork offered 'to endeavour for to get you a burgess place in parliament'.

63. Cork to Goring, Oct. 1629 (Chatsworth, Cork Letter Book 1, f.8); Grosart, ed., *Lismore Papers*, 1st series, V, p. 159.

64. Grosart, ed., *Lismore Papers*, 1st series, V, pp. 82, 89.

65. Cork to Goring, 26 Oct. 1629 (Chatsworth, Cork Letter Book 1, f.10).

66. Croker, ed., *Some Specialities in the Life of Mary Warwick*, p. 21.

67. Nicholas Canny, 'Dominant Minorities; English Settlers in Ireland and Virginia, 1550–1650', in A. C. Hepburn, ed., *Minorities in History* (London, 1978), pp. 51–69.

68. This point will be discussed in detail in Chapter 6, but as late as 1634 Cork was considering the purchase of an estate on the Severn 'so seated as I may have conveniency to transport any thing by sea to either my houses at Youghal and Lismore', Cork to Sir John Jephson, 24 Feb. 1634 (Chatsworth, Cork Letter Book 1, f.739).

69. See for example Walley to Cork, 27 Jan. 1640 (Chatsworth, Lismore Papers, XX, no. 143).

70. Grosart, ed., *Lismore Papers*, 1st series, V, p. 176.

71. Grosart, ed., *Lismore Papers*, 1st series, V, p. 216.
72. For evidence of the renewed confidence of the English in Munster after the battle of Liscarroll see anonymous, *A True Relation of God's Providence in the Province of Munster* (London, 1642).
73. The activities of Broghill in Ireland can be traced in T. W. Moody, F. X. Martin and F. J. Byrne, eds., *A New History of Ireland* (Oxford, 1976), III, pp. 336–86, 420–53; see also the entry in the *D.N.B.* under Boyle, Roger.
74. This bias in Cork's letters could be explained by the fact that when confronted by Wentworth he was forced to cultivate individuals such as Lord Holland who were known to be Wentworth's enemies. In writing to the Earl of Bristol in 1636 Cork also revealed something of his sympathies when he emphasised that the £3,600 he paid in subsidy was more than 'ever any subject in England *by a parliamentary way* was rated at' (my italics), Cork to Bristol, 4 June 1636 (Chatsworth, Cork Letter Book 2, f.128).
75. See under Boyle, Richard in *D.N.B.* In 1644 this son was created Baron Clifford in the English peerage, and following the Restoration became first Earl of Burlington.
76. Webster, *The Great Instauration*, pp. 62–3.
77. The best evidence of her religious position is her unpublished diary (B.L., Add. Ms. 27,351–5).
78. Birch, ed., *The Works of Robert Boyle*, I, p. xxvii.
79. C. V. Wedgwood, *The King's Peace, 1637–1641* (London, 1955), pp. 310–11.
80. Grosart, ed., *Lismore Papers*, 1st series, V, pp. 144, 164.
81. Walley to Cork, 12 Dec. 1640 (Chatsworth, Lismore Papers, XXI, no. 75); Castle to Bridgewater, 1 July 1641 (San Marino, Huntington Library, Ellesmere Ms. no. 7,841).
82. Fenton to Boyle, 25 July 1606 (Chatsworth, Lismore Papers, II, no. 27). In this Fenton sent a copy of the proclamation for defective titles advising Boyle to keep it for future use since Irish lawyers considered it 'to be a sovereign salve to cure the breaches in men's titles, and to settle their estates against all future vexation'.
83. Cork to Dungarvan, 24 Feb. 1643 (B.L., Egerton Ms. 80, ff.15–16).
84. Clark, *English Provincial Society*, pp. 149–84.
85. Webster, *The Great Instauration*, Chapter 1.
86. See for example Sir William Parsons to Cork, 7 May 1643 (Chatsworth, Lismore Papers, XXIV, no. 21) where in congratulating Cork on his victory over Strafford he advised him

not 'to be discouraged with the cross ways of the age, and let the world see, and our own consciences tells us, we are the same men to the king and his service'.

4. SOCIAL ASCENT AND SOCIAL ADJUSTMENTS IN THE CAREER OF RICHARD BOYLE

1. This certainly explains the reference made to Boyle in Kamen, *The Iron Century*, p. 57.
2. Stone, *Crisis*, pp. 81, 113, 116, 428, 571, 580.
3. The historian who seems to have been most convinced by Wentworth is, understandably, C. V. Wedgwood who drew so heavily on the Strafford material. See for an example of her understanding of Boyle, *The King's Peace*, pp. 310–11, 404. In the second of these she referred to Sir John Borlase and Sir William Parsons as 'veteran jackals who ran in Lord Cork's pack'.
4. Cork's concern that the English planters in Ireland be given an opportunity to render service to the crown is best exemplified in his letter to the English privy council, 12 Feb. 1631 (Chatsworth, Cork Letter Book 1, f.259) where he pronounced: 'I am not so wholly wedded to my own will or ease, or so meer a stoic as to prefer my particular before the interest which the public hath and may justly challenge in me.'
5. Cork to Sir John Cook, 2 Jan. 1639 (Chatsworth, Cork Letter Book 2, ff.320–1).
6. Cork to Laud, 12 March 1639 (Chatsworth, Cork Letter Book 2, f.342).
7. Cork to Dungarvan, 10 Dec. 1633 (Chatsworth, Cork Letter Book 1, ff.720–4).
8. Grosart, ed., *Lismore Papers*, 1st series, IV, p. 121. In 1635 Cork bestowed this ring on his nephew John Boyle who represented the senior line of the family, being the son of Cork's eldest brother Bishop John Boyle of Cork.
9. Cork to Dungarvan, 10 Dec. 1633, as in n. 7.
10. Grosart, ed., *Lismore Papers*, 1st series, I, p. 259.
11. 'True Remembrances', 1623 edition, in Grosart, ed., *Lismore Papers*, 1st series, II, p. 117; Cork made mention of this as evidence 'for the antiquity of the earldom of Cork'.
12. Wentworth to Laud, 29 Jan. 1634 (Sheffield City Library, Strafford Papers, Letter Book 6, f.14).
13. See under Fenton, Sir Geoffrey in *D.N.B.*, Cork's regard for Fenton is clear from the fact that he preserved his official

correspondence, and prided himself in the possession of his translation of Guicciardini.

14. See under Weston, Robert in *D.N.B.* Cork's reverence for the Fenton and Weston ancestry was also expressed in the *Musarum Lachrymae*, a collection of verse composed by the fellows of Trinity College, Dublin, on the occasion of the death of the Countess of Cork. In this (sig. A4ʳ) Geoffrey Fenton was recalled as

> Sir Geoffrey Fenton whose approved wit
> Deep judgement, loyal heart made him most fit
> To be state secretary of this realm
> And privy counsellor.

Lady Cork's maternal grandfather was recalled even more fulsomely as (sig. A3ʳ)

> Thrice learned Dr. Weston! Whose clear light
> Of Law, and conscience shined so bright
> (The while that noble Sidney ruled this ancient Isle)
> That he was made Lord Chancellor of this land
> And weighed proceedings with so equal hand
> And conscionable poise, that mongst the rest
> This kingdom's annals ranked him with the best
> For learning, law and virtue.

15. Laud to Wentworth, 11 March 1635 (Sheffield City Library, Strafford Papers, Letter Book 6, f.32).

16. Grosart, ed., *Lismore Papers*, 1st series, II, p. 294 where Cork arranged in 1629 for a tomb over his parents' grave at Preston Church near Faversham 'with all his father's children's pictures, matches and arms cut in alabaster'; reference to Cork's relatives being buried in his 'tomb in Youghal church' is to be found in Grosart, ed., *Lismore Papers*, 1st series, I, pp. 167, 253; II, p. 75; and for the monument at Deptford see Grosart, ed., *Lismore Papers*, 1st series, II, p. 283 where Cork mentioned a visit to his uncle Brown at Deptford, and a visit to the church to view the monument erected to his eldest son Roger. On that occasion Cork noted with some satisfaction that his wife's uncle, Captain Edward Fenton, was also buried in Deptford Church, Kent. See also the references in n. 17 to Chapter 1.

17. The extent of kinship contact that a yeoman might have had is discussed in Macfarlane, *The Family Life of Ralph Josselin*, pp. 126–44.

18. 'True Remembrances', 1623 edition, in Grosart, ed., *Lismore*

Papers, 1st series, II, pp. 100, 137; we get some notion of the wealth achieved in Ireland by Smith from T.C.D. Ms. 820 f. 116.

19. Grosart, ed., *Lismore Papers*, 1st series, I, pp. 44, 167; *Alumni Cantabrigiensis*, I, p. 196, under Boyle, John.

20. Grosart, ed., *Lismore Papers*, 1st series, I, pp. 62, 227, 253, III, pp. 4, 35, IV, p. 185; see *Alumni Cantabrigiensis*, as above, under Boyle, Richard.

21. This pessimistic outlook can be judged from Cork's low level of expectations from his servants, and his laconic remarks when many of these proved disloyal. See for example Grosart, ed., *Lismore Papers*, 1st series, III, p. 333, IV, p. 219.

22. Grosart, ed., *Lismore Papers*, 1st series, IV, p. 185 where Cork records the transfer of spiritual lands to 'the perfidious R. Bp of Cork my faithless and unthankful kinsman whom I had raised from being a poor schoolmaster at Barnett where he had but a stipend of £20 ster. p.a., and hath been by my only favour advanced to all that he is now come into hath by false inventions done all this'.

23. Cork to Joshua Boyle, 13 Jan. 1639 (N.L.I., Lismore Castle Papers, Ms. 13,238).

24. Grosart, ed., *Lismore Papers*, 1st series, I, p. 100, II, pp. 29, 141, 317, III, p. 154, IV, pp. 26, 122, 123, 203, V, pp. 38, 41, 98.

25. Grosart, ed., *Lismore Papers*, 1st series, I, pp. 37, 48, 131, 232, II, pp. 77, 216, 228, III, pp. 134, 180, IV, pp. 67, 109, 219.

26. Grosart, ed., *Lismore Papers*, 1st series, II, pp. 75, 170, 228, III, p. 214, IV, pp. 122, 147, V, p. 41.

27. Thomas Burt to Cork, 20 Apr. 1637 (Chatsworth, Cork Letter Book 2, f. 194).

28. Indeed, as will be seen from the discussion of marriage alliances in this and the next chapter, the Barrymore and Kildare matches were arranged simultaneously with English and New English matches.

29. Walley to Cork, 30 May 1640 (Chatsworth, Lismore Papers, XXI, no. 20) where Walley regrets that Cork's instructions 'to send to Sir Arthur Hide for grafts of his great pearmeane and to take grafts of Sir Walter Rawley's apple in Lisfynny orchard' arrived too late. Other planters in Munster were equally concerned with grafts and we find Sir Thomas Standish of Bruff writing to Cork in 1624 (Chatsworth, Lismore Papers, XIV, no. 277) requesting 'some grafts of your Imperial plum, musk plum and date plum'.

30. Grosart, ed., *Lismore Papers*, 1st series, I, pp. 174, 268, II, p. 21.
31. Grosart, ed., *Lismore Papers*, 1st series, II, p. 33. That the antiquity of the Barry family was important to Boyle is suggested by the reference in *Musarum Lachrymae* (sig. A4) as 'Earl Barrymore that ancient honoured peer'.
32. Lady Barrymore to Cork, 20 Apr. 1634 (Chatsworth, Cork Letter Book 2, f.32).
33. Barrymore to Cork, 20 Apr. 1634 (Chatsworth, Cork Letter Book 2, ff.30–1); same to same, 1 June 1634 (*ibid.*, ff.35–6); Grosart, ed., *Lismore Papers*, 1st series, II, p. 223, III, pp. 87, 102, IV, pp. 208, 209.
34. Grosart, ed., *Lismore Papers*, 1st series, IV, pp. 208, 209.
35. The principal evidence of resistance is to be found in Grosart, ed., *Lismore Papers*, 1st series, III, p. 87 where Cork complained of Barrymore's failure to thank him for hospitality extended to himself, wife and children in Dublin over an eighteen-month period. Three years later in 1634 Barrymore had complied with his father-in-law's wishes by agreeing to look to none other than Cork himself for help in his financial difficulties, Barrymore to Cork, 1 June 1634 (Chatsworth, Cork Letter Book 2, ff.35–6).
36. Grosart, ed., *Lismore Papers*, 1st series, III, p. 132, IV, p. 197; Cork to Walley, 21 Feb. 1639 (Chatsworth, Cork Letter Book 2, ff.332–4).
37. Cork to Barrymore, 6 June 1634 (Chatsworth, Cork Letter Book 2, ff.36–8).
38. Grosart, ed., *Lismore Papers*, 1st series, V, pp. 56–7.
39. Grosart, ed., *Lismore Papers*, 1st series, V, pp. 79, 103, 215; Webster, *The Great Instauration*, p. 63. The Ranelagh household was also frequented by Andrew Marvell, see Hugh Brogan, 'Marvell's Epitaph on—', in *Renaissance Quarterly*, XXXII, no. 2. I am grateful to John Elliott for this reference.
40. Grosart, ed., *Lismore Papers*, 1st series, II, p. 336; Cork to Owen Hodges, steward of Duchess of Lennox, 13 Oct. 1629 (Chatsworth, Cork Letter Book 1, ff.4–5).
41. Cork to Kildare, 13 Oct. 1629 (P.R.O.N.I. Letter Book of George, Earl of Kildare, letter no. 4); same to same, 25 March 1630 (*ibid.*, letter no. 5); same to same, 20 Oct. 1629 (Chatsworth, Cork Letter Book 1, ff.5–6).
42. Grosart, ed., *Lismore Papers*, 1st series, III, p. 182.
43. Grosart, ed., *Lismore Papers*, 1st series, III, p. 212.
44. Cork to Sir Adam Loftus, 3 Apr. 1640 (Chatsworth, Cork Letter Book 2, f.426).

45. Grosart, ed., *Lismore Papers*, 1st series, III, pp. 174–5, 179.
46. Grosart, ed., *Lismore Papers*, 1st series, IV, p. 151.
47. Grosart, ed., *Lismore Papers*, 1st series, III, p. 164.
48. *Ibid.*, p. 165.
49. Grosart, ed., *Lismore Papers*, 1st series, III, p. 134, IV, p. 6.
50. Grosart, ed., *Lismore Papers*, 1st series, IV, p. 45.
51. Grosart, ed., *Lismore Papers*, 1st series, IV, pp. 42–4.
52. In 1638, for example, Cork, seemingly despairing of Kildare's ineptitude, offered to accommodate his children with their nurses and servants at Lismore (Grosart, ed., *Lismore Papers*, 1st series, V, pp. 45–6).
53. Cork to Lady Kildare, 18 March 1639 (Chatsworth, Cork Letter Book 2, f.344).
54. Cork mentioned the three genealogies he had traced in 'True Remembrances', Grosart, ed., *Lismore Papers*, 1st series, II, p. 100, and in 1634 he made further mention of one of them in Grosart, ed., *Lismore Papers*, 1st series, IV, p. 15. That his was no idle antiquarian quest is clear from the mention made in *Musarum Lachrymae* (sig. A4ᵛ) to the marriage with:

> Renowned Kildare, prime earl of this isle
> Whose ancient race, and still continued style
> Of honour, virtue, valour (from the time
> His ancestors bare sway within this clime)
> Filling the writings mouths and hearts of men,
> Command a silence to my worthless pen.

55. Grosart, ed., *Lismore Papers*, 1st series, II, p. 38 where on 6 March 1622 Cork refused to marry younger daughters to the heirs to the lordships of the Decies and Muskerry. The request was made by the Earl of Thomond, then president of Munster, and one of the suitors proffered was Thomond's grandchild and the other his niece's son.
56. Sir John Blennerhasset to Boyle, 19 Nov. 1617, with Boyle's reply (Chatsworth, Lismore Papers, VIII, no. 165); Grosart, ed., *Lismore Papers*, 1st series, I, p. 256, II, pp. 21, 97.
57. Grosart, ed., *Lismore Papers*, 1st series, III, p. 186.
58. Sir William Parsons to Cork, 8 March 1640 (Chatsworth, Lismore Papers, XX, no. 154).
59. Grosart, ed., *Lismore Papers*, 1st series, II, pp. 130, 195, III, p. 125.
60. Grosart, ed., *Lismore Papers*, 1st series, III, p. 24, IV, p. 39.
61. Boyle's reply to the letter of Sir John Blennerhasset, 19 Nov. 1617 (Chatsworth, Lismore Papers, VIII, no. 165); 'True Remembrances', in Grosart, ed., *Lismore Papers*, 1st series, II, p. 104.

62. Strafford to Sir Adam Loftus, 15 Dec. 1640 (Sheffield City Library, Strafford Papers, Letter Book 34).
63. *Ibid.*
64. Grosart, ed., *Lismore Papers*, 1st series, IV, p. 88; Sir William Parsons to Cork, 8 March 1640 (Chatsworth, Lismore Papers, XX, no. 154). It is significant that this last judgement was passed in 1640 and the hope that Cork placed in the Loftus as well as the Jones match can be judged from the lines treating of these in *Musarum Lachrymae* (sig A4ᵛ–B):

> Next Viscount Ranelagh's right noble heir
> Whose Grandsire erst these honoured titles bare
> Dublin's Archbishop and of all this land
> Lord Chancellor, who ruled with great command.
> The third is to be joined in Hymens rite
> Unto the issue of that noble knight
> Sir Adam Loftus counsellor of state
> His worthy heir, whose great grandfather sate
> In that same chair of double government.

65. Cork to Stafford, 20 March 1632 (Chatsworth, Cork Letter Book 1, f.448); Cork to Wentworth, 1 July 1632 (Sheffield City Library, Strafford Papers, Letter Book 1, ff.44ᵛ–45ʳ).
66. Cork to Stafford, 20 March 1632 (Chatsworth, Cork Letter Book 1, f. 448); Grosart, ed., *Lismore Papers*, 1st series, II, p. 182; Dungarvan to Cork, 17 Aug. 1632 (Chatsworth, Lismore Papers, XVII, no. 108).
67. Even if Cork did not see the possibilities in a Villiers connection (and we know from his letter to Stafford noted in 66 above that he did), Falkland, in writing to Cork 31 Dec. 1624, gave him advance notice of the appointment of Sir Edward Villiers as president in Munster 'which for his sake, your sake and my own I am glad of', Grosart, ed., *Lismore Papers*, 2nd series, III, pp. 137–9.
68. Grosart, ed., *Lismore Papers*, 1st series, II, p. 182; the letter to Stafford (mentioned in n. 66 above) makes it clear that the dissolution was not as amicable as is suggested by Cork's diary entry.
69. Grosart, ed., *Lismore Papers*, 1st series, II, p. 329. The offer was made on 26 June 1629 and Lady Southwell acted as intermediary.
70. Cork to Bedford, 17 June 1631 (Chatsworth, Cork Letter Book 1, f.315); Cork to Bristol, 6 Dec. 1633 (Chatsworth, Cork Letter Book 1, ff.714–15).
71. Grosart, ed., *Lismore Papers*, 1st series, II, 325, III, p. 54 where mention is made of Richard, Viscount Dungarvan

having gone to study at Oxford in June 1629, and being back in Munster, Sept. 1630.

72. Cork to Goring, 16 Oct. 1631 (Chatsworth, Cork Letter Book 1, f.345); Cork to Stafford, 20 March 1632 (Chatsworth, Cork Letter Book 1, f.448).

73. Cork to Wentworth, 1 July 1632 (Sheffield City Library, Strafford Papers, Letter Book 1, ff.44^v–45^r).

74. Goring to Cork, 23 Aug. 1631 (Chatsworth, Cork Letter Book 1, f.642).

75. Goring to Cork, 2 Feb. 1632 (Chatsworth, Cork Letter Book 1, f.674).

76. Goring to Cork, 28 Aug. 1632 (Chatsworth, Cork Letter Book 1, f.677).

77. Dungarvan to Cork, 16 July 1632 (Grosart, ed., *Lismore Papers*, 2nd series, III, pp. 184–7); Cork to Stafford, 20 March 1632 (Chatsworth, Cork Letter Book 1, f.448). It is evident from each of these letters that the Fielding match was being foisted on Dungarvan by the king, but the Boyles seem to have been reluctantly bending before the royal will. It may have been to escape this pressure that Dungarvan proceeded on his continental tour.

78. Cork to Sir William Beecher, Oct. 1632 (Chatsworth, Cork Letter Book 1, ff.487–9) where Cork alleged that one noble at court had proffered an only daughter with a portion of £20,000, while another (obviously Somerset) offered £40,000 on the day of marriage and £40,000 on his own death.

79. Cork to Wentworth, 1 July 1632 (Sheffield City Library, Strafford Papers, Letter Book 1, ff.44^v–45^r); the terms of the Clifford match with Cork's comments, 5 Oct. 1632 (Chatsworth, Cork Letter Book 1, ff.481–3); Cork to Clifford, 10 Dec. 1633 (H.M.C., *Cal. Salisbury Mss*, XXII, pp. 272–4).

80. Cork to Sir William Beecher, Oct. 1632 (Chatsworth, Cork Letter Book 1, ff.487–9); Cork to Dungarvan, 10 Dec. 1633 (Chatsworth, Cork Letter Book 1, ff.720–4). It is significant that as early as August 1632 Dungarvan was of the opinion that the Cliffords could not perform the conditions, and he certainly thought that they would 'hardly compass' their commitment to secure him an English barony. Dungarvan to Cork, 17 Aug. 1632 (Chatsworth, Lismore Papers, XVII, no. 108).

81. In so far as any party was mercenary it was Lord Clifford who made his purpose plain to Salisbury, 10 Jan. 1634 (H.M.C., *Cal. Salisbury Mss.*, XXII, pp. 275–7); the comparative nobility of Cork's motives is apparent from his letter to Dungarvan, 10 Dec. 1633, mentioned in n. 80.

82. The Boyle family were in residence at Sir Thomas Stafford's house at the Savoy from 1 Oct. 1639 to 8 July 1640 (Grosart, ed., *Lismore Papers*, 1st series, V, pp. 111, 149).
83. Grosart, ed., *Lismore Papers*, 1st series, V, pp. 101, 106, 112.
84. Grosart, ed., *Lismore Papers*, 1st series, V, p. 87.
85. Grosart, ed., *Lismore Papers*, 1st series, V, pp. 112, 117, 119.
86. Cork to Marcombes, 18 Jan. 1640 (Chatsworth, Cork Letter Book 2, f.406); Grosart, ed., *Lismore Papers*, 1st series, V, p. 121; Croker, ed., *Some Specialities in the Life of Mary Warwick*, p. 5.
87. Grosart, ed., *Lismore Papers*, 1st series, V, p. 168.
88. Grosart, ed., *Lismore Papers*, 1st series, V, p. 182.
89. The subject of dowries is discussed in Stone, *Crisis*, pp. 637–45.
90. The circumstances of Stafford's birth by a Gaelic Irish mother are given in 'True Remembrances', in Grosart, ed., *Lismore Papers*, 1st series, II, pp. 103–4, and Stafford's mother was a tenant of Cork in Carbery (Chatsworth, Cork Letter Book 2, f.137).
91. The intimacy of the relationship can be judged from Cork to Stafford, 10 Jan. 1631 (Chatsworth, Cork Letter Book 1, f.221); in 1628 Stafford, who served in the Queen's household, presented Lady Cork and daughters at court. Grosart, ed., *Lismore Papers*, 1st series, II, p. 266.
92. Perez Zagorin, *Court and Country: The Beginning of the English Revolution of the Mid-seventeenth Century* (New York, 1969), pp. 40–73.
93. Cork to Stafford, 20 March 1632 (Chatsworth, Cork Letter Book 1, f.448).
94. Cork to Stafford (as in n. 93 above); Grosart, ed., *Lismore Papers*, 1st series, II, pp. 26, 49, 140. It is significant that the terms of this match were agreed on before the double Villiers match was dissolved which means that Cork was prepared to risk all on a Buckingham connection.
95. Grosart, ed., *Lismore Papers*, 1st series, II, p. 277. Cork's remark in full was: 'I find my self in danger to be cozened by my said wife's cousin who with her kindred and friendship drew me much against my disposition to yield to that unfortunate match.'
96. 'True Remembrances', in Grosart, ed., *Lismore Papers*, 1st series, II, p. 110; furthermore, on p. 105, Cork recorded the death on 8 Feb. 1625 of 'Sir Thomas Beaumont, Kt, Lo. Viscount Beaumont of Swords, my honoured Lordship and brother'.

97. Cork to Stafford, 20 March 1632 (Chatsworth, Cork Letter Book 1, f.448).
98. Cork to Stafford (as in n. 97 above). This is an obvious exaggeration since this is the same Catherine who, as Lady Ranelagh, became noted for her dedication to religion and learning.
99. Cork to Stafford (as in n. 97 above). The precise date on which Cork withdrew his daughter from the Beaumont house at Coleoverton in Leicestershire cannot be established, but she certainly did accompany her father to London on 7 October 1629, Grosart, ed., *Lismore Papers*, 1st series, II, p. 275.
100. Cork to Stafford (as in n. 97 above); Grosart, ed., *Lismore Papers*, 1st series, II, p. 277.
101. Grosart, ed., *Lismore Papers*, 1st series, II, p. 263 (where Cork records being dined at court by Buckingham on 17 May 1628 and being presented to the king), p. 265 (where Cork on 26 May 1628 presented Buckingham with a gift of a horse), p. 266 (where Cork on 3 June 1928 presented Lady Buckingham with a similar gift), pp. 269, 270 (where on 6 and 8 July 1628 Buckingham assisted Cork in his differences with Lord Chancellor Loftus), p. 277 (where Cork recorded a stay from 20–23 August at Lady Beaumont's house in Leicestershire). It was there, probably on 23 August 1628, that Cork revealed his dissatisfaction with how he had been treated, but this date was significantly the same on which Buckingham was assassinated, the news of which seemingly reached Cork on 26 August 1628.
102. Grosart, ed., *Lismore Papers*, 1st series, II, pp. 98, 118, 138. This match was proposed to Cork by the king with Lord Carew as an intermediary. No reason is given why it did not come to fruition.
103. Grosart, ed., *Lismore Papers*, 1st series, II, p. 212.
104. Grosart, ed., *Lismore Papers*, 1st series, II, pp. 199, 203, 227, 254.
105. Grosart, ed., *Lismore Papers*, 1st series, III, p. 104, V, p. 87. The modesty of the match in Cork's eyes is suggested by the scant reference in *Musarum Lachrymae* (sig A4^v) to 'noble Digby'.
106. Thomas Cross to Cork, 19 Dec. 1637 (Chatsworth, Cork Letter Book 2).
107. Cork to Stafford, 10 Jan. 1631 (Chatsworth, Cork Letter Book 1, f.221); Grosart, ed., *Lismore Papers*, 1st series, II, p. 327; Cork to Colonel Goring, 14 Jan. 1636 (Chatsworth, Cork Letter Book 2, ff.122–4).

108. Cork to Goring, 9 Oct. 1633 (Chatsworth, Cork Letter Book 1, ff. 704–6).
109. Cork to Goring, 9 Oct. 1633 (as in n. 108 above).
110. Grosart, ed., *Lismore Papers*, 1st series, III, p. 105.
111. Cork to Colonel Goring, 14 Jan. 1636 (Chatsworth, Cork Letter Book 2, ff.122–4).
112. Wentworth to Carlisle, 20 May 1633 (Sheffield City Library, Strafford Papers, Letter Book 8, f.1).
113. Cork to Colonel Goring (as in n. 111 above); Cork to Colonel Goring, 4 Sept. 1635 (Chatsworth, Cork Letter Book 2, ff.98–9).
114. Goring to Sir Thomas Stafford, 6 April 1633 (Chatsworth, Cork Letter Book 1, ff.631–3).
115. This point was clearly understood by Wentworth who in writing to Goring assured him that Cork had no legitimate cause for grievance; on the contrary, as he put it to Goring, 'I conceived your lordship had therein done him a mighty office ...he proffered a daughter and you purchased her a portion'. Wentworth to Goring, 19 Aug. 1633 (Sheffield City Library, Strafford Papers, Letter Book 8, f.8).
116. Goring to Sir Thomas Stafford, 6 April 1633 (Chatsworth, Cork Letter Book 1, ff.631–3).
117. Cork to Sir Percy Smith, 13 Sept. 1639 (Chatsworth, Cork Letter Book 2, ff.383–4).
118. Cork to Stafford, 10 Jan. 1631 (Chatsworth, Cork Letter Book 1, f.221).
119. Cork to Walley, 13 Sept. 1639 (Chatsworth, Cork Letter Book 2, ff.384–6); Cork to Goring, 10 Dec. 1638 (Chatsworth, Cork Letter Book 2, f.309). In July 1639 Cork referred even to the colonel as 'my noble son-in-law Goring'. The difficulty between Cork and the Gorings is explained by Cork's, as it proved inaccurate, calculation that Goring would fill the void left at court by the death of Buckingham and would be able to deliver the very high demands that Cork was making of him. That such was Cork's calculation is suggested by the reference to this match in *Musarum Lachrymae* (sig. A4ᵛ) as one with 'the hopeful heir of Great Lord Goring'.
120. In writing to Sir Henry Wotton 22 Dec. 1636 (Chatsworth, Cork Letter Book 2, f.137), Cork referred to Ireland as 'this barren and remote kingdom', and in writing to Wotton the previous year, 4 Sept. 1635 (Chatsworth, Cork Letter Book 2), Cork described himself as 'your poor remote countryman that bestows my times in Ireland'. Such comments, as will be mentioned in Chapter 6, need to be balanced against those devoted to the praise or defence of Ireland.

121. Carew, George, Earl of Totnes in *D.N.B.*
122. See Chapter 3, pp. 26–7.
123. Brief autobiographical note by Totnes from birth in 1555 to 1626 when appointed treasurer and receiver general to Queen Henrietta Maria (Chatsworth, Lismore Papers, XVI, no. 165). This sketch shows that Carew's social advance came quite late in his career, but that he came to the royal attention through his service in Ireland. The note lacks, however, the colourful rationalisations that are the most arresting features of the 'True Remembrances'.
124. A catalogue of the nobility of England and the administration with fees attached to each office, taken 1617 (Chatsworth, Lismore Papers, VIII, no. 207); Grosart, ed., *Lismore Papers*, 1st series, I, p. 166: on 27 Sept. 1617 Cork paid 40s. to 'Mr Wallys that presented me with a book of fees of all the King's officers in England'.
125. I owe this information to Dr G. E. Aylmer, who in turn cites Professor Lawrence Stone as the author of this point.
126. Chr. Browne to Sir William Fenton at Youghal, 20 Jan. 1618 (N.L.I., Lismore Castle Papers, Ms. 13,240). The office in question had already been disposed to Sir Foulke Conway, but May supposed that Conway, who had paid £800 but who was encumbered with a large family, would re-sell the office for £1,000.
127. Grosart, ed., *Lismore Papers*, 1st series, I, p. 180.
128. Henry Vaughan to Boyle, 26 Aug. 1612 (Chatsworth, Lismore Papers, IV, no. 28) who looked forward to Boyle's return to Gloucestershire which would be 'a great fortune to all your poor friends in these parts'. Vaughan was proffering a property owned by his nephew in Gloucestershire which was available for £7,000, and he regretted that he had not been sooner 'acquainted with the contents of your letter sent to my brother Boyle of Massmore'. Richard Boyle to Sir Richard Boyle, 12 June 1613 (Chatsworth, Lismore Papers, IV, no. 63).
129. Cork to Thomas Cross, 1 Feb. 1637 (Chatsworth, Cork Letter Book 2, f.164).
130. Grosart, ed., *Lismore Papers*, 1st series, I, pp. 194, 234, II, p. 64, III, pp. 102–3, 164, 185, 200, IV, pp. 19, 74.
131. Sherlock to Cork, 15 July 1623 (Chatsworth, Lismore Papers, XIV, no. 49).
132. Cork to Sir Edward Villiers, 21 Oct. 1621 (Chatsworth, Lismore Papers, XII, no. 66).
133. Goring to Cork, 16 Nov. 1630 (Chatsworth, Cork Letter Book 1, f.683).

134. Cork to Sir John Jephson, 24 Feb. 1634 (Chatsworth, Cork Letter Book 1, f.739); Cork to Henry Wotton, 22 Dec. 1636 (Chatsworth, Cork Letter Book 2, f.137).
135. Cork to Bristol, 4 June 1636 (Chatsworth, Cork Letter Book 2, f.128). Cork then claimed that a purchase in the west country was 'an ambition I have in my thoughts long had'.
136. Grosart, ed., *Lismore Papers*, 1st series, IV, pp. 192–3; Cork to Walley, 21 Feb. 1639 (Chatsworth, Lismore Papers, XVI, no. 156); Walley to Cork, 26 Apr. 1639 (Chatsworth, Lismore Papers, XX, no. 16); Grosart, ed., *Lismore Papers*, 1st series, V, p. 182.
137. Peter Roebuck, 'The Making of an Ulster Great Estate: the Chichesters, Barons of Belfast and Viscounts of Carrickfergus, 1599–1648', in *Proceeding of the Royal Irish Academy*, LXXIX (1979), pp. 1–25.
138. Chichester after his elevation to office in England occasionally kept Boyle informed of continental happenings, Lord Chichester to Boyle, 17 Aug. 1623 (Chatsworth, Lismore Papers, XIV, no. 84). In this letter Chichester also expressed gratitude to Boyle for the generous marriage portion he had provided his daughter to marry Adam Loftus who was Chichester's son-in-law.
139. Cork to Sir William Beecher, 21 Apr. 1631 (Chatsworth, Cork Letter Book 1, ff.301–4).
140. Cork to Goring, 1629 (Chatsworth, Cork Letter Book 1, f.8).
141. Cork to Wotton, 22 Dec. 1636 (Chatsworth, Cork Letter Book 1, f. 137); Wotton like Cork was from Kent which is what Cork referred to when he described himself to Wotton, 4 Sept. 1635, as 'your poor remote countryman' (Chatsworth, Cork Letter Book 2, ff.97–8).
142. Cork to Mr James Fry, 24 Nov. 1633 (Chatsworth, Cork Letter Book 1, ff.710–11); Dungarvan to Cork, 18 Dec. 1633 (Chatsworth, Lismore Papers, XVII, no. 113).
143. Grosart, ed., *Lismore Papers*, 1st series, II, pp. 274, 277, 283, 303, 337; Cork to Wotton, 22 Dec. 1636 (Chatsworth, Cork Letter Book 2, f.137). Their social position is discussed in Clark, *English Provincial Society*.
144. Cork to Wotton, 4 Sept. 1635 (Chatsworth, Cork Letter Book 2, ff.97–8).
145. Grosart, ed., *Lismore Papers*, 1st series, V, pp. 101–2.
146. Cork to Wotton, 22 Dec. 1636 (Chatsworth, Cork Letter Book 2, f.136).
147. Cork to Wm Perkins, 20 June 1635 (Chatsworth, Cork Letter Book 2, ff.82–4).

148. Cork to Wotton, 4 Sept. 1635 (Chatsworth, Cork Letter Book 2, ff.97–8).
149. Cork to Perkins, 5 Jan. 1639 (Chatsworth, Cork Letter Book 2, f.326).
150. Grosart, ed., *Lismore Papers*, 1st series, II, p. 293.
151. Cork to Perkins, 20 June 1635 (Chatsworth, Cork Letter Book 2, ff.82–4); Sir John Leek to Cork, 14 Aug. 1624 (Chatsworth, Lismore Papers, XV, no. 65).
152. Cork to Barrymore, 6 June 1634 (Chatsworth, Cork Letter Book 2, ff.36–8).
153. Dermod McCarthy to Boyle, Jan. 1615 (Chatsworth, Lismore Papers, V, no. 104). Walley to Cork, 27 Jan. 1640 (Chatsworth, Lismore Papers, XX, no. 143); same to same, 30 May 1640 (Chatsworth, Lismore Papers, XXI, no. 20); same to same, 12 Dec. 1640 (Chatsworth, Lismore Papers, XXI, no. 75).
154. Cork to Dungarvan, 21 July 1634 (Chatsworth, Cork Letter Book 2, ff.40–42); Grosart, ed., *Lismore Papers*, 1st series, IV, p. 210.
155. Birch, ed., *The Works of Robert Boyle*, I, introduction, p. 20; Croker, ed., *Some Specialities in the Life of Mary Warwick*, pp. 4, 19; Cork to William Perkins, 6 March 1637 (Chatsworth, Cork Letter Book 2, f.168) where the earl boasts: 'I may depart Ireland not oweing any man a penny as I did the last time I went over into England'; Grosart, ed., *Lismore Papers*, 1st series, V, p. 110.
156. Clifford to Wentworth, 15 July 1635 (Sheffield City Library, Strafford Papers, Letter Book 8, ff.252–3).
157. Grosart, ed., *Lismore Papers*, 1st series, IV, pp. 6, 24, 80, 109–10.
158. Grosart, ed., *Lismore Papers*, 1st series, IV, pp. 146, 150.
159. Macfarlane, *The Family Life of Ralph Josselin*, p. 6, discusses the role of the diary as conscience keeper. Cork's diary is for the most part a record of account, but he occasionally used it for checking his own moral lapses.
160. Dungarvan to Cork, 17 Aug. 1632 (Chatsworth, Lismore Papers, XVII, no. 108).
161. Goring to Sir Thomas Stafford, 6 April 1633 (Chatsworth, Cork Letter Book 1, ff.631–3).
162. In writing to Walley, 21 Feb. 1639, Cork complained of his children 'for they do think all is good purchase they can get from me' (Chatsworth, Cork Letter Book 2, ff.332–4).
163. Pembroke and Salisbury to Cork, 20 March 1638 (Chatsworth, Cork Letter Book 2, f.274).

164. Castle to Lord Bridgewater, 1 July 1641 (San Marino, Huntington Library, Ellesmere Ms. no. 7,841).

5. THE FAMILY LIFE OF RICHARD BOYLE

1. 'An Account of Philaretus [Robert Boyle] during his Minority', in Birch, ed., *The Works of Robert Boyle*, I, pp. xii–xxvi; Croker, ed., *Some Specialities in the Life of Mary Warwick*; see also the Diary of Mary, Countess of Warwick (B.L., Add. Ms. 27,351–5), and Collections out of Lady Warwick's Papers (B.L., Add. Ms. 27,358). The last-mentioned relate to Mary Boyle's career during the 1670s but she reflects occasionally on her childhood years and on her parents.
2. W. S. Clark, ed., *The Dramatic Works of Roger Boyle, Earl of Orrery* (2 vols., Cambridge, Mass., 1937).
3. Thomas Birch, ed., *The Works of the Honourable Robert Boyle* (6 vols., London, 1772). The most recent appraisal of Robert Boyle as a scientist and philosopher is J. R. Jacob, *Robert Boyle and the English Revolution: a Study in Social and Intellectual Change* (New York, 1977).
4. The key role played by Catherine, Lady Ranelagh, in the formation of the 'Invisible College' is referred to repeatedly in Professor Jacob's book referred to in n. 3 above; in Webster, *The Great Instauration*; and in Christopher Hill, *The Intellectual Origins of the English Revolution* (Oxford, 1965). For a further insight into her role as patron see Hugh Brogan, 'Marvell's Epitaph on —', in *Renaissance Quarterly*, XXXIII, pp. 197–9.
5. This is the constant theme in her diary (B.L., Add. Ms. 27,351–5).
6. J. C. MacErlean, ed., *Duanaire Dháibhidh Uí Bhruadair* (London, 1910), II, poem xii where reference is made to the Oliver Stephenson who slew Kinalmeaky, in battle, an action that is portrayed as particularly gallant.
7. Francis, Viscount Shannon, *Discourses Useful for the Vain Modish Ladies and their Gallants* (London, 1696).
8. For a classic exposition of this traditional view of the family see Bernard Bailyn, *Education in the Forming of American Society: Needs and Opportunities for Study* (Chapel Hill, N.C., 1960).
9. This is the argument that is discussed and refuted in Peter Laslett, *The World we Have Lost* (London, 1965). More recent studies have shown that extended families have existed in, for example, southern France. I wish to thank Lawrence Stone for reminding me of this.

10. *Ibid.*, and Peter Laslett, ed., *Household and Family in Past Time* (Cambridge, 1972).
11. Laslett, *The World we Have Lost*, pp. 95–6.
12. See for example P. Gibbon and C. Curtin, 'The Stem Family in Ireland', in *Comparative Studies in Society and History*, XX, pp. 429–53.
13. The initial result was to stimulate a series of case-studies, the most notable being the cluster of publications on New England townships that appeared in 1970. The most influential of these were: John Demos, *A Little Commonwealth: Family Life in Plymouth Colony* (Oxford, 1970); Philip Greven, *Four Generations: Population, Land, and Family in Colonial Andover* (Ithaca and London, 1970); Kenneth Lockridge, *A New England Town: The First Hundred Years: Dedham, Massachusetts, 1636–1736* (New York, 1970). All these were based on Ph.D. theses which to some degree had been inspired by the work of the Cambridge Group.
14. Stone, *Crisis; The Family, Sex and Marriage*.
15. Stone, *The Family, Sex and Marriage*, p. 124.
16. *Ibid.*, pp. 85–119.
17. *Ibid.*, pp. 123–218.
18. *Ibid.*, pp. 221–69.
19. Philip Greven, *The Protestant Temperament: Patterns of Child-Rearing, Religious Experience, and the Self in Early America* (New York, 1977).
20. *Ibid.*, pp. 17–18, 25–8, 265–8. Greven also drew heavily on psychology to support his case.
21. *Ibid.*, pp. 269–74.
22. Greven (*The Protestant Temperament*, p. 265) claims that 'the emergence of a native American gentry throughout the colonies, which began in the mid-seventeenth century, coincided with the development of distinctive patterns of family life that set many families of wealth, eminence, and power apart from their contemporaries'. These he claims 'conformed to the models of gentility developed in England and eagerly emulated throughout the colonies'. From this it would seem that the crucial factor for Greven was the maturing of colonial society.
23. Stone, *The Family, Sex and Marriage*, p. 148.
24. *Ibid.*, pp. 168, 187, 204; Stone, *Crisis*, pp. 608, 657, 659, 684.
25. See Chapter 2, pp. 15–16.
26. 'True Remembrances', Birch, ed., *Works of Robert Boyle*, I, introduction, p. vii.
27. Grosart, ed., *Lismore Papers*, 1st series, I, p. 224, II, pp. 4, 137.

28. Grosart, ed., *Lismore Papers*, 1st series, I, p. 179, II, p. 130. Sir John Leek to Cork, 1 Aug. 1624 (Grosart, ed., *Lismore Papers*, 2nd series, III, pp. 120–5).

29. Grosart, ed., *Lismore Papers*, 1st series, II, p. 316, III, p. 119.

30. See the relevant quotation in n. 95 to Chapter 4.

31. Cork to Ranelagh, 22 Aug. 1639 (Grosart, ed., *Lismore Papers*, 2nd series, IV, pp. 81–6); Grosart, ed., *Lismore Papers*, 1st series, II, p. 277.

32. This can be judged from the comments on the conception of Thomas Stafford (Grosart, ed., *Lismore Papers*, 1st series, II, p. 104). Cork was satisfied that George Carew was the father of Stafford by an Irish mother because the woman in question 'damneth her self if any man knew her carnally in 14 days before her conception that night or in 21 days after, her husband Capt. Stafford being absent from her then above one month'.

33. Cork to Ranelagh, 22 Aug. 1639 (Grosart, ed., *Lismore Papers*, 2nd series, IV, pp. 81–6).

34. On Cork's departure for Dublin from Lismore on 11 Jan. 1635 he left behind Dungarvan and his wife 'at her ladyship's request (conceiving as she conceived that she was with child)'. This was seemingly a false alarm since no child was born to Lady Dungarvan until 14 March 1636, but Dungarvan and his wife made the journey to Dublin in May 1635 and Cork laid out £300 to purchase a carriage for her use in November 1635 when she was clearly pregnant. Grosart, ed., *Lismore Papers*, 1st series, IV, pp. 67, 108, 134.

35. Grosart, ed., *Lismore Papers*, 1st series, I, p. 106, II, p. 84.

36. Cork to Parsons, 6 Dec. 1623 (N.L.I., Lismore Castle Papers, Ms. 13,273(7)). Cork admittedly confessed that he himself was 'overladen with grief from this sorrowful and irrecoverable blow', but he resigned himself to God's will, something that the female members of his household seemingly could not do.

37. The low educational attainment of Lettice Goring can be judged from her barely literate letter to her father, 27 Sept. 1640 (Grosart, ed., *Lismore Papers*, 2nd series, IV, p. 136).

38. Grosart, ed., *Lismore Papers*, 1st series, IV, p. 217.

39. Croker, ed., *Some Specialities in the Life of Mary Warwick*, p. 4, suggests that Mary Boyle was shielded from 'reading plays and romances' prior to her departure for England in 1638, when she was thirteen or fourteen years old.

40. See Table 2 which is based principally on the 'True Remembrances' which gives the dates of birth, and on Cork's diary

where fleeting references are made to the unsuccessful marriage negotiations.

41. *Ibid.*

42. See Table 3, based on similar evidence.

43. Cork to Walley, 13 Sept. 1639 (Chatsworth, Cork Letter Book 2, ff.384–6); Birch, ed., *Works of Robert Boyle*, I, introduction, p. xx.

44. Laurence Parsons to Cork, 3 Dec. 1623 (N.L.I., Lismore Castle Papers, Ms. 13,237(6)); Grosart, ed., *Lismore Papers*, 1st series, II, pp. 21, 97, 108.

45. It should be noted that contrary to common knowledge on this subject Lawrence Stone believes masturbation not to have been a matter of much concern to moralists in the seventeenth century. *The Family, Sex and Marriage*, pp. 512–13.

46. The experiences of Sarah, Dorothy and Alice support this contention. Sarah born 29 March 1609 went to live with her husband 1 October 1623; Dorothy born 30 December 1617 went to live with her husband 13 February 1632 and Alice born 20 March 1608 settled with her husband on 29 July 1621.

47. Cork to Stafford, 20 March 1632 (Chatsworth, Cork Letter Book 1, f.448). It is significant that when Dungarvan was being considered as a party to the proposed double Villiers match (dissolved in 1626 when Dungarvan was still but fourteen), he had an opportunity to see his prospective bride 'and liked her as well as it was possible for one of my age to like a woman'. See Dungarvan to Cork, 16 July 1632 in Grosart, ed., *Lismore Papers*, 2nd series, III, pp. 184–7. Such an opportunity does not seem to have been provided to Cork's daughters whose futures were decided for them while they were still children.

48. Croker, ed., *Some Specialities in the Life of Mary Warwick*, pp. 5–6; Chapter 4 above, p. 58.

49. Croker, ed., *Some Specialities in the Life of Mary Warwick*, pp. 2–3, 14–15.

50. Grosart, ed., *Lismore Papers*, 1st series, I, p. 179, II, pp. 38, 130.

51. Grosart, ed., *Lismore Papers*, 1st series, II, p. 195, III, p. 125.

52. Grosart, ed., *Lismore Papers*, 1st series, II, pp. 195, 217, 315, III, p. 54.

53. Grosart, ed., *Lismore Papers*, 1st series, II, pp. 26, 140.

54. Cork to Stafford, 20 March 1632 (Chatsworth, Cork Letter Book 1, f.448); Chapter 4, pp. 60–1.

55. See Table 2.

56. Philip Greven, *Four Generations*, pp. 72–99, esp. pp. 83–4.
57. Cork to Kinalmeaky and Broghill, 6 Jan. 1637 (Chatsworth, Cork Letter Book 2, ff. 142–3).
58. Greven, *The Protestant Temperament*, pp. 32–43, 159–70; Stone, *The Family, Sex and Marriage*, pp. 167–70.
59. Greven, *The Protestant Temperament* (p. 27) notes that grandparents were specifically excluded from the evangelical household, but he indicates (pp. 152–5) that a role in the upbringing of children was assigned to grandparents by 'moderate' parents. However, Greven does not suggest that even these grandparents were permitted to reside within the household. On the role of Lady Alice Fenton within the Boyle household see for example Cork to Clifford, 25 June 1634 (H.M.C., *Cal. Salisbury Mss.*, XXII, pp. 279–80) where he mentions that 'it was ever my care and his deceased mothers and grandmothers to give him [Dungarvan] a religious, virtuous and civil education'. One important fact is that Lady Fenton was probably closer in age to Cork than was his wife and his affection for her can be measured by his description of her at her death in 1631 as 'a virtuous religious mother-in-law', Grosart, ed., *Lismore Papers*, 1st series, III, p. 85. It should be noted that on this point my disagreement with Philip Greven is sharper than with Professor Stone, since the latter merely claims that the seventeenth century witnessed the emergence of the nuclear family 'not as a unit of habitation, but as a state of mind', *The Family, Sex and Marriage*, p. 148.
60. Lord and Lady Digby together with their children seem to have spent extended periods of time in residence with Cork in Dublin, until Sarah Digby's death there in 1633. Cork to Kildare, 13 Oct. 1629 (P.R.O.N.I., Letter Book of George, Earl of Kildare, letter no. 4); Grosart, ed., *Lismore Papers*, 1st series, III, pp. 192, 202). Then, as was mentioned in the previous chapter, Lady Kildare with her children spent many years in residence with her father, as did Richard Viscount Dungarvan together with his lady and children.
61. The incessant hum of business that must have permeated the Boyle residence can be sensed from even a glance at Cork's diary, Grosart, ed., *Lismore Papers*, 1st series, I – V.
62. If we may select at random 1614 to exemplify Boyle's movements in his pre-Dublin days we find that in March 1614 he returned to his residence after having been in England and Dublin since August 1613; then the month of July was spent in attendance at a christening, supervising his Kerry estates and attending a session at Bandon. Then on 28 July, after

but five days at home, Boyle departed for a business visit to Dublin that lasted until 9 August. Already on 12 September Boyle was again away from home to attend an assize at Cork, and on 6 October he left to attend parliament in Dublin where he seems to have remained until December. Grosart, ed., *Lismore Papers*, 1st series, I, pp. 31, 39, 48–57.

63. Grosart, ed., *Lismore Papers*, 1st series, I, pp. 28, 84.
64. Grosart, ed., *Lismore Papers*, 1st series, II, pp. 304, 325.
65. Grosart, ed., *Lismore Papers*, 1st series, II, pp. 109, 182, 193, 217.
66. Grosart, ed., *Lismore Papers*, 1st series, III, pp. 54, 140. The phrase 'leaven of Ireland' was in fact used by Cork in the context of providing a continental tour of his second and third sons Kinalmeaky and Broghill. See Chapter 4, p. 71.
67. Grosart, ed., *Lismore Papers*, 1st series, III, p. 210, IV, p. 221.
68. The subject of wet-nursing is discussed in Stone, *The Family, Sex and Marriage*, pp. 426–30, and, as will be shown later in this chapter, the Boyle family conformed to the English aristocratic norm in this matter.
69. Grosart, ed., *Lismore Papers*, 1st series, III, pp. 30, 200.
70. Grosart, ed., *Lismore Papers*, 1st series, IV, pp. 64, 67, 157. The grand return to Lismore on 17 Dec. 1634 was after Cork had been displaced in government by Wentworth.
71. Cork left Lismore for Dublin on 21 Jan. 1635 and remained there until July 1635. His summer at Lismore was interrupted by a visit to the lord deputy at Portumna, and on 21 Oct. 1635 Cork again left for Dublin and remained there until 21 July 1636. Grosart, ed., *Lismore Papers*, 1st series, IV, pp. 120, 123, 129, 202.
72. 'An Account of Philaretus [i.e. Mr R. Boyle] during his Minority', in Birch, ed., *Works of Robert Boyle*, I, introduction, pp. xii–xxvi.
73. Grosart, ed., *Lismore Papers*, 1st series, II, p. 84
74. *Ibid.*, p. 258.
75. *Ibid.*
76. Grosart, ed., *Lismore Papers*, 1st series, IV, pp. 64, 67, 125.
77. Grosart, ed., *Lismore Papers*, 1st series, II, p. 207.
78. 'An Account of Philaretus', p. xiii.
79. Grosart, ed., *Lismore Papers*, 1st series, IV, p. 195.
80. On birth intervals see Table 1. 'An Account of Philaretus', pp. xiii, xiv. One gets the impression that Robert Boyle had no recollection of his mother and he considered 'it amongst the chief misfortunes of his life, that he did never know her that give it him'. Since his parents were absent in England

for a considerable part of 1628 and 1629, and resided in Dublin after their return, it is likely that Robert never again met his mother from the time he was first committed to a wet-nurse.

81. 'An Account of Philaretus', p. xiv.
82. *Ibid.*
83. Cork left Lismore for England on 21 April 1628 and was absent until 1 July 1635 except for a short break in the summer of 1631 and a month at Christmas 1634. Grosart, ed., *Lismore Papers*, 1st series, II, p. 340, III, pp. 98, 102, IV, pp. 64, 67, 120.
84. 'An Account of Philaretus', p. xiv.
85. Grosart, ed., *Lismore Papers*, 1st series, IV, pp. 67, 125; 'An Account of Philaretus', p. xv.
86. 'An Account of Philaretus', p. xvii.
87. *Ibid.*, pp. xvii–xviii; Grosart, ed., *Lismore Papers*, 1st series, V, pp. 61, 64.
88. 'An Account of Philaretus', p. xviii; Grosart, ed., *Lismore Papers*, 1st series, V, p. 65.
89. 'An Account of Philaretus', pp. xviii, xix.
90. *Ibid.*
91. *Ibid.*
92. 'An Account of Philaretus', p. xx; Grosart, ed., *Lismore Papers*, 1st series, V, p. 112; Croker, ed., *Some Specialities in the Life of Mary Warwick*, p. 4.
93. Stone, *Crisis*, p. 659.
94. Stone, *The Family, Sex and Marriage*, pp. 426–30.
95. Croker, ed., *Some Specialities in the Life of Mary Warwick*.
96. Some confusion exists as to her birth date. The usually reliable Cork entered the date as 11 November 1624 in the 'True Remembrances', while Mary Boyle (Croker, ed., *Some Specialities in the Life of Mary Warwick*, p. 1) claimed 8 November 1625 as her date of birth. The latter is taken to be the more likely because it is clear from her autobiography that she had no recollection of her mother who died on 16 Feb. 1630, and she certainly would have had some memory of her if she had been born in November 1624.
97. Croker, ed., *Some Specialities in the Life of Mary Warwick*, p. 2; Grosart, ed., *Lismore Papers*, 1st series, II, p. 258, V, pp. 56–7. During her stay at Mallow, Mary Boyle seems to have returned to Lismore for only ten days in October 1637; Grosart, ed., *Lismore Papers*, 1st series, V, p. 35.
98. Grosart, ed., *Lismore Papers*, 1st series, II, p. 317, IV, pp. 26–7.
99. Grosart, ed., *Lismore Papers*, 1st series, V, p. 17.

100. Croker, ed., *Some Specialities in the Life of Mary Warwick*, p. 2. Lady Cleyton's husband Sir Randal Cleyton purchased for £200 from Boyle in Jan. 1612 the office of clerkship of the council in Munster. Grosart, ed., *Lismore Papers*, 1st series, I, p. 5. Mary Boyle also recalled Lady Cleyton in her diary (B.L., Add. Ms. 27,358, f. 84).

101. Grosart, ed., *Lismore Papers*, 1st series, I, p. 79.

102. Table 4

103. Cork to Kildare, 25 March 1630 (P.R.O. N.I., Letter Book of George, Earl of Kildare, letter no. 5).

104. This description, which seems to have been cultivated by Cork himself, was used freely by Robert Boyle in referring to his father. 'An Account of Philaretus', pp. xv, xvii, xx.

105. A marriage to the son of Lord Justice Sarsfield was arranged for Lettice Boyle in 1617 when she was aged eight, and the agreement was dissolved in 1621 when she was eleven. Then, in January 1624, she became engaged to Lucius Cary, Lord Falkland's son, but this was also dissolved. It is evident that if either of these matches had materialised she too would have left home as a child. Grosart, ed., *Lismore Papers*, 1st series, I, p. 180, II, pp. 24–5, 118. Joan Boyle, born June 1611, was a party to the double Villiers match dissolved in April 1626 so it appears that she was contracted before her twelfth birthday. See Chapter 4 above, pp. 54–5, 60.

106. Grosart, ed., *Lismore Papers*, 1st series, II, pp. 120, 199, 203, 254. These citations show that after the marriage to Digby in December 1626, Sarah and her husband remained in residence at Lismore until 25 March 1628.

107. The closeness with which Cork supervised from a distance the upbringing of his children can best be gathered from the correspondence with M. Marcombes, when he served as tutor to Robert and Francis Boyle, most of which is presented in full in Grosart, ed., *Lismore Papers*, 2nd series, IV.

108. Cork to Kinalmeaky and Broghill, 6 Jan. 1637 (Chatsworth, Cork Letter Book 2, ff.142–3).

109. *Ibid.*

110. Walley to Cork, 16 July 1641 (N.L.I., Lismore Castle Papers, Ms. 13,237(26)).

111. *Ibid.*

112. Cork's admiration for Kinalmeaky can be judged by his reaction to his death on the battlefield of Liscarroll, September 1642. Grosart, ed., *Lismore Papers*, 1st series, V. 214.

113. The details of this can best be followed in Croker, ed., *Some Specialities in the Life of Mary Warwick*, pp. 2–14.

114. Grosart, ed., *Lismore Papers*, 1st series, V, p. 116.
115. *Ibid.*
116. Stone, *The Family, Sex and Marriage*, p. 187.
117. Croker, ed., *Some Specialities in the Life of Mary Warwick*, p. 12.
118. *Ibid.*, p. 14.
119. *Ibid.*, pp. 11, 12, 13, 14.
120. *Ibid.*, pp. 8, 15.
121. Cork to Walley, 21 Feb. 1639 (Chatsworth, Cork Letter Book 2, ff. 332–4); Walley to Cork, 18 March 1639 (Chatsworth, Calendar of the Lismore Mss., 1396–1774, XIX, no. 129).
122. Cork to Kildare, 25 March 1630 (P.R.O.N.I., Letter Book of George, Earl of Kildare, letter no. 5).
123. *Ibid.* It seems that Kildare had requested that his young sister be fostered in the Boyle household and Cork responded that his own wife's recent death 'makes this kingdom more unfit for your sister's education'.
124. Nicholas Canny, 'Dominant Minorities: English Settlers in Ireland and Virginia, 1550–1650', in A. C. Hepburn, ed., *Minorities in History* (London, 1978), esp. pp. 54–6.
125. It would appear from the depositions taken subsequent to the 1641 rebellion that Sir Randal Cleyton enjoyed freehold land worth £140 per annum, and his castle and property at Mallow were valued at £450 (T.C.D., Cork Depositions, Ms. 822, f.90). The Parsons family were related by marriage to the Boyles and the various members looked consistently to Cork for direction.
126. Croker, ed., *Some Specialities in the Life of Mary Warwick*, pp. 1–2; Collections out of Lady Warwick's Papers, 8 Nov. 1675 (B.L., Add. Ms. 27,358, f. 84).
127. 'An Account of Philaretus', p. xiii.
128. *Ibid.*, p. xv.
129. *Ibid.*, p. xviii.
130. Croker, ed., *Some Specialities in the Life of Mary Warwick*, p. 2.
131. Stone, *The Family, Sex and Marriage*, pp. 66–82.
132. Examples of this astrological interest can be found in Grosart, ed., *Lismore Papers*, 1st series, II, pp. 110, 111, 112, 207, 227, 317, III, pp. 174–5, IV, pp. 45, 165–6, V, pp. 102, 169, 189. This concern to establish the star under which individuals were born has thus been interpreted by Thomas, *Religion and the Decline of Magic*, pp. 384–5.
133. 'An Account of Philaretus', p. xiv.
134. The first-born Roger, and after his death the eleventh child

Roger, who became Baron Brogill, were called after Cork's own father. The second child Alice was called after her grandmother who was also her godmother Lady Alice Fenton. The third child Sarah was seemingly called after one of her godmothers. The fourth child Lettice was called after Lady Lettice Chichester, wife of Sir Arthur Chichester, who was her godmother. The fifth child Joan was called after Cork's mother. The sixth child Richard was called after Cork himself. The seventh child Catherine was called after Lady Cork. The eighth child Geoffrey was called after Geoffrey Fenton, his maternal grandfather. The ninth child Dorothy was called after Dorothy, wife of the Bishop of Waterford, who was a godparent. The tenth child Lewis is unaccounted for, his godparents being called John and William. The twelfth child Francis was called after his godfather Lord Francis Aungier. The thirteenth child Mary was called after her aunt and godmother Lady Mary Smith. The fourteenth child Robert was called after his brother-in-law and godfather Lord Robert Digby. The fifteenth child Margaret was presumably called after a godparent.

135. Grosart, ed., *Lismore Papers*, 1st series, II, p. 111.
136. Grosart, ed., *Lismore Papers*, 1st series, III, p. 132.
137. Cork to Sir Henry Wotton, 4 Sept. 1635 (Chatsworth, Cork Letter Book 2, ff.97–8).
138. 'An Account of Philaretus', pp. xvii–xviii. The other explanations were that old people customarily give 'their eldest children the largest proportion of their fortunes, but the youngest the greatest share of their affection', and that up to the time of his father's death, he had not reached an age when he might run into debt or other evil courses.
139. Grosart, ed., *Lismore Papers*, 1st series, III, p. 199; this contrasts with his entry on the death of Geoffrey Boyle when he merely prayed God 'to make me patiently thankful'. Grosart, ed., *Lismore Papers*, 1st series, I, p. 140.
140. Grosart, ed., *Lismore Papers*, 1st series, II, p. 299.
141. Grosart, ed., *Lismore Papers*, 1st series, I, p. 262, II, p. 193, III, pp. 62, 132.
142. Grosart, ed., *Lismore Papers*, 1st series, II, p. 194, IV, p. 227.
143. Croker, ed., *Some Specialities in the Life of Mary Warwick*, pp. 15, 17 and p. 27 where she referred to Cork as 'my own, dear, deserving father'.
144. Orrery to Countess of Dorset, 7 April 1677 (N.L.I., Orrery Ms. 33). In this Orrery is making the point that he has left his son far better provided for than his father left himself,

this despite the fact that his father was the richest subject in the king's dominions. I wish to thank Mr Liam Irwin for this reference.

145. Clifford to Salisbury, 28 June 1635 (Chatsworth, Cork Letter Book 2, f.88).

146. We find that Lewis and Roger Boyle were educated together and then sent on the Grand Tour together; so also were Francis and Robert Boyle: and of the daughters we know that Mary and Margaret Boyle were together assigned to the fosterage of Lady Cleyton. Richard did not have a male sibling close in age to him which may explain why his education was linked to that of Arthur Loftus.

147. See for example Cork to Kinalmeaky and Broghill, 6 Jan. 1637 (Chatsworth, Cork Letter Book 2, ff.142–3).

148. See for example, Grosart, ed., *Lismore Papers*, 1st series, IV, p. 219, V, pp. 39, 46.

149. Grosart, ed., *Lismore Papers*, 1st series, II, p. 221.

150. Croker, ed., *Some Specialities in the Life of Mary Warwick*, pp. 6, 9.

151. Grosart, ed., *Lismore Papers*, 1st series, II, p. 182. Cork mentions 'the disparity of our children's ages and growth was such as hindered our intendments'.

152. Grosart, ed., *Lismore Papers*, 1st series, II, p. 110.

153. Francis, Viscount Shannon, *Discourses Useful for the Vain Modish Ladies and their Gallants*, p. 73.

154. Cork to Colonel Goring, 14 Jan. 1636 (Chatsworth, Cork Letter Book 2, ff.122–4).

155. Grosart, ed., *Lismore Papers*, 1st series, II, pp. 212, 216, 277.

156. 'An Account of Philaretus', p. xiii; Croker, ed., *Some Specialities in the Life of Mary Warwick*, p. 1.

157. *Musarum Lachrymae*, sig. d⁴; 'True Remembrances', in Birch, ed., *The Works of Robert Boyle*, I, introduction, p. ix.

158. See the note on p. ix of the 'True Remembrances' which makes reference to this myth being prevalent in the 1670s.

159. This is based on the assumption that seventeenth-century women did not produce children before they were eighteen, of after they were forty. It is of interest that Mary Boyle thought it reasonable to expect that she could bear children when she was 'not much more than thirty-eight years old'. That she was concerned to bear further children at that point of her career is explained by the death of her son which deprived the Warwick family of a male heir, Croker, ed., *Some Specialities in the Life of Mary Warwick*, pp. 32–3.

160. Grosart, ed., *Lismore Papers*, 1st series, III, p. 18; 'An account of Philaretus', p. xiii.
161. This is the principal theme of Stone, *The Family, Sex and Marriage*, but see pp. 221–269. Philip Greven in *The Protestant Temperament* (pp. 265–331), while citing evidence of the affectionate family only from the mid-eighteenth century, does allow for the possibility that it might have existed in other societies at an earlier date. Its appearance in America is seen by him to coincide with the development for the first time of social and economic elites.
162. Cork to William Perkins, 20 June 1635 (Chatsworth, Cork Letter Book 2, ff.82–4).
163. From 1622 onwards when Cork entered in his diary 'This day God bless me I am 56 years old', he seems to have accepted that death was imminent. Grosart, ed., *Lismore Papers*, 1st series, II, p. 57.
164. Cork to Sir Henry Wotton, 22 Dec. 1636 (Chatsworth, Cork Letter Book 2, f.137). In *Musarum Lachrymae* (sig. 13ᵛ) death is addressed as: 'Thou awe of bad men, comfort of the good.'
165. In 1629 for instance Cork mentioned that he had within his household, besides his 'poor wife', 'the Lord Digby and his Lady with little Katie'. Cork to Kildare, 13 Oct. 1629 (P.R.O.N.I., Letter Book of George, Earl of Kildare, letter no. 4).
166. Stone, *The Family, Sex and Marriage*, pp. 64–6, 159.
167. Among the depositions taken subsequent to the 1641 rebellion there are, for example, three such references from County Leitrim alone (T.C.D., Ms. 831, ff.6ʳ, 15ʳ, 12ᵛ). I wish to thank Brian McCuarta for these references which I am assured by Professors Aidan Clarke and Michael Maxwell, who have worked most closely on the despositions, are by no means exceptional.
168. Nicholas Canny, 'Dominant Minorities', in Hepburn, ed., *Minorities in History*, esp. pp. 54–6.
169. Edmund Morgan, *The Puritan Family* (New York, pb. edition, 1966), p. 77. This book was originally published in 1944.
170. Lawrence Parsons to Cork, 17 Dec. 1623 (N.L.I., Lismore Castle Papers, Ms. 13,237(8)).

6. RICHARD BOYLE: ANGLO-IRISHMAN

1. Henry Peers to Boyle, 18 Nov. 1619 in Grosart, ed., *Lismore Papers*, 2nd series, II, pp. 166–7.
2. See the works of Ranger cited in Chapter 1, nn. 2, 15.

3. It is significant that Cork himself, although brought on to the English privy council, was not elevated to the English peerage. That Cork sought an English title seems certain, and that it was denied him is suggested by the extraordinary decision in November 1640, when Cork's presence was required by the English parliament, to have him 'by writ called into the Upper House by his Majesties great grace' rather than have him created an English peer. Grosart, ed., *Lismore Papers*, 1st series, V, p. 164.

4. In writing to Walley in 1638 Cork complained of being in debt and remarked that: 'I would neither wrong mine own honour *nor the reputation of Ireland* by appearing there [at court] in a poor condition' (my italics), Cork to Walley, 30 Nov. 1638 Chatsworth, Cork Letter Book 2, ff.301–3).

5. See Ranger, 'Richard Boyle and the Making of an Irish Fortune', pp. 273–4.

6. See Chapter 4, pp. 65–70.

7. The latter was certainly a factor since even after his fortune was made Cork gave serious consideration to every possibility of obtaining land in Ireland by purchase or otherwise. See for example Cork to Arundel, 20 Nov. 1630 (Chatsworth, Cork Letter Book, 1, f.204) where he is mooting the purchase of Killybegs in Co. Donegal.

8. Cork to Clifford, 21 July 1634 (Chatsworth, Cork Letter Book 2, ff.42–3). It should be mentioned that, at this point, Cork may have been striving to convince Clifford that he had acted wisely in marrying his daughter to Dungarvan.

9. Ranger, 'Richard Boyle and the Making of an Irish Fortune', pp. 273–4.

10. Sir Francis Foulkes to Countess of Orrery, 21 Aug. 1672 (N.L.I., Orrery Ms. 33, f.178ᵛ), where Foulkes advises against the Earl of Orrery continuing 'to keep a papist butler though he is a good serviceable man, yet the papists are so wicked that they would be glad to have my lord out of the way on any terms, for the Irish look on his lordship as the greatest bar to all their damned designs'. I owe this information to Mr Liam Irwin. The Earl of Cork also continued to employ some Irish servants to the end of his career but we cannot be certain that they were Papists since previous to the 1641 rebellion many Irish, and more probably many who had close associations with planters, conformed to the established church. Nonetheless, at least one servant Donogh Mac Teigh Carty caused Cork embarrassment when in February 1636 he gave vent to 'treasonable words (which in his madness and drink he spake against his sacred

Majesty)', Grosart, ed., *Lismore Papers*, 1st series, IV, pp. 158–9. On the question of religious conformity see Nicholas Canny, 'Why the Reformation failed in Ireland: une Question Mal Posée', in *Journal of Ecclesiastical History*, XXX (1979), pp. 423–50.

11. During the course of rebellion in 1642 John Walley fretted for the safety of Tallow because 'Thomas the last sovereign hath stored his house with Irish...which nest will be the destruction of that place', Walley to Cork, 22 Jan. 1641 (N.L.I., Lismore Castle Papers, Ms. 13,237(27)); the self-same Walley, however, saw the economic necessity of having the Irish as sub-tenants on the land and he was alarmed at the havoc wreaked by the English soldiers on the Irish tenants living close to Lismore. These he described as 'poor people that live peaceably and endeavour to pay their rents' who were so harassed that he feared there would 'not be an Irish tenant left upon any of these lands where your Lordship planted them', Walley to Cork, 22 Apr. 1642 (Chatsworth, Lismore Papers, XXIII, no. 7). The Irish at Bandon lived in an Irish town, seemingly in cabins and thatched houses, and Cork's agent Augustine Atkins recommended repeatedly that these be given the choice of departing the town or building with stone chimneys and slate roofs since their 'cabins and old rotten houses [were] very dangerous for firing the town'. Atkins to Cork, 30 May 1636 (Chatsworth, Lismore Papers, XVIII, no. 131); same to same, 1 Sept. 1639 (Chatsworth, Lismore Papers, XX, no. 105); John Langton to Cork, 17 May 1642 (Chatsworth, Lismore Papers, XXIII, no. 43). This evidence shows the falsity of Cork's claim to the English house of commons that Bandon was a town of 'at least 7,000 souls all English Protestants, and no one Irishman nor Papist dwelling therein', Cork to Speaker, 25 Aug. 1642 (Chatsworth, Lismore Papers, XXIII, no. 119).

12. Dermot Moriertagh to Cork, 22 July 1623 (Chatsworth, Lismore Papers, XIV, no. 55); Walter Nagle to Cork, 28 Sept. 1623 (Chatsworth, Lismore Papers, XIV, no. 134).

13. Barrymore to Wentworth, 26 May 1639, in Grosart, ed., *Lismore Papers*, 2nd series, IV, pp. 37–9. Barrymore's complaint was that Sir Piers Crosby had frightened away those who had volunteered 'by multitudes' by amazing them with 'tales of Scottish witchcrafts and enchantments'.

14. Information of David Murdoe of Lismore, 6 Apr. 1643 (Chatsworth, Lismore Papers, XXIV, no. 8).

15. John Walley to Cork, 22 Apr. 1642 (Chatsworth, Lismore Papers, XXIII, no. 7).

16. Sir Thomas Browne to Boyle, 7 Apr. 1610 (Chatsworth, Lismore Papers, III, no. 41); the plausibility of this explanation will be evident from the discussion in Chapter 5 of the upbringing of the Boyle children.

17. On Gaelic wet-nurses see the references relating to Co. Leitrim, already referred to in Chapter 5, in T.C.D., Ms 831, ff.6ʳ, 12ᵛ, 15ʳ. The Eton reference comes from Grosart, ed., *Lismore Papers*, 2nd series, III, p. 224, and I wish to thank Michael McCarthy-Morrogh, a research student at London, for calling it to my attention. My information on Matthew de Renzi comes from Brian MacCuarta, 'Newcomers in the Irish Midlands, 1540–1641' (M.A. thesis, University College, Galway, 1980). On the necessity of clergymen knowing the language see Grosart, ed., *Lismore Papers*, 2nd series, I, pp. 39–40; William Herbert, *Croftus sive de Hibernia*, ed., W.E. Buckley (London, 1887), esp. pp. 50–2; and Memorandum by the Lord Bishop of Kilmore (Chatsworth, Lismore Papers, XVII, no. 58).

18. Edmond Ferriter to Cork, 7 July 1623 (N.L.I., Ms. 13,237(3)) who in seeking the renewal of his lease professed that 'under God and the king I rely only upon your honour'; Walter Nagle to Cork, 28 Sept. 1623 (Chatsworth, Lismore Papers, XIV, no. 134); Walley to Cork, 30 May 1640 (Chatsworth, Lismore Papers, XXI, no. 20).

19. Dermot Moriertagh to Cork, 22 July 1623 (Chatsworth, Lismore Papers, XIV, no. 55) where the author is seeking to have Piaras Feiritéir, 'a wilful idle young man', deprived of his lease in favour of Moriarty's own son. A letter of John Hampton to Cork, 9 Aug. 1623 (Chatsworth, Lismore Papers, XIV, no. 76) shows that Cork had resisted the Moriarty request and renewed the Feiritéir lease.

20. Authority of martial law was extended to Piaras Feiritéir and Dermot Dingle at the outset of rebellion, and it was alleged that 'the one cut off men's ears and punished as he pleased and the other put up gallows at Ballinacurtie'. Feiritéir was further appointed a captain by Lord President St Leger but then deserted to the enemy, took Castlemaine and ransacked Tralee. On this, see John Fitzgerald to Cork, 26 Feb. 1642 (B.L., Egerton Ms., 80, ff.5–6). The poetic reference comes from P. Ua Duinnín, ed., *Dánta Phiarais Feiritéir* (Dublin, 1934), p. 105.

21. Cork on 20 Feb. 1620 recorded the loan of his new harp to William Barry the blind harper (Grosart, ed., *Lismore Papers*, 1st series, I, p. 241).

22. The gift was seemingly of a different instrument, 'a fair new

Irish harp' sent to him by his 'cousin' William Ryan and which
Cork sent on 10 Oct. 1632 to the Lord Keeper of England
(Grosart, ed., *Lismore Papers*, 1st series, III, p. 162). Cork to
Lord Keeper, 10 Oct. 1632 (Chatsworth, Cork Letter Book 1,
f.500). It seems that planters generally took to Irish music
and provided patronage in their houses for harpists. See Luke
Gernon, 'A Discourse of Ireland', in C.L. Falkner, *Illustrations
of Irish History and Topography, mainly of the Seventeenth
Century* (London, 1904), pp. 360–2, and anonymous, *The
Present State of Ireland Together with Some Remarks upon the
Ancient State Thereof* (London, 1673), esp. pp. 121–3, 152–3.

23. See for example Cork's diary entry for 10 Oct. 1632 where
gifts of whiskey to the lord keeper, lord privy seal, the Archbishop of Canterbury and the Bishop of London are recorded,
and a gift of Waterford black frieze to Canterbury 'to make
him a cassock' (Grosart, ed., *Lismore Papers*, 1st series, III,
p. 162).

24. Cork to Bishop of London, 5 Oct. 1632 (Chatsworth, Cork
Letter Book 1, ff. 496–8).

25. This point is developed in Nicholas Canny, 'Why the Reformation Failed in Ireland: une Question Mal Posée', cited in n. 10
above.

26. Cork to Dorchester, 10 May 1631 (Chatsworth, Cork Letter
Book 1, 312–13); on the background to this thought see Canny,
The Elizabethan Conquest, pp. 117–36. It is important to
recognise that much of this analysis derived from traditional
Anglo-Irish criticisms of Gaelic Ireland as expressed for example
in 'Rowland White's, "Discourse touching Ireland" c. 1569',
ed. Nicholas Canny, in *I.H.S.*, XX, pp. 439–63.

27. Cork to Dorchester as in n. 26 above; same to same 8 Dec.
1630 (Chatsworth, Cork Letter Book, 1, ff. 207–11); Cork to
Secretary Cook, 27 Feb. 1633 (Chatsworth, Cork Letter Book 1,
ff. 606–13).

28. Cork to Arundel, 7 Jan. 1631 (Chatsworth, Cork Letter Book 1,
f. 225).

29. Cork to Secretary Cook, 27 Feb. 1633 (Chatsworth, Cork Letter
Book 1, ff. 606–13).

30. Sir John Davies, *A Discovery of the True Causes why Ireland
was Never Entirely Subdued* (London, 1612).

31. Canny, 'Why the Reformation Failed in Ireland: une Question
Mal Posée'; on the attitude of English missionaries towards the
American Indians see Neal Salisbury, 'Red Puritans: "the
Praying Indians" of Massachusets Bay and John Eliot', in
William and Mary Quarterly, XXXI, pp. 27–54.

32. Cork to Sir William Beecher, 20 March 1631 (Chatsworth, Cork Letter Book 1, f. 265); Cork to Lord Treasurer, 17 Apr. 1631 (Chatsworth, Cork Letter Book 1, ff. 288–9).
33. Cork to Dorchester, 8 Dec. 1630 (Chatsworth, Cork Letter Book 1, ff. 207–11) where he expresses fear of the admiration for Spain that was fostered by seminary priests.
34. Cork to Secretary Cook, 27 Feb. 1633 (Chatsworth, Cork Letter Book 1, ff. 606–13). It should be mentioned that Cork on other occasions despaired of Irish craftsmen, as when he sought to import cut stone from England for the construction of Gill Abbey 'our masons here [being] bunglers and slow', Cork to George Hyllard, 21 Nov. 1637 (Chatsworth, Cork Letter Book 2, f.244).
35. Ranger, 'The Career of Richard Boyle, First Earl of Cork', p. 96.
36. Cork to Carlisle, 7 Jan. 1630 (Chatsworth, Cork Letter Book 1, ff. 23–5).
37. Brendan Bradshaw, 'Sword, Word and Strategy in the Reformation in Ireland', in *Historical Journal*, XXI (1978), pp. 475–502. See also the criticism of this article advanced in Nicholas Canny, 'Why the Reformation in Ireland Failed: une Question Mal Posée'.
38. Moody, Martin and Byrne, eds., *A New History of Ireland*, III, pp. 241–2. Terence Ranger ('The Career of Richard Boyle, First Earl of Cork', pp. 273–4) treated Cork in 1629–31 as the leader of 'an aggressively Protestant-planter party on national lines' but he also recognised the more positive side to Cork as a Protestant reformer.
39. The efforts by planters at developing manufacturers in the period prior to 1641 are best described in Gerard Boate, *Ireland's Natural History* (London, 1652).
40. Nicholas Canny, 'Why the Reformation Failed in Ireland: une Question Mal Posée'.
41. Sir John Leak to Cork, 18 Dec. 1624 (N.L.I., Lismore Castle Papers, Ms. 13,237(9)) mentions one Clarke, a schoolmaster at Bandon, who had taught '12 English and often 8 Irish children, 4 of Mr. Supples and divers others'. The school at Lismore, taught by Mr Goodrich, with Mr Hulet as usher, was a thriving institution of seventy pupils before it was reduced to thirty-five by the harsh regime of Goodrich. See Chapter 5, p. 108.
42. This description was applied to Cork's foundation of the school at Lismore. Hardress Waller to Cork, 21 Jan. 1639 (Chatsworth, Cork Letter Book 2, ff. 330–1).

43. See Canny, *The Elizabethan Conquest of Ireland*, pp. 116–36; and specifically in relation to Cork see Cork to Dorchester, 8 Dec. 1630 (Chatsworth, Cork Letter Book 1, ff.207–11).
44. Mervyn James, *English Politics and the Concept of Honour* (*Past & Present*, supplement no. 3).
45. This was, in fact, the essential point at issue between the New English and the Old-English Catholics in Ireland throughout the first half of the seventeenth century. See Moody, Martin and Byrne, eds., *A New History of Ireland*, III, pp. 187–242.
46. Cork to Lord Treasurer of England, 10 May 1630 (Chatsworth, Cork Letter Book 1, ff.109–10) where, in objecting to the suggestion that impropriated church property be granted in reversion to the spiritual incumbents, Cork professed that 'his Majesties lands are in effect all passed away; his Majesties titles and impropriations are the only remain he has in this kingdom to reward his servitors withall'.
47. Wallop to Walsingham, 1 March 1581 (P.R.O., S.P. 63/81/2).
48. Robert Paget to Cork, 15 Nov. 1634 (N.L.I., Lismore Castle Papers, Ms. 13,237(19)).
49. Captain Robert Gore to William Freke, 24 May 1620 (Chatsworth, Lismore Papers, XI, no. 38).
50. Cork to Goring, 26 Oct. 1629 (Chatsworth, Cork Letter Book 1, f.10).
51. See for example Cork to Joshua Boyle, 28 Sept. 1639 (Chatsworth, Cork Letter Book 2, f.390) where he directs that a case in star-chamber be commenced against Dr Thomas, a former chaplain, who, not satisfied with the curacy provided him by Cork, had sued for a patent appointing him vicar. As Cork put it: 'I much desire to have that man know me and himself.'
52. Cork to Captain Price, 2 March 1631 (Chatsworth, Cork Letter Book 1, ff.268–9).
53. Cork to Sir George Horsey, 13 Apr. 1624 (Grosart, ed., *Lismore Papers*, 2nd series, III, pp. 107–12) where the earl justified the price he has paid for the Grenville estate in Munster, 'the dearest bargain that ever was made in Ireland', on the grounds of 'conveniency with strength and making my estate entire'. This dimension to Cork's aggressiveness, particularly in relation to Sir William Power is discussed in Ranger, 'The Career of Richard Boyle, First Earl of Cork', pp. 223–5. On the St Leger episode see Walley to Cork, 21 Apr. 1639 (Chatsworth, Lismore Papers, XX, no. 11); Joshua Boyle to Cork, 14 July 1641 (Chatsworth, Lismore Papers, XXII, no. 37).
54. James Wale to Cork, 10 Apr. 1624 (N.L.I., Lismore Castle Papers, Ms. 12,237(9)).

55. Cork to Alderman Parkhurst, 12 Feb. 1632 (Chatsworth, Cork Letter Book 1, f.526).
56. Canny, 'The Permissive Frontier', in Andrews, Canny and Hair, eds., *The Westward Enterprise*, pp. 17–44.
57. James, *English Politics and the Concept of Honour*, pp. 87–8, where it is argued that military men remained attached to traditional personal bonds of loyalty that were coming into disrepute in civil society.
58. Cork to Sir William Beecher, 14 March 1631 (Chatsworth, Cork Letter Book 1, ff.274–6); Cork to Stafford, 10 Jan. 1631 (Chatsworth, Cork Letter Book 1, f.221).
59. Cork to Sir William Beecher, 20 March 1631 (Chatsworth, Cork Letter Book 1, f.265).
60. For the Anglo-Irish in the late eighteenth century see A. P. W. Malcomson, *John Foster: the Politics of the Anglo-Irish Ascendancy* (Oxford, 1978), esp. Chapter 7, pp. 281–349.
61. Anonymous, *Several Passages of the Late Proceedings in Ireland* (London, 1642). Even before the rebellion of 1641 some planters were conscious of what Hardress Waller termed 'much baseness and treachery among our selves'. Thus all misfortunes, such as a 'great mortality' at Lismore in 1639, were attributed to 'God's heavy wrath' on Lismore which had 'grown one of the most dissolute towns in Ireland', Waller to Cork, 21 Jan. 1639 (Chatsworth, Cork Letter Book 2, ff.330–1); Dean Robert Naylor to Cork, 23 May 1639 (Chatsworth, Lismore Papers, XX, no. 36).
62. Tristram Whitcombe, *A Most Exact Relation of a Great Victory* (London, 1642); the author had been a merchant at Kinsale prior to the 1641 rebellion and claims to have lost property to the value of £5,565 (T.C.D., Ms. 822, f.26).
63. Sir William Parsons to Cork, 7 May 1643 (Chatsworth, Lismore Papers, XXIV, no. 21).
64. Cited in Ranger 'The Career of Richard Boyle, First Earl of Cork', p. 265.
65. Cork to Wotton, 22 Dec. 1636 (Chatsworth, Cork Letter Book 2, f.137).
66. Anonymous, *The Present State of Ireland Together with Some Remarks upon the Ancient State Thereof*. I wish to thank Dr David Dickson for having drawn my attention to this pamphlet, and Professor Aidan Clarke for having identified John Temple as the author of the passage quoted.

7. CONCLUSION: THE BOYLES, IRELAND AND THE 'NEW SCIENCE'

1. To his credit it must be stated that Lawrence Stone made frequent reference to Ireland in his treatment of social mobility in *The Crisis of the Aristocracy*, but most of his information was drawn from C. R. Mayes, 'The Early Stuarts and the Irish Peerage', in *English Historical Review*, LXXIII (1958), pp. 227–51. Mayes was correct in assuming that the 'Inflation of Honours' in Ireland was partly occasioned by the government's need for a Protestant aristocracy on which it could depend, but no study has yet been done of the interconnection between the English and the Irish peerages during the course of the seventeenth century.

2. It is intended that the general problem of self-perception among colonial groups in the Atlantic world be the subject of a collection of essays by several hands to be jointly edited by the present writer and Dr A. R. D. Pagden.

3. The best source known to the present writer is the De Renzi family collection in the P.R.O., London, but information suited to the study of social and economic affairs is also to be found among the Thomond Mss. at Petworth House; the Drogheda Papers in the National Library of Ireland; the Perceval Papers in the British Library and the Sackville Mss. in the Kent Archives Office.

4. The thirty-two volumes of depositions, organised on a county basis, are available in the library of Trinity College, Dublin. Professor Clarke's lecture has not yet been published.

5. Ranger, 'The Career of Richard Boyle, First Earl of Cork'.

6. For a summary account of the debate see Chapter 1, above.

7. The citation is from Nicholas Canny, 'Early Modern Ireland: an Appraisal Appraised', in *Irish Economic and Social History*, IV (1977), pp. 56–65, esp. p. 60. For a discussion of Gaelic attitudes see Nicholas Canny, 'The Formation of the Irish Mind: Religion, Politics and Gaelic Irish Literature 1580–1750', in *Past & Present*, no. 95 (May, 1982), pp. 91–116.

8. Moody, Martin and Byrne, eds., *A New History of Ireland*, III.

9. The books that will be discussed in this section are Charles Webster, *The Great Instauration: Science, Medicine and Reform, 1626–1660* (London, 1975); J. R. Jacob, *Robert Boyle and the English Revolution: a Study in Social and Intellectual Change* (New York, 1977) and T. C. Barnard, *Cromwellian Ireland: English Government and Reform in Ireland, 1649–60* (Oxford, 1975). The nub of the thesis is that English puritans,

and most especially the members of the Hartlib Circle, indulged in a selective reading of the writings of Francis Bacon which enabled them to dovetail his views on scientific enquiry into their own millenarian prognostication. The author is aware that this central element of the thesis has been called into question, most notably in John Morgan, 'Puritanism and Science: a Reinterpretation', in *Historical Journal*, XX (1979), pp. 535–60, but it is not the purpose here to discuss the merits of the case being made for a Baconian influence on puritan thought. A book on which the several authors drew heavily is G. H. Turnbull, *Hartlib, Dury and Comenius* (Liverpool, 1947).

10. Webster, *The Great Instauration*, pp. 32–77; Barnard, *Cromwellian Ireland*, pp. 212–16; Jacob, *Robert Boyle*, p. 28.

11. Jacob, *Robert Boyle*, pp. 16, 21, 24; Webster, *The Great Instauration*, pp. 88–99.

12. This is the thesis of T. C. Barnard, *Cromwellian Ireland*; but see also T. C. Barnard, 'The Hartlib Circle and the Origins of the Dublin Philosophical Society', in *Irish Historical Studies*, XIX (1974), pp. 56–71, where Dr Barnard challenges the explanation for the development of scientific enquiry in late seventeenth-century Ireland as expressed in K. T. Hoppen, *The Common Scientist in the Seventeenth Century* (London, 1970). It is also relevant to mention that the thesis in Barnard's *Cromwellian Ireland* is consistent with the view of Lord Dacre of Glanton as expressed in his essay 'Scotland and the Puritan Revolution', in H.R. Trevor-Roper, *Religion, the Reformation and Social Change* (London, 1967), pp. 392–444, see esp. pp. 411–12. I wish to thank Aidan Clarke for drawing my attention to this point.

13. These points were previously raised in a review of T.C. Barnard, *Cromwellian Ireland*, in *Irish Economic and Social History*, III (1976), pp. 88–9. For an early example of the desire to build a completely new society in Ireland, expressed in exactly these terms, see Geoffrey Fenton to Burghley, 6 Dec. 1583 (P.R.O., S.P. 63/106/4). It is of interest to note that Fenton became father-in-law to Richard Boyle, and was thus Robert Boyle's grandfather.

14. Cited in Dorothea Townshend, *The Life and Letters of the Great Earl of Cork* (London, 1904), p. vi.

15. The best recent work on Roger Boyle is in the thesis of Liam Irwin, 'The Presidency of Munster, 1660–72' (University College, Cork, 1976). See also the following publications by Liam Irwin: 'The Earl of Orrery and the Military Problems of Restoration Munster', in the *Irish Sword*, XIII, pp. 10–19,

'The Role of the Presidency in the Economic Development
of Munster, 1660–72', in *Journal of the Cork Historical and
Archaeological Society*, LXXXII, pp. 102–14, and 'The Sup-
pression of the Irish Presidency System', in *I.H.S.*, XXII,
pp. 31–2. On the career of Roger Boyle outside Ireland see Julia
Buckroyd, 'Lord Broghill and the Scottish Church, 1655–6', in
Journal of Ecclesiastical History, XXVII, pp. 359–68, and
'Scotland and the Puritan Revolution', in Trevor-Roper,
Religion, the Reformation and Social Change, pp. 392–444.

16. Boate, *Ireland's Natural History*. In the preface Arnold Boate
mentioned that it had been his brother's intention to describe
'the great pains taken by the English, ever since the conquest,
for to civilize them [the Gaelic Irish] and to improve the
country'. On p. 89, Gerard Boate praised the efforts of the pre-
1641 planters to stock their lands with superior breeds of live-
stock and he deplored how these had been slaughtered by the
'barbarians', during the 1641 rebellion, who 'endeavoured quite
to extinguish the memory of them [the English] and of all the
civility and good things by them introduced amongst all that
wild nation'. Specific reference to 'scientific' advances promoted
in Ireland by the planters ('the introducers of all good things
to Ireland') are detailed by Boate, pp. 96, 97–8, 114, 121–2,
124–30, 134–5, 136–7, 157, 160.

17. J.R. Jacob, *Robert Boyle.*

18. *Ibid.*, p. 25; Falkland to Cork, 31 Dec. 1624 (Grosart, ed.,
Lismore Papers, 2nd series, III, pp. 137–9); Grosart, ed., *Lismore
Papers*, 1st series, II, pp. 98, 118, 138.

19. J.R. Jacob, *Robert Boyle*, pp. 21–2, 24, 148–9.

20. *Ibid.*, pp. 47–82.

21. Cork to George, Earl of Kildare, 13 Oct. 1629 (P.R.O.N.I.,
Letter Book of George, Earl of Kildare, letter no. 5).

22. See for example Grosart, ed., *Lismore Papers*, 1st series, IV,
p. 218 where Cork mentioned a payment to Mr Jacob Long of
Kinsale, his German physician, who provided him with plasters
and prescriptions for dead palsy, and *ibid.*, V, p. 102 where
Cork mentioned a little glass bottle of spirit of amber that Lady
Stafford had given him for curing palsy.

23. J.G.A. Pocock, *The Ancient Constitution and the Feudal Law:
A Study of English Historical Thought in the Seventeenth
Century* (Cambridge, 1957), pp. 59–63.

24. Brendan Bradshaw, 'Sword, Word and Strategy in the Reformation in Ireland', in *Historical Journal*, XXI (1978), pp.
475–502. The present writer has had occasion to disagree with
some points in Dr Bradshaw's argument but what has been

said reinforces Bradshaw's main point that the Irish experience forced Englishmen to think more critically of strategies for the enforcement of the Reformation. See Canny, 'Why the Reformation Failed in Ireland: une Question Mal Posée', cited in n. 10 above.

25. The principal individuals that were mentioned as having exerted an influence on Richard Boyle were Geoffrey Fenton, Thomas Stafford, George Carew, Viscount Falkland, Archbishop James Ussher, George Downham and Sir Arthur Chichester. Others of advanced opinion who must have exerted some indirect influence on Boyle's thought are Edmund Spenser, Sir John Davies, Fynes Moryson and William Herbert, but it should be noted that some of the more advanced opinions were expressed in letters by obscure men of action and have never been committed to print.

Index

Printed in Great Britain by
Amazon.co.uk, Ltd.,
Marston Gate.